Death Nine

The Dyatlov Pass Mystery

By Launton Anderson

For my Dad,
who shares my love of mysteries,
gave me the gift of curiosity,
and has always been my rock.

Preface

In 2002, I was stationed in England and the Dyatlov Pass mystery was featured on a TV show. At that time, the details sounded far-fetched. Missing eyes? No Tongue? The story resembled an urban legend.

I retired from the US Air Force in 2005. It was that year that I again heard about the Dyatlov Pass mystery. This time it was presented as a true story. How did nine strong young adults die in a cold Russian winter? Why did they leave their warm tent while half-dressed? I researched and found books, news articles, transcripts, descriptions of the hikers, and details of their deaths. This was not an urban legend, it had really happened.

I love puzzles, mysteries, and clues. While in the Air Force, I worked in the cryptographic world. We analyzed problems, developed solutions, and continually asked "How" and "Why". By 2015, I'd collected an extensive file of information. I learned about the hikers, their hiking experience, how these winter hikes were conducted, and endless details about their final fatal hike.

I gathered my notes and prepared to write a paper. My initial thought was to create a document that outlined and examined the clues of this mystery while exploring theories. As the material came together, I realized this document was becoming a book. And that's where we are now.

In this book, you'll find an abundance of material. I've included photos from the hikers' own cameras. We'll discuss the hike itself utilizing the hikers' own words from their diaries. We'll analyze the clues revealed during the search for the hikers. We'll review the autopsies and injuries.

While many have dismissed this mystery as the result of a natural event, we'll see that the clues point to so much more than that. This tragedy was not the result of an avalanche or infrasound. The hikers did not panic and run off to their own deaths while recklessly abandoning their warm shelter. No, there was something much more sinister at play than a natural disaster. And here, we'll connect those dots. We'll see how the clues point to a single solution. At the end of this book you'll find the official reports from the original investigation. I've included the hikers' diaries, official witness statements, the official radiation report, and the official autopsies.

While the clues, official reports, and photos are important, the most important aspect of this tragedy is the hikers themselves. Igor, Zina, Rustem, George, Yuri, Alexander, Nicholas, and Simon were all healthy athletes who died brutal deaths on a cold, dark, winter night. The mystery of how and why they died remains unsolved to this day.

Thank you for joining me on this journey while we explore this tragedy. Perhaps together we can solve the Dyatlov Pass mystery.

Launton Anderson

Acknowledgements

To the talented Aleksander from Taina: Your devotion to flawless maps clarified the scene and situation like no other.

Alexey Rakitin: Your book *'Dyatlova Pass. The Mystery of the Death of Sverdlovsk Tourists in February 1959'* provided a fascinating insight into the complex details of this case. It's an inspirational work of art.

Walton Mendelson: Your professional technical knowledge is invaluable. Without it, this book would not have been possible. You have no idea how many late nights I pored over your advice, fiddling with this format until it worked. Thank you, thank you, thank you.

For my family and friends: You've each imprinted a part of yourselves into my heart. Whether near or far, you shine a positive light in my life. I love you all so much. Thank you for being there and thank you for being you.

And for you, dear reader: Without you, this book is just words on a page. But with you, it becomes a journey of exploration and discovery. Thank you for sharing your time and this journey with me.

Table of Contents

Chapter
1

The Hikers

*"Our life is not just a call of nature,
it is an attempt to find our place in the universe.
And when life becomes a search for a place,
search for immortality."*

~Igor Dyatlov~

In January 1959, ten hikers departed from their university in Sverdlovsk, Russia to begin a long anticipated winter hike through the Ural Mountains. Led by a radio engineering student named Igor Dyatlov, the group traveled by train, bus, truck, and sleigh to their final destination: an uninhabited mining village called 2nd North.

While the destination was 'final' in their travel itinerary, it was actually the beginning of their adventure. It was here that their hike would actually begin. From this point forward, they would be on their own and many miles from civilization.

It was also here, in the 2nd North, where one of the hikers turned back to go home. Yuri Yudin, who suffered from a painful nerve condition, chose to leave the group rather than slow them down. He made the difficult decision to return with the sleigh rather than continue forward with the hike.

The nine remaining members reorganized and re-packed their backpacks with the items that Yuri Yudin would have carried. Then, as he turned back with the horse and sleigh driver, the other nine set out into the wilderness. Together, these nine hikers had a combined 55 years of outdoor survival experience. They were never seen alive again.

By the end of February, searchers found five of their partially clothed, frozen bodies scattered a mile away from their destroyed tent. Igor had cuts on his hands and face, Zina had a bruise that wrapped halfway around her waist. Rustem had a cracked skull. Yuri Doroshenko had burned hair and George had a piece of skin in his mouth that had been torn off his own hand. The last four were found as the snow melted in May. Alexander had a broken neck. Simon had crushed ribs. Luda's eyes and tongue were missing and Nicholas had a head injury so severe that parts of his skull were embedded in his brain.

What happened? How did nine able-bodied and experienced people end up half naked, severely injured, and frozen a mile away from their tent? Why was the tent destroyed?

These and many questions have remained unanswered for years. In the immediate aftermath, a grieving Yuri Yudin was tasked with identifying their items. He also gave a clear picture of 'life on the trails'. But he didn't know what happened. No one did. It was a mystery with no one left to tell the tale. But those nine hikers did leave clues. They left rolls of film. They left diaries. We have their autopsy reports and radiation tests. So, there is something to see. We may never know what happened, but we can look at their legacy and maybe, just maybe catch a glimpse of the horror that unfolded on that dark winter night.

Igor
(Igor Dyatlov)

Igor was a radio engineering student entering his 5th and final year of studies at the Ural Polytechnic Institute University (UPI) located in Sverdlovsk, Russia.

At 23 years old, he was a talented engineer, inventor, and athlete. He was a popular student at the university and had joined the UPI hiking club during his first year of studies. Over the years, he'd been on many school sponsored hikes during all types of weather. All the hikes were challenging, but the winter hikes were especially grueling. Winter hikes entailed the hikers to use skis, carry all equipment in backpacks, and hike during what was often difficult weather conditions. Hikers would camp in blizzards with temperatures often plummeting to 30 below. Most summer and winter hikes took place throughout the Ural mountain area in Siberia.

As Igor grew more experienced in hiking, he began leading the hikes. UPI gave numerical values to the hikes dependent upon difficulty. A category '1' was the easiest, with '2' being medium and '3' being the most difficult. Igor had completed several category 3 hikes and had advanced to the point of being a leader of these difficult hikes. He was considered the most experienced athlete of the UPI hiking club.

Not only was Igor a valuable hiking leader, he was also an inventor who modified specialty items for hikes. One of those items was a radio.

Igor spent many hours in UPI's radio department rebuilding and modifying radios. He made them lighter, more durable, and portable. Igor's radios were often requested and included during hikes for communication purposes.

Another thing Igor invented was the portable tent heater also called a stove. (Note: From Russian to English, the word 'heater' translates to 'stove'. In studies of this mystery, this item is often called a stove. However, this device was only to be used for heat and was never intended for cooking. It was a portable source of heat for the winter hikes).

4

This stove invention was a small metal box shaped like a muffler with a long pipe attached. This device would be hung inside the top of the tent. The box would be filled with wood, lit, and then burn through the evening generating heat inside the tent. The long pipe would vent dangerous fumes outside through the back of the tent. The stove could be completely disassembled for easy transportation.

A rule with the use of the stove was that someone stayed awake to keep an eye on it. Normally, this duty was rotated among the hikers.

A third invention of Igor's was the 'double tent'. Igor sewed two tents together and created a large tent that could accommodate up to 12 hikers. He added hooks at the top of the tent for ease of hanging the stove.

In November 1958, Igor submitted a request through the UPI Hiking Club to lead and manage a category 3 winter hike. This hike would take place during the winter break which was scheduled from mid-January through mid-February.

Per protocol, Igor's request was routed through the UPI Hiking Club and ultimately the UPI administration. Permission was granted with the expectation that UPI would review and approve the hike's individual members to ensure they were capable of a level 3 hike.

With the approval in place, word quickly got out that Igor would be leading a category 3 winter hike. Several students and alumni applied to participate. By the end of December, Igor's group hike consisted of 10 team members.

One of the first members to join the hike was Zina. She and Igor had been dating for months. They'd gone on group hikes together and completed difficult hikes before. Everyone who knew the couple agreed that their dating didn't change the dynamic of the hike. Both were capable, experienced, and mature enough to place the safety and success of the hike above their feelings for each other.

Igor was a leader, inventor, and loyal friend. He created many items that were useful and helpful while hiking in difficult situations. Even after the tragedy, no one doubted Igor's leadership qualities. The mountain pass, where the deaths occurred, had no name. Afterwards, it was named 'Dyatlov Pass'.

Zina
(Zinaida Kolmogorov)

At 22 years old, Zina was in her 4th year at UPI majoring in Radio Engineering. She'd been a member of the UPI hiking club since she started school. She'd completed several complex and difficult hikes. She was considered the soul of the UPI hiking club. They were very proud of her and she was a welcome addition to any hiking group. She always carried her load and took on any extra responsibilities.

Just the previous year, during a hike, Zina was bit by a viper snake. She came perilously close to death and was only saved when the group came upon a family living in the forest. The family applied local herbal remedies to Zina's wound. She survived but suffered weeks of painful healing.

In the moments immediately after the snake bite, Zina was more worried about the group than she was about herself. She apologized profusely to her team mates when they carried her out. She didn't want to be a burden and she didn't want to hinder them from completing the hike.

By all accounts, Zina is remembered as a natural leader. She was very involved in extra-curricular activities such as taking children out to day camps. She also participated in student concerts and sports events. She was a generous and gentle person and very popular in the university.

Zina almost died during an earlier hike when she was bit by a viper. She had to be carried out and apologized for being a burden. Despite being close to death for several weeks, Zina recovered and continued to complete the most rigorous hikes

---

Yuri
(Yuri Doroshenko)

Yuri was 21 years old and a 4th year student at UPI majoring in Radio Engineering. He had a long history of hiking experience. He'd been a member of the UPI hiking club since his first year at the university.

He'd completed several hikes including the most rigorous category 3's. Yuri was strong, reliable, and had great endurance. He was considered the hardest worker of the team. His dependability and strength made him a welcome member of any hike.

A favorite UPI story is about Yuri and a bear. One time, while Yuri was on a group hike, a bear ran towards the group's campsite. Yuri saw it, jumped up, grabbed a hammer, and ran yelling at the bear. The bear turned and ran away.

Yuri had dated Zina for a while. After their break-up they remained on good terms. Yuri got along very well with Igor and they were close friends. There weren't any difficulties with the fact that Igor was now dating Zina. The three of them had completed many hikes together.

Yuri was a legend in the UPI hiking club. During a previous hike, a bear wandered into camp. Yuri didn't hesitate. He lunged at it with a hammer and chased it away.

Alexander
(Alexander Kolevatov)

Alexander was a 24 year old 4th year student at UPI majoring in Physics and Technology.

Prior to this, he had attended a university in Moscow and had been a member of that hiking club. He'd completed several difficult hikes including one to the polar Urals. He received a degree in Metallurgy. Afterwards, he worked in Moscow as a senior lab assistant in a classified institute called the Ministry of Medium Machine Building. This institute conducted research into the development of material for the nuclear industry. After three years he enrolled in UPI.

At UPI, Alexander became a member of the hiking club and completed several difficult and complex hikes.

His friends said he was a cautious, diligent, and studious man. One of his hobbies was collecting and smoking antique pipes.

Alexander was a well- liked and admired member of the club. He was strong, orderly, methodical, and had natural leadership skills. He was described as reasonable and confident. Hiking groups enjoyed having him on their team.

Alexander had a degree in Metallurgy. He worked in Moscow for three years conducting classified nuclear research. He then moved to Sverdlovsk and enrolled in UPI to study for a degree in Physics and Technology.

Luda
(Lyudmila Dubinina)

At 20 years old, Luda was the youngest of the group. She was a 3rd year student at UPI majoring in Engineering and Economics. One of the first things Luda did at the university was join the hiking club. She'd completed several hikes up to the category 2. No one doubted that she'd be able to complete this one which would be her first category 3.

In 1957, during a hike, Luda was accidentally shot in the leg by a hunter. Her team carried her out on a stretcher in what turned out to be a very painful ordeal for Luda. Even so, she apologized to the group continuously. A few months later, as soon as she was healed, Luda started hiking again.

During a hike in 1958, Luda helped carry the stretcher of a wounded team member. They had to travel through mountain passes and steep slopes. Luda remained cheerful and dependable through it all.

She was a known merry maker and would find a way to make a fun time out of any situation. She was part of the UPI ice dancing club and an avid photographer. She was also a gifted athlete and singer.

Luda came from a family of solid communists and was raised in the spirit of the party. She was an avid supporter of the government and was vocal about her opinion and stances. She wasn't afraid to state her opinion.

Everyone agreed that Luda was a hard worker. She was a welcome member of any group. She was reliable, independent, strong, and brave.

Although Luda was the youngest in the group, she handled herself well. She was accidentally shot by a hunter during an earlier hike. After several months of healing, she started hiking again. She was a welcome member of any group.

George
(Yuri (Georgy) Krivonischenko)

George was 23 years old and had graduated from UPI in 1957 with a degree in Civil Engineering. He currently worked as an engineer in Plant 817. Prior to this, he worked in a sensitive position at the Mayak nuclear plant.

In September 1957, there was a nuclear contamination accident called "The Kyshtym Disaster". George helped with the clean-up. Up until Chernobyl, the Kyshtym nuclear disaster was the worst in the world. Today it ranks as number three, right behind Chernobyl and Fukushima.

After his work with the Kyshtym clean-up, George was promoted to a supervisory position. He was due to start his new job on February 21st. During the time of the hike, George was on a month-long break from work and was going to start the new supervisory position upon his return.

Both during and after his time at UPI, George had completed several category 3 hikes. He and Igor were close friends and had done almost all of their hikes together. George was a skilled artist and musician. He played the mandolin and often brought it along on hikes.

George was a dependable, reliable, and valuable team member. He was often the comic relief and could find humor in most situations.

He was well-liked and well known to all the members of the hiking club. During the planning phase of the hike, there were several group meetings at his house.

George worked in Kyshtym nuclear plant. He helped with clean-up after, what was at that time, the worst nuclear disaster in the world.

Rustem
(Rustem Slobodin)

Rustem was 23 years old and had graduated from UPI in 1958 with a degree in Mechanical Engineering. He worked as an engineer in Plant 817 and worked alongside George until George's upcoming promotion. Rustem, however, was not part of the nuclear disaster clean-up.

Rustem was very athletic, agile, strong, and resilient. He was a strong athlete and enjoyed long distance running. He was active in a variety of sports. He led, organized, and participated in numerous sporting events.

Rustem was also an avid and experienced hiker. He had completed numerous category 3 hikes over the years. Friends said he was reliable and would readily come to the rescue and help anyone who needed help. He and was considered one of the strongest members of the hiking group.

In addition to his athleticism, he was also musically inclined and played the mandolin. Quite often, he would play while everyone was gather around the campfire in the evening.

He was a strong, athletic, reliable, and welcome member of the group.

Rustem was considered the most athletic of the group. He was a long distance runner and played a variety of sports. He was also musically inclined and played the mandolin. During hikes, he would often play while everyone was gathered around the campfire.

11

Yuri
(Yuri Yudin)

Yuri Yudin was 22 years old and a 4th year student at UPI majoring in Engineering and Economics. He made several hikes over the years including the category 3's.

Yuri Yudin had a nerve condition called sciatica that frequently caused severe pain. The symptoms are described as tingling, numbness, weakness, and pain that originate in the lower back and travel down the large sciatic nerve in the back of each leg.

Yuri was originally a member of Igor's winter hike. But Yuri's sciatica flared up and prevented him from continuing. Reluctantly, he withdrew from the hike.

The plan was for him to stay in a nearby town until the end of the hike. Then the whole group would return home together. Ultimately, that never happened. The sciatica flare-up saved Yuri Yudin's life. He never saw his friends alive again.

Although the mystery of what happened to the group is still unsolved, Yuri Yudin provided insight to the group's personalities and dynamic. Yuri's observations and involvement in the investigation was invaluable. His knowledge answered some questions that to this day would be unresolved if not for him.

Yuri Yudin passed away in 2013 and according to his last wishes, he was buried in St. Michael cemetery near some of the other hikers.

Yuri Yudin never fully recovered from the trauma of losing his nine friends. He always thought he might save been able to save them if he'd continued on the hike. He often said: "All my life I wanted to be the tenth."

Yuri Yudin's sciatica flared up and he turned back at the last minute. He was invaluable during the investigation. Even so, he always felt like he could have saved them.
"All my life I wanted to be the tenth"

Nicholas
(Nikolay Thibault-Brignoles)

Nicholas was 23 years old and had graduated UPI in 1958 with a degree in Civil Engineering. He was working as an engineering foreman in construction.

Nicholas' mother was Russian and his father was French. Nicholas was born in an internment prison camp. His father was accused of being active in the revolutionary party and convicted of crimes against the state. The family was sent to the camp and Nicholas' father was sentenced to 10 years hard labor working in the mines. Nicholas' father died when Nicholas was only 9 years old.

Despite his difficult upbringing, Nicholas was cheerful, reliable, and self-confident. He was a valued member of the group and had participated in hikes for years. He'd completed several complex hikes including the category 3's. Nicholas was generous with his time and energy. If a team member needed help or was struggling with a heavy load, Nicholas would transfer some items to his own backpack to alleviate his friend in need.

Nicholas was extremely popular, energetic, and well-liked at both the university and at his engineering job. He had a great sense of humor and was a welcome addition to the hike.

Nicholas as born in an internment camp, while his father was being held there as a political prisoner. Despite this difficult upbringing, Nicholas was cheerful, reliable, and confident. If any member ever needed help with anything, Nicholas was the first one there. He often sacrificed his time and energy to benefit others.

13

Simon
(Semyon (Alexander) Zolotarev)

At 37 years old, Simon was by far the oldest of the group. He was a soldier in WW2, serving from 1941 through 1946 earning four combat awards. By the end of WW2 97% of Russian males born in 1921, who served in the war, perished as casualties of the war. Simon was one of the 3% who survived.

After the war, Simon joined the Moscow School of Military Engineers, but had to quit due to a forced reduction of students. He then went to the Leningrad Military Engineering School, but had to quit there. Again due to student reductions. He then attended the Minsk Institute of Physical Education and graduated in 1951.

He worked as an athletic and hiking instructor in the mid 50's. By the time he joined Igor's hiking group, he was a top candidate for an instructor position at UPI. Completing a category 3 hike would improve his credentials and improve his chances for the position.

On a personal note, he planned on visiting his mother right after the hike was complete. The hike would end in a village called Vijay and Simon planned on continuing on to his mother's from there.

In considering Simon for the instructor position, the UPI administration contacted Igor and requested that Simon join his group. Igor had little choice except to accept the request and include Simon on the hike.

The other members of the group were alarmed to hear a stranger was joining them. They'd all hiked together in various groups over the years. They knew each other well and knew they could depend on each other.

Being out in the dangerous winter weather, traveling on skis and carrying everything to survive in a backpack required complete group unity and trust. There's no way to contact anyone for help. If someone gets hurt, not only would it be dangerous, it could be potentially deadly for the whole group. There is no extra equipment if a ski or ski pole breaks. Food is rationed. Everyone must pull his or her own weight. There's no room for error.

So, it wasn't surprising that the other members weren't thrilled to have this stranger join them. Simon knew he needed to be trusted and accepted. He met members of the group in various settings.

Despite being the oldest- and having military experience- he never insisted on being the one in charge. That role belonged to Igor Dyatlov.

Simon slowly started making friends with the group members. Nicholas in particular became a close friend. Eventually, after group meetings and social get-togethers, the others warmed up to Simon. He began to fit in and as the hike start date approached, the 10 person group began to feel like a cohesive unit.

Although they'd had no choice in whether Simon's inclusion, the group members didn't hold that against Simon.

As they packed and prepared, Simon pulled his weight and it became apparent that he would be an asset during a cold, remote winter hike.

By the end of WW2 97% of Russian males born in 1921, who served in the war, perished as casualties of the war. Simon was one of the 3% who survived. He was a highly decorated war veteran and had extensive outdoor survival skills

---

Chapter 2

The Hike

*"I wonder what awaits us in this trip.
What will be new?"*

~Zina~

Zina

After Igor was approved to lead the hike, he submitted his equipment request and route information to UPI. Among the equipment requested was the double-tent, the portable stove, and one of the portable two-way radios. UPI approved the tent and the stove, but disapproved the request to take the radio. Their reasoning was that since hike was of the highest difficulty, the luxury of radios would not fit into the challenges of surviving in the wilderness carrying only the bare necessities.

We can only wonder what the outcome would have been if a radio had been available to call for help. Or maybe whatever happened, happened so suddenly that even a radio would have been useless. This is an answer we may never know.

As was custom, in addition to the tent and stove, UPI provided skis, poles, tools, coats, and other equipment necessary for a winter hike. No extra skis or ski poles were provided, so if a hiker broke a ski or lost a pole, the entire hike would be in jeopardy. The snow was often up to 10ft deep. Skiing allowed a hiker to move forward, but walking without skis would be nearly impossible.

Each hiker carried a backpack with their own personal items as well as group items, such as the tent, tent poles, rope, axes, compasses, and cameras. This also included food, alcohol (although prohibited on hikes, no one ever really cared as long as it was consumed in moderation), and other supplies.

UPI also approved Igor's hike route through the Ural Mountains which would cover 217 miles in 16 days in a circular route. The route would take them through wilderness, valleys and up Mt. Otorten and Mt. Gora Oykachakhl. The route ended with them back at the village of Vijay where Igor would send a telegram to UPI announcing that they'd made it safely.

That telegraph was never sent.

Here we'll look at the Dyatlov group's last days as was witnessed by those who interacted with them up until they stepped into the forest on January 28th. From there, we have their photos and diaries dated up to January 31st. Then tragedy struck triggering a mystery that has endured for more than 50 years.

January 23rd

The Dyatlov group and another UPI hiking group lead by a student named Yuri Blinov took a train from the city of Sverdlovsk to the town of Serov.

January 24th

When the two groups arrived in Serov around dawn on January 24th, the train station was empty. No shops were open and the hiking groups were told they couldn't wait in the train station for their evening train which was scheduled to depart at 6:30pm.

Before the groups could decide what to do with their time, George, in a spontaneous moment, started singing and waving his hat around. He jokingly begged strangers for candy. Everyone was surprised, but George was known to be the comic relief, so it wasn't totally out of his character. It was a goofy and small attempt at lightening up the mood. But soon enough, a police officer arrived. He informed both groups that Serov was a 'good communist town' and that there was 'no crime here and certainly no disruption of the peace'. George was swiftly arrested and taken away.

An arrest could mean detention for days while the matter was sorted out. The rest of Dyatlov's group had no choice but to wait and see. Fortunately, after a few hours, George was released and free to go as long as he promised to not be disruptive. Grateful and relieved, the group joked that George was now assigned 'extra duties' for his crazy antics.

A school was located near train station. The group was given permission to wait there until their train in the evening. The custodian secured their equipment in an unused room to keep it safe. She also brought them hot water for their tea.

That afternoon, the Dyatlov group got to meet with the school children and answer questions about hiking. The group, especially Zina, was such a hit that the school children begged for them to stay and talk to them longer. But, the group needed to gather their equipment for the next leg of their journey.

The Dyatlov group and the Blinov group met back up at the train station to await their evening train. Amazingly, they had another encounter with the police after a drunk young man accused the Dyatlov group of stealing his vodka and wallet. The police escorted the young drunk away.

Both groups were more than relieved to board the train. They arrived at a town called Ivdel around midnight. Here there were no rules against sleeping in the station, so the groups spread out the equipment and rested until morning when they were scheduled to take a bus to a village called Vijay.

January 25th

On the morning of January 25th, after spending the night in the train station in Ivdel, the two groups boarded a bus to the village of Vijay. They arrived around in Vijay at 2pm. They spent the night in a hotel which provided relief from sleeping in the train stations.

It was also in Vijay where the two groups separated. The Blinov group was a group of ten students who were on a hike sponsored by UPI just like the Dyatlov group. Both hikes were through the Ural Mountains. Dyatlov's hike was to be 16 days long, while Blinov's hike was planned to last 25 days. Both hikes would run parallel to each other, but be separated by several miles.

After the death of the Dyatlov group, the Blinov group became important witnesses during the official investigation. One interesting fact is the Blinov group saw 'orange fireballs' while out on their hike and wrote of it in their diary. This event was recorded well before the Blinov group knew of the Dyatlov tragedy. It's unknown what these fireballs were or how or if they even affected the Dyatlov group. The Blinov group would also report that there was heavy snow during the weeks of their hike.

January 26th

The Dyatlov group left Vijay riding in the back of an open truck. After traveling three hours in the freezing cold, they finally arrived at their destination: a logging settlement called the 41st Quarter. They were greeted warmly by the men living there and promptly given warm quarters in the local hostel (A hostel is a dorm style hotel).

The 41st Quarter was the last inhabited town for the hikers. Their next move would be onto an uninhabited mining camp the next day.

The stay in the 41st Quarter proved to be a happy and comfortable one. The logging men were hospitable and good company. The Dyatlov group sang songs, Rustem played a mandolin, and many of them watched movies. Conversation lasted well into the night.

The ride to the 41st Quarter in the back of an open truck.
From left: Yuri Doroshenko, Yuri Yudin, Igor, Nicholas, Zina (sitting, almost hidden), Luda, Simon, Rustem (far right). George is taking the picture and Alexander is in unseen behind the group.

Four of the loggers. The one on the left is Ognev who was nicknamed 'Beard'. The other names are unknown.

Some of the Dyatlov hikers with some of the loggers.
From left: Yuri Yudin, Igor, unknown logger, and Beard. Luda is standing between the unknown logger and Beard. Nicholas is sitting in front of Luda, Zina is next to Nicholas, and Alexander is in the very front. All other names are unknown.

The hikers and the loggers shared a loaf of bread on the day the hikers left. From left: Luda, Igor, behind Igor is Beard, and George is on the far right. All the other names are unknown.

These two group photos were taken one right after the other. At the far left is Yuri Doroshenko (Standing), Luda is standing in front of him, Zina is in the middle wearing a scarf, Alexander is center-right with his hood up, and Igor is second from the right.

Preparing to leave the logging town. Zina is at the top of the stairs.
Foreground: Some of the hikers backpacks.

January 27th

The hikers packed their gear and left for the old, uninhabited mining camp called 2nd North.

One of the loggers offered to transport their backpacks in a horse drawn sleigh. By the time the sleigh was packed and the horse made ready, it was almost 4pm before the group left.

By this time Yuri Yudin had decided he could not endure the rigors of the hike because his sciatica had flared up. However, he did continue with the group on to 2nd North because he wanted to collect rock and mineral specimens to take back to UPI for further study.

2nd North was an abandoned mining camp consisting of 24 houses in various states of disrepair. Beard had told them that there was one house that was in suitable shape to provide shelter for the night.

The trek from 41st Quarter to 2nd North was 15 miles. Between the late start and several stops for the horse, the group finally made it to the mining camp at 11pm.

It was completely dark, but they were able to find the habitable house and get a good fire going. The nine hikers and the driver, whose name was Velikyavichusk, settled in for the evening. They all stayed up talking and joking until 3am when they finally bedded down for sleep.

The horse drawn sleigh carrying all the backpacks
From left: Yuri Doroshenko, Zina, Luda, Velikyavichusk
(the driver), Yuri Yudin, Igor, Nicholas, and Rustem.

Luda, Simon, and Zina resting on crosses used to dry fish

January 28th

After the group woke up and had breakfast, Yuri Yudin, Yuri Doroshenko, and Alexander went to collect rock and mineral samples. Meanwhile the others packed. From this point forward, they would be hiking on skis, carrying all their belongings on their backs, and sleeping in the large tent.

As Yuri Yudin prepared to depart, he conversed with Igor. Yuri had noticed that Igor previously had a spirited conversation with one of the loggers. Igor claimed the conversation was not important, but that the group may need a few extra days to complete the hike.

So, instead of the group arriving in Vijay on February 12th, their arrival was pushed back to February 14th. Yuri didn't press Igor for more details. Once Yuri got home, he told UPI that the Dyatlov group may not return until February 14th.

Yuri passed items to the group, giving them some of his socks and mittens. He gave a sleeveless vest to Alexander

So, with the items distributed and the return date pushed back, Yuri Yudin said good-bye to his group of friends. He and the sleigh driver left at 10am.

Igor, George, Rustem, Zina, Yuri Doroshenko, Alexander, Simon, Luda, and Nicholas were never seen alive again.

Nicholas and his backpack.

Luda saying good-bye to Yuri Yudin with Igor in the background.

Zina saying good-bye to Yuri Yudin with Simon in the background.

Leaving the abandoned mining camp called the 2nd North. It's unknown who is in the center of this picture.

From this point forward, we can surmise the group's movement based on their diaries and photos.

We'll pick up from where we left off on the day the group left the abandoned village.

January 28th Continued

The nine remaining hikers packed their backpacks and greased their skis. The left the 2nd North at 11:45am.

They stopped at 4pm for a lunch break and then stopped for the evening at 5:30pm. They set up the tent and started a campfire to heat dinner.

After dinner, they sat around the campfire talking and singing songs. Alexander was on duty for the night to keep watch over things. All in all it was a good day. Everyone was in good spirits and looking forward to the next day.

The hikers kept a group diary as an official record of their travels. Each evening, after chores and dinner, someone would write the details from the day. Everyone took turns writing in the group diary, while some of the hikers kept personal diaries, too.

The group diary was discovered in the abandoned tent, along with Luda, Zina, and Rustem's diaries. A fifth diary was also found, but it wasn't signed. To this day, we don't know who authored the 'Unknown diary'.

Zina Diary
January 28
Driver today leaves, and Yuri Yudin. Took a few samples. I saw them for the first time this breed after drilling. Here a lot of chalcopyrite and pyrite. Last night boys stupid they joked. In my opinion, there is no need to pay attention, they might be less rude. And so far, nothing. Already it's time to go, and still and rummage rummage. I don't understand how you can so long to assemble.

Here's the first 30 min. Of course, nothing heavy backpack. But you can go. The first day it is always difficult.
left forward
Alexander tested his device then quit.
The second halt.
Yesterday without backpacks much lighter
snow, snow, snow, snow
on the banks of the frozen.
rivers snow snow
Broom sweeps clean.
Lunch was hours in 4
After lunch, made only one move and halt stood
I zashivala tent
Settled to sleep. Igor bad mood all evening
I just didn't recognize it. Had to sleep with wood from the oven.

The Group Diary
January 28
We were awaken by the rumbling voices of George and Alexander. Weather so far is smiling at us. It's only -8C outside.

After breakfast, some of the guys lead by Yuri Yudin, our well-known geologist, went to look for local minerals. They didn't find anything except pyrite and quartz veins in the rock. Took them long time to wax their skis and adjust the mounting. Yuri Yudin goes back home today. It is a pity, of course, that he leaves us. Especially for me and Zina, but nothing can be done about it.

Started hike at 11.45. We go up the river Lozva. We take turns to head the group for about 10 minutes. Snow cover is significantly less than last year. We have to stop and scrape the wet, melting snow from the bottom of the skis. George is behind and makes sketches of the route. The bank of the river near Second North (especially the right bank) are limestone cliffs that rise high at places. Overall the terrain becomes flatter, entirely covered by forest.

We stop for the night at 5:30 pm on river Lozva. Today we spend our first night in the tent. The guys are busy with the stove, sewing curtains out of sheets. With somethings completed and others not, we sit at dinner. After dinner we sit for long time around the campfire and sing heartfelt songs. Zina even tries to learn to play mandolin under guidance of our musician Rustem.

Then we resume our discussions, mostly about love. Someone comes up with an idea that we need a special notebook for ideas that we might come up with. Conspiring, we started going into the tent two people at a time.

The suspended stove radiates heat and divides the tent in two sections. The further section is occupied by me and Zina. Nobody wants to sleep by the stove. We agree that George will sleep there. On the other side sleeps the person on duty- Alexander.

George couldn't stand the heat and after laying down for 1-2 min, he got up and moved to the second section cursing and accusing us of treason. After that they still argued about something for a long time, but at the end all was quiet.

~ Luda ~

Nicholas and Simon

31

Luda, George, Nicholas, and Rustem

Luda, Rustem, Nicholas, and Zina

Nicholas

Rustem

The Manis are nomadic natives who live in the Ural Mountains. They're a peaceful people who subsist from fishing, hunting, and gathering. They move with the weather and the availability of food.

Many student hiking groups had interacted with the Mansi over the years. The Mansi would often offer food and shelter and any necessities to help the group.

There had never been an instance of Mansi violence towards hiking groups, hunters, or anyone else who traveled through their land. And while the Mansi do have holy sites, the area where the Dyatlov group perished is of no spiritual importance to the Mansi.

After the Dyatlov tragedy, one of the early theories was that Dyatlov's group had trespassed on a Mansi religious site and triggered the Mansi to kill the group.

Mt. Otorten- where the Dyatlov group was headed- means 'Do Not Go There' in Mansi. Mt. Kholat Syakhl- where the Dyatlov group tent was found- means 'Dead Mountain' in Mansi.

While they may sound like warnings, these names 'Do Not Go There' and 'Dead Mountain' are merely reminders to the Mansi themselves that these areas are not good hunting areas.

Although the Mansi were officially investigated, they were soon cleared. Official investigators have formally discounted the Mansi as the cause of the Dyatlov tragedy

January 29th

On January 29th, the men of the party took turns leading the group and breaking the trail to make it easier for the others to follow. Each turn took 10 minutes and every 70 minutes after each man had a turn, the group rested. They stopped for lunch midway. Then they followed a Mansi ski trail and noted the Mansi signs carved into tree. They also saw a Mansi storage platform. They stopped and camped for the night near the Auspiya River.

Today was Yuri Doroshenko's birthday. He turned 21.

The Group Diary
1.29.59

Second day of our hike. We made our way from the Lozva river to the Auspiya river. We walked along a Mansi trail. The weather is −13C. The wind is weak. We often find ice on the Lozva river. That's all.
~Nicholas~

Zina's Diary
29.1.59

Today is Yurka's birthday. We go first to Lozva then we turn to Auspiya. Surroundings are beautiful. Along the Auspiya Mansi have passed. A trail is visible, grooves, a path is visible. We often see Mansi signs on the trail. I wonder what they write about? Now the Mansi trail goes South.

Now we sit the three of us: Rustem, Yuri and I Waiting for the rest. For the night stopped near the ski tracks. We are burning firewood with Yuri. We talked about the past. Such a playboy.

Mansi carving on a tree

The tent. Notice the pipe at the back. This was used to vent the portable stove that was used for heat. The tent was built on a layer of branches on top of the snow.

From left: Simon, Luda, and George in front of the tent. George is emptying ashes from the stove before packing it away. It's unknown which of the hikers is in front of Simon.

Alexander and Nicholas in front of the tent.

Yuri turned 21 on January 29th, 1959.

January 30th

The portable stove keeps the group warm through the night and there's a discussion about how they could build steam heat into the tent.

The group starts hiking around 9:30am. The weather is getting colder. They follow a deer trail that soon ends, so they must break a trail through 4ft deep snow. The trees are thinning and the group is ascending above the tree-line. They can feel the altitude change.

At 2pm they stop for a lunch of dried meat, crackers, sugar, garlic, and coffee.

They stop for the night around 5pm, pitch the tent on some fir branches, and start the fire. Nicholas and Luda argue over chores and Luda goes into the tent.

Yuri's extra coat and mittens get burned somehow (this incident is not further explained).

Zina mentions in her diary that they are going to build a storage site soon. This site will be where the group will leave extra gear to lighten their loads for the summit up the mountain. They'll stash their extra things and keep a few days worth of supplies with them. After the summit, they would return to the storage site to collect their items.

The storage site itself is any type of shelter. Whether an actual above-ground structure (like the Mansi storage platform) or a hole covered with branches, it was very common with the long distance hiking groups back then.

Today the group celebrates Alexander's birthday and give him a tangerine. He divides the tangerine into 8 parts and shares it with the group.

However, Alexander's real birthday is November 16th. It's unknown why Alexander told the group his birthday was today.

The Group Diary
30 January 1959
Diary is written in the cold on the go.
Today is a third cold night on the bank of Auspiya river. We are getting used to it. The stove does a great job. Some of us (Thibeaux (Nicholas) and Krivonischenko (George)) think we need to build steam heat in the tent. The curtains in the tent are quite justified. We get up at 8:30am. After breakfast we walk along the Auspiya river, but the ice again doesn't allow us to move forward.

We went on the bank on a sledge-deer trail. In the middle of the road the saw Mansi shed. Yes, Mansi, Mansi, Mansi. This word comes up more and more often in our conversations. Mansi are people of the North. Small Hanti-Mansijskiy nation located in Salehard with 8 thousand population. Very interesting and unique people that inhabit the North Polar Urals, close to the Tyumen region. They have a written language, and leave characteristic signs on forest trees.

Weather: temperature in the morning - 17 C

day - 13 C

night - 26 C.

The wind is strong, south-west, snow begins to fall, heavy clouds, drop in temperature. The temperature is normal for Northern Urals.

This is a story about the forest. Mansi signs tell about animals they saw, resting stops and other things. It is particularly interesting to solve its meaning for the tourists as well as historians.

Deer trail turns into a trodden path, and then ends. To go without a trail is very hard, snow is 120 cm (4 feet) deep. The forest gradually thins and trees get smaller. Lots of dwarf birches and pines. You can feel the altitude. It is impossible to walk on the river. It is not completely frozen, there is ice and water under the snow. We have to go back on the bank of the river. The day is over and we have to find a place for bivouac. That's the stop for the night. Strong west wind. It blows the snows off the cedar and pine trees, creating the impression of a snow fall.

As usual we quickly start a fire and pitch the tent on some fir branches. We are warmed by the fire and go to sleep.

(Unsigned)

Unknown Diary

January 30

In the morning it was 17 ° now it is getting colder. "Volunteers" Alexander and Nicholas are repeating their duties as a punishment for slowing the group yesterday took a long time to start a fire. In the evening it was decided that we will leave the tent exactly 8 minutes after waking up. Therefore, all have been awake and waiting for the command. But it is useless. Around 9:30 in the morning we began the passive preparation. Nicholas is joking about something in the morning. Everyone is reluctant to get up.

And the weather! In contrast to the rest of the warm days –

today is a sunny cold day. The sun appears playful.

Today as yesterday were are following the path of Mansi. Sometimes Mansi writings appear on trees. In general, all sorts of obscure mysterious characters. There is slogan for our campaign, "In a country of mysterious signs." If we knew these letters, it would be possible, without any doubt, to go down the path, confident that it would lead us to the right place. Here the trail takes us to the shores of the river. We lose track. In the future, the trail follows the left bank of Auspii River, but the team of deer crossed the river and we are going through the woods. At the first opportunity we will turn back to the river. As it is easier to follow it.

At approximately 2 pm we stop for a lunch. Dried meat, guest crackers, sugar, garlic, coffee, stocked in the morning - that's our lunch.

Good mood.

A couple more hours - and we will stop at 5 pm for the night. We have been looking for a place, then we returned about 200 meters back. Charming place. Deadwood, high pines, in short, everything you need for a good night.

Part 2.

Luda quickly got tired and sat down by the fire. Nicholas changed his clothes. He began to write a diary. The law is that until all the work is done, do not approach the fire. And so they had a long argument, of who will sew the tent. Finally Nicholas gave up and took a needle. Luda remained seated. And we sewed the hole (and there were so many that there was enough work for all except two attendants and Luda). Guys are terribly outraged.

Today is the birthday of Alexander. Congratulations. We give him a tangerine, which he immediately divided into 8 pieces (Luda went into a tent and did not come out until the end of the dinner). So another day of our trek went well.

Zina's diary
30.1.59
We go on Auspiya. Cold. Mansi trail ended. Pine forest. There was sun in the morning, now is cold. All day long we walked along Auspiya. Will spend the night on a Mansi trail. Nicholas didn't get to be a watchman so me and Rustem will stay on duty today. Burned mittens and Yuri's second quilted jacket. He cursed a lot. Today, probably, we will build a storage.

The January 30th entry was the last entry in both the Unknown diary and Zina's diary. However, on the very last page of Zina's diary is a single word: 'Rempel'. This is the name of a local hunter.

Zina writing in her diary. Simon is seen behind her also writing in a diary.

From left: Nicholas, Rustem, and Simon.
Igor is in the foreground.

Rustem modeling Yuri's burned coat.

Igor

January 31st
This is the last entry in the group diary.

The Group Diary
31 January 1959
Today the weather is a bit worse wind (west), snow (probably from the pines) because the sky is perfectly clear.

Came out relatively early (around 10 am). Took the same Mansi sled trail. Till now we walk along a Mansi trail, which was crossed by a deer hunter not long ago.

Yesterday we apparently came across his resting stop. Deer didn't go much further. The hunter didn't follow the beaten trail and we are now in his steps.

Today was surprisingly good accommodations for the tent, air is warm and dry, despite the low temperature of -18C to -24C. Walking is especially hard today. Visibility is very low. We can't see the trail and sometimes we have to advance gropingly. All we can do is 1.52 km (1 mile) per hour.

We are forced to find new methods of clearing the path for the skis. The first member leaves his backpack on the ground and walks forward, then returns and rests for 10-15 minutes with the group. Thus we have a non-stop paving of the trail. It is especially hard for the second to move down the new trail with full gear on the back. We gradually leave the Auspiya valley, the rise is continuous, but quite smooth. Fir trees are replaced by wispy birch-wood. We came out of the tree line. Wind is western, warm, penetrating. The speed of the wind is similar to the air draft created by a taking off airplane. Firn, open spaces. I can't even start thinking of setting up a storage. It's close to 4. We have to start looking for a place to pitch the tent. We are going south in Auspiya river valley. This apparently is the place covered with the deepest snow. Wind is not strong, snow cover is 1,22 m. Tired and exhausted we started the preparations for the night. Not enough firewood. Frail damp firs. We started fire with logs, too tired to dig a fire pit. We had supper right in the tent. It's warm. It is hard to imagine such a comfort somewhere on the ridge, with a piercing wind, hundreds kilometers away from human settlements.

~Igor~

From left: George, Luda, and Yuri.
Zina is in the foreground and Alexander is on the far right

Simon

From left: Igor, Alexander, and Simon with the rest of the hikers.

February 1st

As noted earlier, after a day of hiking they would complete their chores, eat dinner and then write in their diaries. Since there are no further diary entries, that means that something happened after they set up the tent on February 1st.

When the abandoned tent and campsite were found, there was no sign of a campfire, but food was found in the tent. There were pieces of meat, bread, crackers, a sandwich, and a cup of cocoa. Apparently, the group hiked for the day, set up camp, decided to not build a fire and prepared to eat in the tent. So, whatever happened, must have happened while they were eating but before they went to sleep for the night.

Sometime during their last day, the Dyatlov group did build a storage site. It was eventually found during the search.

There are no more diary entries, but there are a few photos of the hikers from that final day. Some of these photos were found 'loose' in the official file and some were found in the film developed from the hiker's cameras.

These two photos of the hikers are believed to be taken on their last day hiking.

These two photos were contained in the official file, but not attributed to any particular roll of film. Due to location and placement of the ski poles, these two pictures are thought to be the very last taken of the group.

The last picture on one of the rolls of film. It's unknown who is in this picture.

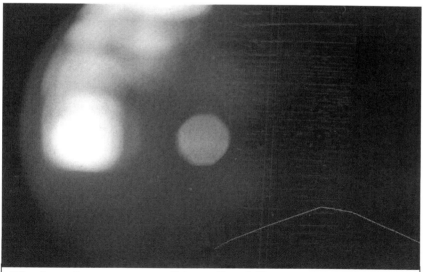

The last picture on one of the rolls of film.

Chapter 3

The Search

"A Land of Mysterious Signs"

~Dyatlov Group Slogan~

February 12th

Back at UPI in Sverdlovsk, no one was concerned when there was no telegram from the Dyatlov group. Delays happen during hikes, and Yuri Yudin had passed the message that they group might be delayed. Meanwhile, Blinov's group returned and announced there was heavy snow in the region during the last days of their hike. This news supported the fact that the Dyatlov group was delayed due to weather.

February 17th

Luda and Alexander's families were worried and called the UPI administrators to voice their concerns. The families were assured that the Dyatlov group was fine and delayed due to the weather. After a few more days, with still no word from the Dyatlov group, the families elevated their concerns and called the Sverdlovsk City Committee demanding answers.

February 20th

An emergency meeting was held between the City Committee and the UPI administrators. It was decided to immediately launch a search party for the missing Dyatlov group. This search party consisted of UPI students, instructors, and experienced winter outdoorsmen. (Note: Back then no formal organized search groups existed. Searches consisted of whoever was available and willing to help). Businesses and nearby universities donated money and supplies to supplement the search.

February 21st

A plane carrying volunteers and supplies circled the area of the Dyatlov route hoping to spot the missing hikers or some type of SOS. They did not spot any signs of the missing group.

February 22nd

Another search flight was launched and, yet, there was still no sign of the Dyatlov group. Local officials provided search dogs, two-way radios, and sent in local professional forest rangers. Mansi trackers joined the search teams.

February 23rd

A new plan was formed to have a helicopter drop off searchers and supplies in various locations of the Dyatlov group's route. The search teams did find several different ski trails and began to follow them.

February 24ᵗʰ and February 25ᵗʰ

The search teams followed several trails, yet found no sign of the missing hikers.

February 26ᵗʰ

Late in the afternoon, with a winter storm approaching, one of the search teams found the Dyatlov group's campsite.

The tent was collapsed but visible. The back entrance was covered with a few inches of snow. The front entrance was halfway open.

A pair of skis stood up right next to the tent. An ice axe was stuck in the snow near the front entrance.

A flashlight was laying on top of the tent with a dusting of snow on it. The flashlight was switched off and turned on when switched on indicating the battery was still good.

Igor's coat was just outside the tent entrance. In the pockets were a pocketknife and a picture of Zina. Several socks, hats, loose change, and other small objects were scattered around the campsite.

About 50 ft. away from the campsite were several sets of footprints leading away from the tent. It was apparent that whoever made the foot prints were either barefoot or were wearing only socks.

Some of the footprints were indented tracks, while others were raised tracks- like a column.

These footprint 'columns' are created when a warm foot- such as a bare foot- steps on the snow. Body heat from the foot melts the snow and then this refreezes into ice. As the wind blows the looser snow away, this footprint 'column' remains behind.

The tracks were a mix of indented footprints and raised footprints. There were also several unusual marks mixed in with the footprints which resembled drag marks or signs of a struggle. There was also a handprint nearby.

Near the tent, the tracks were grouped together. But as they moved downslope and away from the tent, they grew further apart. There were spots where a single set of tracks would veer off by themselves, only to re-join the main set of tracks after a short distance.

Witnesses disagreed on how many sets of tracks there were. Some said there were eight, while others said there were nine or more. Unfortunately, there are very few pictures of the footprints and no photos of the complete set of tracks.

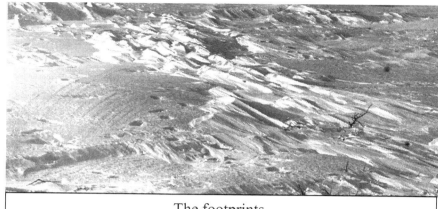

The footprints.

Footprints in the foreground.

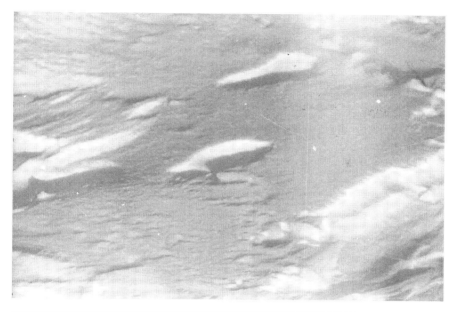

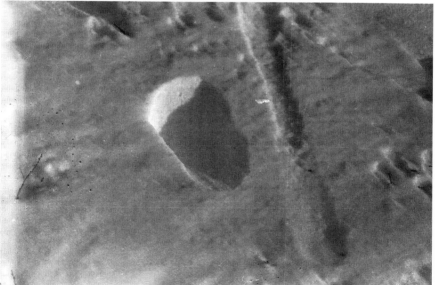

Two pictures of the footprints. Notice the unusual marks next to the footprint in the 2nd picture.

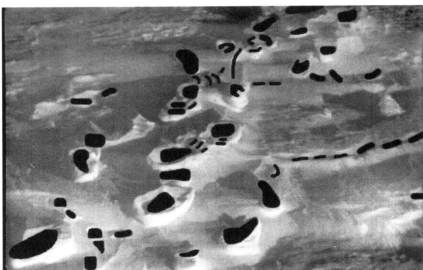

These two pictures are identical. Here the prints made columns rather than indents. The unusual marks along with the footprints indicate a struggle. It also looks like an object was being dragged. The 2nd photo shows the footprints and marks colored in.

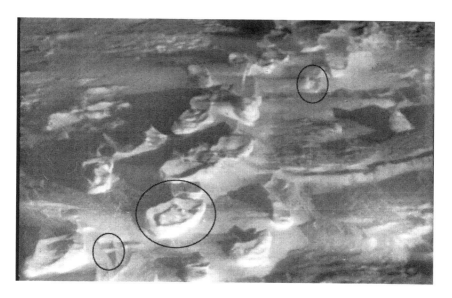

The same two pictures again with a few of the many unusual tracks circled.
From left to right: A boot heel track, a barefoot track, and a handprint.

The tent was frozen to the ground, thus initially preventing searchers from seeing inside. To open the tent, the searchers took the pick axe and chopped a hole in the top. Then they peeled the canvas away revealing the contents.

There were no bodies in the tent, but there were many other items such as food, boots, blankets, backpacks, cameras, diaries, buckets, and a metal box.

By this time, the weather was worsening and it was getting dark, so a more thorough search of the tent and area wasn't immediately possible.

Before leaving for the main camp, the searchers collected the ice axe, Igor's coat, the cameras, a flask of vodka, the diaries, and the metal box.

That evening, back at the main camp, the searchers read the diaries. They were encouraged when they read about the Dyatlov group's intention to assemble a storage site. This meant that the missing hikers possibly had access to food and supplies. They were also happy to read that the group had reported no problems in the January 31st entry (the last entry in any diary).

The contents of the metal box brought even more good news. In it was Igor's passport, the return train tickets, and 700 rubles- which was a considerable amount of money back then. The discovery of the money meant that the missing hikers weren't victims of criminals. A criminal would have taken the money and probably the food and vodka too.

These good signs were celebrated by passing the Dyatlov group's vodka flask around and toasting to the good health of all.

The next day a large number of searcher returned to the tent area. Some followed the footprints, some searched for the storage site, and others investigated the tent.

Additional items were found outside the tent. A pair of socks and slippers were wrapped up in a checkered shirt that was later identified as Igor's. A urine stain in the snow near the tent was another indication that the missing hikers had been there.

Notable items discovered in the tent were: Whole crackers and uncrushed tins of food. These are a sign that there was no avalanche or evidence of an act of nature crushing the tent and causing it to collapse.

If there had been an avalanche, then these items would have surely been crushed.

Also inside the tent were buckets, a saw, a flashlight, three axes, a knife, two kettles, a first aid kit, three compasses, a pocket watch, and four cameras. All items were undamaged.

On the floor of the tent were signs of dinner in progress such as chopped, cured meat, bread, biscuits, sugar, and a cup of cocoa. Condensed milk and other tins of food were found stored at the back of the tent.

The stove was found in the tent full of unburned kindling. There's dispute over whether the stove had been assembled or not. Some searchers say it was assembled, while others say it was disassembled but laid out on the floor of the tent. Either way, it was found in the tent as if being made ready for the night.

Just inside the tent and laying on top of other items was a cut-up ski pole. According to witnesses, the top had been cut off. A notch had been carved into the remaining piece. There has been no explanation as to why one of the ski poles was cut up. There were no extra ski poles with the hikers and destroying one would mean someone be short one. Another important note about the ski pole is that it was bamboo. A very difficult wood to cut.

An ominous sign that didn't seem significant at first was that there were nine coats, eight jackets, several coat liners, a fur coat, two fur vests, four ski pants, a pair of cotton pants, four scarves, 13 pairs of gloves, seven boots (three pair plus one extra boot), eight pair of shoes, six pair of ski boots, three winter hats, a fur hat, and several pair of slippers. In other words, much of their protective outer clothing was found in the tent. Yet, the hikers were missing. If their coats and boots were in the tent, what were they wearing out in the cold winter weather?

In addition to the items found in the tent, it looked like the tent had been prepared for the evening. Blankets were out. Some were folded and some were spread out on top of the backpacks. All nine backpacks were in the tent. At night, the backpacks were used as a cushion and layer between the ground and the hikers. Blanket and jackets were spread out on the backpacks and used for addition cushion and warmth.

Neither the front nor that back of the tent was blocked. The front entrance was found halfway unbuttoned (these tents used buttons to secure the entrances).

Long cuts in the canvas were found on the downslope side of the tent (to the right of the entrance). They assumed the missing hikers would provide an explanation for this.

Inside, near the tent entrance, was an entertaining flyer made by the hikers before they disappeared. It was a newspaper spoof and contained funny news articles.

There is no picture of the flyer, but the contents were typed out and placed in the official file during the investigation.

Here's a copy of the contents:

EVENING Otorten" №1:

February 1, 1959 edition of the trade union body of the "Khibiny"

Editorial
We will greet XXI Congress with an increase in tourists!

PHILOSOPHICAL SEMINAR on Love and tourism takes place daily in the room tent (main building). Lectures are presented by Dr. Thibault (Nicholas) and candidate of Love Sciences Dubinina (Luda).

Armenian riddle
Can one stove and one blanket warm 9 tourists?

THE SCIENCE
In recent years, the scientific community is a lively debate about the existence of a snow man. According to recent reports, snow man lives in the Northern Urals, near Otorten mountain.

TECHNICAL NEWS.
Tourist sled.
Good while riding on the train, by car and on horseback. For cargo transportation on snow is not recommended.
For advice contact the chief constructor comrade Kolevatov (Alexander).

SPORT
A team of radio technicians comrade Doroshenko (Yuri) and comrade Kolmogorova (Zina) set a new world record in the competition for the assembly of the stove in just 1 hour 02 minutes 27.4 seconds.

The tent contents were removed and the tent was disassembled revealing that it had been originally been properly assembled for an overnight stay. The snow beneath had been leveled. On top of the snow was 3 pairs of skis for support. The tent canvas was on top of the skis. Backpacks were spread out over the tent floor on the inside. On top of the backpacks were blankets and padded jackets. On top of the blankets were the rest of the items. The tent itself was fastened to ski poles. This was normal tent set-up at the time.

After removing the tent contents and disassembling the tent, the backpacks were dumped out and those items were inspected for clues. There was nothing noteworthy in any of the backpacks. The backpacks and their contents were added to the tent pile. Then the whole pile was packed and loaded for transport to Ivdel for further investigation.

At the Ivdel airport a distraught Yuri Yudin was tasked with the difficult chore of identifying the objects and determining what item belonged to which hiker.

Meanwhile, the tent was hung in an office of the building used as a 'headquarters' for the search operation.

Purely by chance, a seamstress was called into that same office to repair some uniforms. She looked over the tent and closely examined the long cuts. She was confident that the cuts were made from the inside of the tent. This statement caused quite a stir and the tent was immediately sent off to Sverdlovsk for further investigation.

An examination of the tent was conducted in the Sverdlovsk Research Crime Lab. It was confirmed that the cuts were indeed made from the inside of the tent. It was also confirmed that the cuts were just that- cuts. They were not a small slice and then a long tear as if someone was trying to tear the canvas with their bare hands. In addition to the actual cuts, there was further evidence of knife scrapes inside the tent. As if several unsuccessful attempts had been made to cut the canvas but the cuts had not penetrated the heavy canvas.

Rather than provide answers, this study raised even more questions. Why were they cutting up the tent? It wasn't done in haste because there was time for many attempts- both successful and unsuccessful at cutting the canvas. If it was to exit the tent, why couldn't they use the front or back entrance? Neither was blocked by snow and in fact, the front entrance was partially open. The answers to these questions have never been found. The cuts in the tent remain one of the most baffling questions of this mystery. Why cut up the tent from the inside?

The tent.

The tent and all the items in a big pile.

The stove (circled) among the other tent items.

Left: A close-up picture of George emptying the stove earlier in the hike.
Right: A close-up picture of the stove laying on top of the pile of tent items.

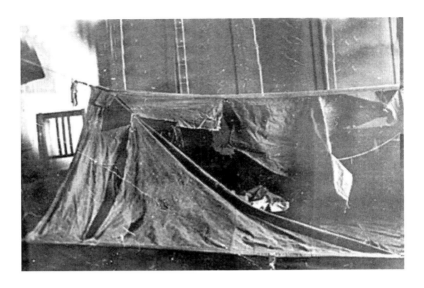

The tent as it hangs in the Search Operations Center
Top Picture: The left half of the tent with the entrance is on the left.
Bottom picture: The right half of the tent.

The tent as it hangs in the Search Operations Center
The entrance to the tent is on the left. The cut side was facing down slope.

Searchers looking for more clues. The tent and tent items are in the foreground.

A search group of three students and two Mansi trackers found the missing hiker's storage site. It was 1/3 of a mile southwest of the tent. The storage site was a hole dug in the snow and lined with cardboard and logs. Extra food and items were stashed inside and then covered up with logs and branches. A pair of upright skis marked the spot.

The contents were removed and evaluated for clues. It was apparent that the items hadn't been touched since they were initially placed. So, none of the Dyatlov group had returned to the storage site for provisions.

An inventory of the provisions included: condensed milk, canned meat, sugar, butter, cooked sausage, oatmeal, cocoa, coffee, tea, loin, milk powder, crackers, and noodles, a pair of boots, a pair of shoes, an ice pick, a hat, a checkered shirt, firewood, extra batteries, and George's mandolin.

The searchers removed the items and took them to their main camp. It's unknown whose pair of skis were 'marking' the storage site. The Dyatlov group did not have any spare skis with them.

The storage area. The skis marking the spot are in the middle of this picture.

Both of these pictures are of the searchers removing items from the storage area.

Chapter
4

The Bodies

"My mother was worried and I promised her this would be my last hike."

~Nicholas~

February 27th

Searchers found Yuri and George. Their bodies were in a clearing under a large cedar tree.

This area was a mile away and in a direct line of sight to the Dyatlov campsite.

However, to get to this area from the campsite, George and Yuri would have had to walk away from the tent, through the woods, and then climb a 15 ft. cliff.

The mystery deepened as searchers inspected the cedar area. The ground was trampled and looked like several people had gathered there, yet only George and Yuri's bodies remained.

A few feet from the bodies were the remnants of a campfire. However, several logs were only partially burned while others nearby were not burned at all.

Experienced outdoorsmen estimated that the fire had burned for 90 minutes at the most. They saw no reason for the fire to have gone out by itself, so that meant that it was extinguished on purpose.

Another oddity was that the campfire site was on the side of the cedar tree facing away from the Dyatlov campsite. In other words, it did not seem possible that the fire was used as a signal to the campsite, because the cedar tree would have blocked most of the light from the campfire.

Scattered around the area were several socks, a partially burned woman's handkerchief, a hat, a cuff torn off a sweater, and other pieces of torn clothing. Next to the cedar tree was an intact button-up shirt with 8 rubles in the pocket. Searchers also found a long strip of cloth that measured 30 inches long and 4 inches wide. This unusual item was not torn clothing. Later, Yuri Yudin and other witnesses would describe this item as similar to a military winding. These windings were strips of cloth that soldiers used to wind around their boots for insulation.

Small trees within the area, and up to 60 feet away, had their tree tops and branches cut off. This wood was green and unusable for a fire. The tree tops and branches were nowhere to be found.

The large cedar tree itself had branches broken and cut off of it up to a height of 14 ft. The side of the tree in a direct line-of-sight to the Dyatlov tent was almost clear of branches. Some of these branches were scattered on the ground, while others were caught and just hanging off the tree. Traces of blood were found on the tree.

George and Yuri were under the cedar tree and about three feet from the campfire.

George was on his back. He was wearing an undershirt, a button-up shirt, and torn pants. His right foot was barefoot. On his left foot was a burned, torn sock.

His left hand was bloody with skin torn off the back of it. Skin was also torn off his index finger and his lower left leg. Both of which were bloody also.

Next to him was Yuri. Yuri was on his stomach. He was dressed in a button-up shirt, shorts, and torn pants. Torn and burned socks were on both feet. Yuri's ear, nose, lips, and left hand were bloody.

Cedar branches were under both bodies.

The searchers noted descriptions of the bodies and took pictures before removing them from the area.

The Cedar tree with branches cut.

George and Yuri.
From left: Yuri laying on his stomach, George laying on his back. The tall cedar tree is on the far right.

George and Yuri. George is on his back. Yuri is on his stomach.

George and Yuri.
George is on his back. Yuri is on his stomach.

George and Yuri.
George is on his back. Yuri is on his stomach.

A partially burned log.

The cedar area after the bodies were removed.
To the left is the campfire area.
To the right is the tall cedar tree.
The bodies were in front and to the right of the tree.

The cedar area from the side that faces the tent.
The campfire area is directly behind the cedar tree.
Notice the broken branches and tree tops.
The shirt is on the right near a broken branch.

The cedar area from another angle.
The bodies were to the left of the tree.
The campfire area is to the right of the tree.
Notice the tree in the foreground is missing its top.

February 27th (Continued)

Searchers following the footprints discovered a flashlight 1/3 of a mile from the Dyatlov campsite. The flashlight was found in the 'on' position, but was not lit, so the batteries had died at some point.

Searchers followed the footprints down to the woods where all the prints disappeared. There they found Zina. Her body was ½ mile from the campsite and halfway between the campsite and the cedar area.

Zina was laying on her right side. She was wearing a pink hat, a flannel shirt, a coat, underwear, leggings, and ski pants. She had socks on both feet. There was blood on her back from a deep abrasion on her waist.

Then they found Igor.

His body was located halfway between Zina and the cedar area. He was ¾ of a mile away from the campsite.

Igor was laying on his back with his head near a tree trunk. His hands were pressed against his chest and his left arm was wrapped around a tree branch. He was wearing a sweater, a flannel button-up shirt, a coat, long underwear and ski pants. He had a cotton sock on one foot and a wool sock on the other.

March 5th

After nearly a week of searching between the Dyatlov campsite and the cedar area, the searchers found another body. It was Rustem.

Rustem is described as laying in a 'corpse bed'. Meaning he remained alive for a while after he fell in the snow. His body heat had melted some of the snow around him and then re-froze into a 'bed' of ice. None of the other bodies were found in a corpse bed. Meaning they were already dead when their bodies were placed in the snow or someone moved the bodies around or turned them over after they died.

Rustem was on his stomach with his right arm at his side and his left arm extended. He was wearing a t-shirt, a button-up shirt, a sweater, a jacket, long underwear, and ski pants. He had four socks on each foot and a boot on his right foot. His other boot was left behind in the tent. His passport, 310 rubles, a penknife, a pencil, a pen, a comb, and a box of matches were found in his pockets.

The cedar area, Igor, Rustem, and Zina were in a straight line to the campsite. Igor, Rustem, and Zina were all found under six inches of snow and they were all facing head first towards the campsite. It looked like they were going that direction when they died.

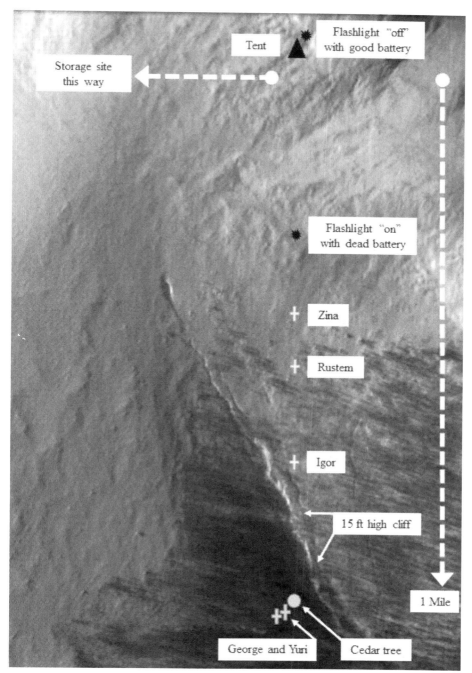

Tent

Flashlight "off" with good battery

Storage site this way

Flashlight "on" with dead battery

+ Zina

+ Rustem

+ Igor

15 ft high cliff

1 Mile

++ George and Yuri

Cedar tree

(Map copyright: Google Earth and Digital Globe)

Search teams searching between the campsite and the woods. The Dyatlov tent is in the foreground surrounded by skis.

Search teams searching between the campsite and the woods. At first the searchers used ski poles to check for bodies under the snow. Soon, the ski poles were replaced by 'avalanche probes', which were 10 ft long poles with barbs at the end.

Zina

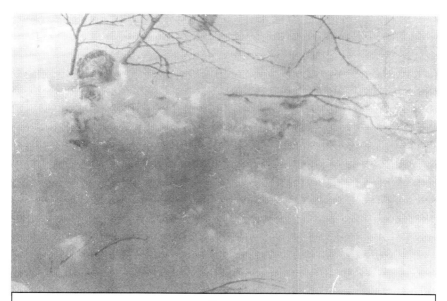

Igor

81

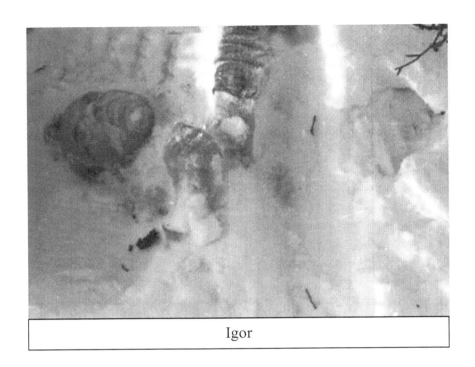

Igor

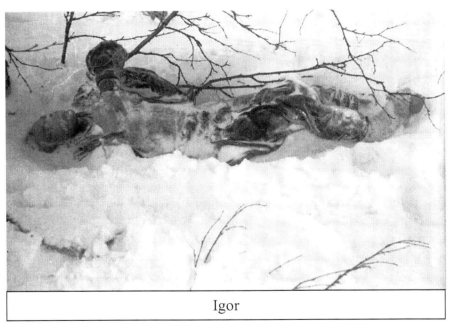

Igor

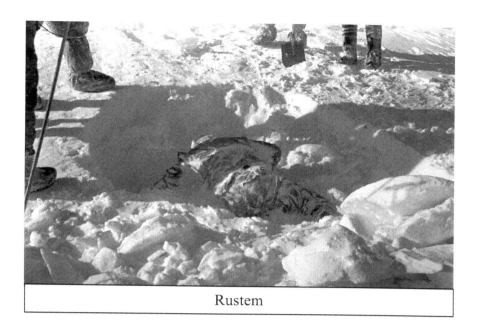

Rustem

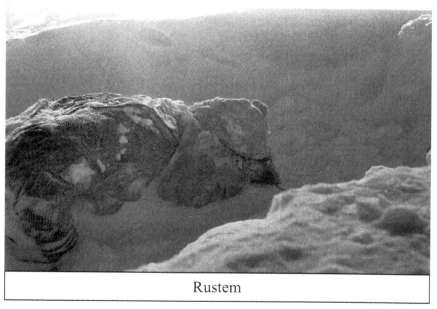

Rustem

May 5th

Throughout March and April, the search teams continued to look for the last four hikers. When the search first started back in February, the searchers used ski poles to check for bodies under the snow. Soon, the ski poles were replaced by 'avalanche probes', which were 10 ft. long poles with barbs at the end. In some places, the drifts were too deep for even the avalanche probe to reach all the way down.

As warmer weather thawed some of the snow, more of the Dyatlov group's items were revealed. A knife sheath, coins, and other small items were found at the campsite. The knife sheath belonged to Alexander. His knife had been found in the tent in February.

In the cedar area they found George's knife and Simon's compass. Also, in the cedar area, the melting snow revealed a trail of the broken tree tops, branches, and small broken trees that had previously been buried in the snow.

Following the broken branches trail, searchers found a pair of black cotton sweatpants. Upon closer inspection, it was discovered that one of the legs of the sweatpants had been cut off with a knife. The missing leg was nowhere to be found. Nearby, they found half of a woman's wool sweater. Like the sweatpants, the sweater had been cut in half and the other half was still missing. This sweater was Luda's.

It was logical to assume that these objects indicated that the bodies would be nearby. However, searchers could see that there were no bodies in the cedar area or nearby forest. So, they continued along the trail of broken branches to a field that was 200 ft. away from the cedar.

In that open field, the snow had drifted to well over 15 feet during the winter. It was slowly melting during the warmer spring weather, but the actual drift was still quite deep.

The avalanche probes were not long enough to probe to the very bottom of the drift, so a few areas were randomly selected to be dug out. In one of these areas, at a depth of about 9 ft., the searchers came to a makeshift type of flooring which is frequently called a snow den in the official documents.

This snow den was comprised of the missing tree tops and branches from the cedar area and measured 10 sq. ft. On each corner of the flooring was a piece of clothing. In one corner was the missing leg from the sweatpants, in another corner was the other half of Luda's sweater, a pair of pants was in another corner, and a shirt in the last corner.

Search teams using the 10 ft avalanche probes.

The trail of broken trees and branches.

Some of the clothes found between the Cedar and the snow den.

The field where the snow den was found.
The searchers used the avalanche probes, but the snow was too deep. The indent in the middle of the field is from a stream under the snow. The skis mark a spot to dig.

The edge of the field.

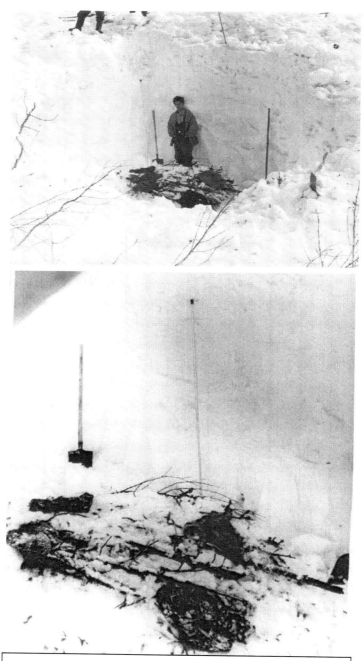

Both photos are of the flooring in the snow den

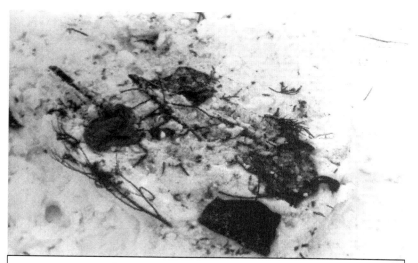

The snow den flooring up close.

The snow den flooring after it thawed. This is what it would have looked like when it was first built and before the snow flattened the branches.

Another large hole was dug 20 ft. from the snow den. This hole was directly above the stream that ran through the middle of the field. A search dog alerted to a body. There was no body in that hole, so another hole was dug along the stream. At a depth of 14 feet under the snow, they found the body of Luda.

The searchers carefully dug out the area around Luda and revealed the last three hikers- Simon, Alexander, and Nicholas.

All four were in a stream. Nicholas, Simon, and Alexander were laying right next to each other. Their upper bodies were in the stream while their legs were still encased in the snow on the bank.

Luda was face down in the stream close to Nicholas. But, rather than laying across the stream like the others, Luda was perpendicular to them on a small waterfall.

They were all so close together that it was impossible to get to the men without moving Luda's body first.

Luda was dressed in two sweaters and a button up shirt. She had on stockings and torn burnt pants which ended up being the pair that were cut off of George in the cedar area. She had a pair of torn, brown socks on her feet.

Nicholas had two hats on, one of which was tied tightly under his chin. He also wore a t-shirt, a torn sweater, a coat, sweat pants, and wool pants He had matching socks and boots on both feet. On his left wrist were two watches.

Simon was wearing two hats, a t-shirt, a long sleeved t-shirt, a sweater, a fleece jacket, a coat, long underwear, two pairs of ski pants, a pair of canvas pants, two socks on his left foot, one sock on his right, and a pair of boots.

His hands were badly frostbitten (as were all the hiker's), but he held a pencil in his right hand and a notebook in his left. He also had a camera around his neck. Earlier in the search, four cameras were found in the tent. They belonged to Igor, Rustem, George, and Simon.

This camera found with Simon was an unknown fifth camera. Since it was immersed in water with Simon, the film was ruined, but no one knows why Simon had two cameras.

Alexander was dressed in a t-shirt, a button up shirt, a sweater, a fleece jacket and a coat with a burn on one sleeve and a tear on the other. He was also wearing shorts, two pairs of pants, a pair of wool socks, with another sock on his right foot, and three additional socks on his left foot.

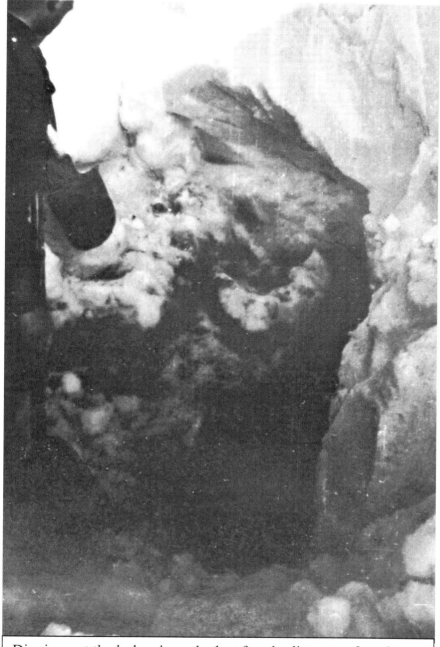

Digging out the hole where the last four bodies were found.

An exploratory hole dug in the ravine. The search dog alerted to a body nearby.

Searchers are standing in front of the hole where the last four bodies were found. The exploratory hole is behind them.

The field where the snow den and the last four bodies were discovered. The bodies were found in the hole in the center of this picture. The snow den hole is on the right.

A composite of the area where the snow den and the last four bodies were discovered. The bodies were found in the hole in the center of this picture. The snow den hole is on the right.

Luda was found first. Her body was so close to the others that they had to remove her before they could remove the others. The other three are in the stream above her head.

After removing Luda's body, they covered the hole with a tarp for the night. The other three are still in the stream and covered up by the snow.

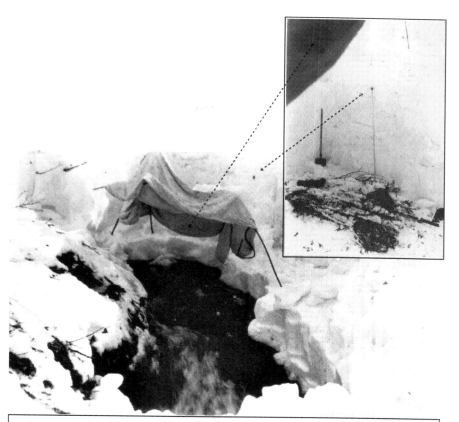

This is another picture of the tarp covered hole with a picture of the snow den inserted.

What this shows is how close the snow den was to the hole where the four bodies were found. The dot behind the tarp is the top of the avalanche probe left in the snow den (marked with arrows).

In the upper left of the snow den picture a dark spot. This is part of the tarp from the hole (also marked).

Removing Luda's body. Her body was removed the same day the bodies were found. Searchers had to remove her body before they could dig further to reach the other three. Nicholas, Simon, and Alexander's bodies were removed the next day.

From left: Alexander, Simon, and Nicholas- whose head is under water.

This collage shows the way all four were found. There was no picture taken of all four, because searchers had to remove Luda's body before they could dig further to reach the other three. Luda was on a small waterfall and face down in the water. Nicholas' head was under water facing towards Simon and Alexander.

These two pictures show searchers removing Nicholas' body

Searchers removing Alexander's body

Searchers removing Simon's body

Top: Luda on her stomach. The searchers raised her shirt to show the avalanche probe mark on her back.
Bottom: Nicholas

Top: Alexander.
Bottom: Simon. He has a camera around his neck, a pen in his right hand and a notebook in his left hand.

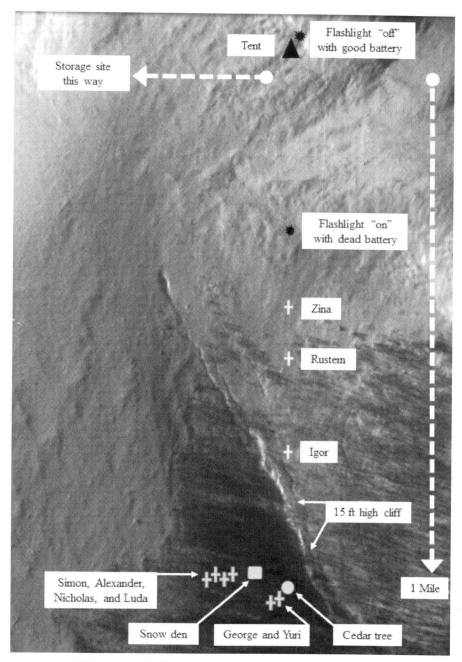

Storage site this way

Tent

Flashlight "off" with good battery

Flashlight "on" with dead battery

Zina

Rustem

Igor

15 ft high cliff

1 Mile

Simon, Alexander, Nicholas, and Luda

Snow den

George and Yuri

Cedar tree

(Map copyright: Google Earth and Digital Globe)

Chapter 5

The Autopsies

"We must remember, these were well-trained, strong, athletic people."

~Dr. Boris Reborn, Chief Medical Examiner~

From the beginning, the case was classified as a criminal investigation. There'd been no signs of an avalanche or other natural event. There were no downed trees and nothing in the tent to suggest anything but a peaceful evening. Even though the tent was sliced up on one side, items inside the tent such as crackers and a cup of cocoa were undisturbed.

From the searchers to the detectives, the consensus was that someone forced them out of the tent. Whether it was a stranger or one of the hikers themselves was unknown.

After the discovery of the first five (Zina, Igor, Rustem, George, and Yuri), their deaths seemed almost predictable. They'd died from the cold. However, upon the discovery of the last four (Luda, Simon, George, and Alexander), the case became more ominous. These four were piled together. Their being in running water was most unfortunate. That water washed away valuable evidence such as original body positions and possible writing in Simon's notebook.

All the known evidence made no sense. The tent was destroyed, hats, gloves, and coats were left abandoned. Some of these items were even found outside the tent. The campfire in the Cedar area only burned for 90 minutes before being extinguished. Lifelong forestry experts and hunters confirmed that there was no reason for the fire to extinguish on its own. The dry logs were only partially burnt. The Cedar area was protected from high winds and the fire should have kept burning. Rustem and Alexander even had matches in their pockets, so there was even a way to re-light the fire. But that didn't happen. The matches stayed unused.

Clothes were cut in half, abandoned, and discarded like a trail from the Cedar to the Snow Den. Branches had been cut off green trees, thus unusable for firewood, and those branches were discarded along the same trail.

Nine people were out in the freezing cold and yet the only one who used the discarded clothing was Luda. She was wearing George's pants which had been burnt (along with his leg) by the campfire. And her left shin and foot were wrapped in a torn grey jacket that probably came from either George or Yuri (both of whom were found in the Cedar area). It is noteworthy that Alexander had a burn on his coat. There is dispute whether it was his coat originally or if it came off Yuri or George.

As investigators searched for clues, the bodies were sent to the morgue. The autopsies for George, Yuri, Zina, and Igor were performed on March 4th. Rustem's was on March 8th, while the autopsies for Luda, Nicholas, Simon, and Alexander were performed on May 9th.

The coroner noted each item of clothing as it was removed from the body. Some items are noted as inside out. This was normal for cold weather winter hiking, as the hikers were wear their clothes in layers to sleep in. They'd often turn the clothes inside out to help with warmth and drying for the next day's wear.

Another thing to note about the clothing is that insoles, balaclavas, and hats were often placed in between the layers of clothing worn at night. The premise for this was the same as turning the clothes inside out. Those items would be warm and, hopefully, dry by the time they were needed for use the next day.

The autopsy notes on the following pages have been transcribed and translated from the official autopsies. Procedures for autopsies were very different in 1959 than they are nowadays. Back then, there was often no explanation offered for unusual injuries. For instance, Luda's tongue and the entire bottom of her mouth is missing. There is no explanation for this and no further description such as cuts from a knife or chew marks from an animal. Many injuries are merely noted. Some were measured and some were not. However, the clothes were described in detail. Many items of clothing were found unzipped or unbuttoned. Items found in pockets were also described.

Other items that were described were skin color and cadaver spots. The cadaver spots are discolored areas on the skin where the blood pooled after the person died. For example, if a person died on their back then their cadaver spots would be found on their back.

One more thing of note that is that the hiker's cameras and films were used to photograph their bodies when found and also while in the morgue. That would be unacceptable by today's standards, but back then it was a common practice. The hiker's skis, ski poles, and supplies were also re-utilized for the searchers. None of those items were kept for further processing nor were the cameras and films kept for further analyzing. Although the investigative technique back then was to dust for fingerprints, none of that was done with any of the items. They were all re-used during the investigation.

Following are the autopsies starting with Zina and ending with Luda. Each one contains a list of injuries, tests performed, a diagram of injuries, and photos of the hiker when found and in the morgue.

Zina (Zinaida Kolmogorov)

DOB: 12 JAN 1937 (22 years old)
Occupation: Student majoring in Radio Engineering

Body Located: In the forest between the tent and the Cedar area
Body Position: Laying on her right side
Cadaver Spots: Greyish-blueish lilac color on her back
Frostbite: On all fingers
Color Overall: Lilac red

Height: 5 ft. 3 inches
Hair: Brown, 12 inches long in two braids each woven with a red ribbon

Clothing
Red wool cap tied to chin with a bow
Blue wool cap underneath red cap
Blue wool hooded sweater with the left cuff torn off
Long sleeved red and green plaid button up shirt with one front pocket
     The pocket is unbuttoned and the left sleeve is torn at the cuff
Red sweater with blue stripes with a patch on each elbow
Balaclava (cold weather mask) in between button up shirt and sweater.
Blue long sleeve t-shirt
Black bra buttoned with two buttons
Black ski pants with fasteners at the side. All pockets are unbuttoned.
     The bottom right cuff has three small cuts.
Blue cotton pants. All pockets are unbuttoned.
     There is a comb and a shoelace in the back pocket.
     The front right pocket is turned inside out.
Natural colored fleece trousers
Black cotton tights
Natural colored cotton shorts with four buttons
Brown wool boots with fur insoles
Pair of blue and brown colored socks

External Injuries
Bloody abrasion and bruise above right eye
Bloody abrasions on both upper eyelids

Zina (Zinaida Kolmogorov)

External Injuries (Continued)
Bruise from right eyebrow to right cheek
Bloody abrasion from the bridge to the tip of her nose
Many small cuts, abrasions, dried blood, and bruises on
      both sides of her face
Scratches and blood under her nose
Both lips are bloody and swollen
Bloody abrasion 12 inches long and 2 inches wide on her right side waist
      from her stomach to her back
Abrasions and bloody knuckles on both hands
Bloody fingernail shaped cuts on the back of her right hand
Skin torn and bloody from outer part of middle finger on right hand

Internal Injuries: None noted.

Sexually Assaulted: No

Alcohol: None detected

Last meal: 6- 8 hours before death

Microscopic Examination: Not noted

Radiation Test: N/A not tested

Official Cause of Death: Freezing. Violent- an accident

Zina (Zinaida Kolmogorov)

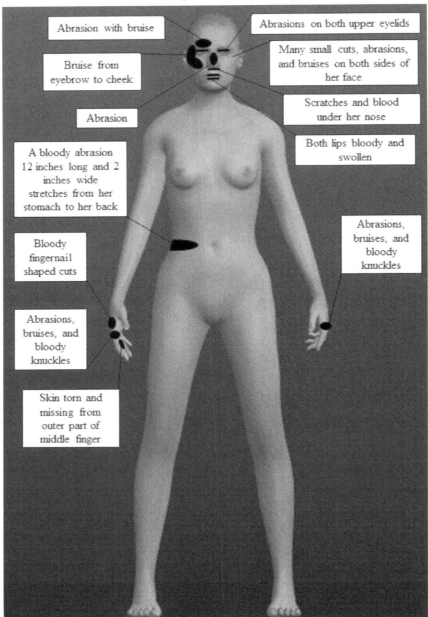

Abrasion with bruise

Abrasions on both upper eyelids

Bruise from eyebrow to cheek

Many small cuts, abrasions, and bruises on both sides of her face

Abrasion

Scratches and blood under her nose

A bloody abrasion 12 inches long and 2 inches wide stretches from her stomach to her back

Both lips bloody and swollen

Bloody fingernail shaped cuts

Abrasions, bruises, and bloody knuckles

Abrasions, bruises, and bloody knuckles

Skin torn and missing from outer part of middle finger

(Copyright: Launton Anderson)

Zina (Zinaida Kolmogorov)

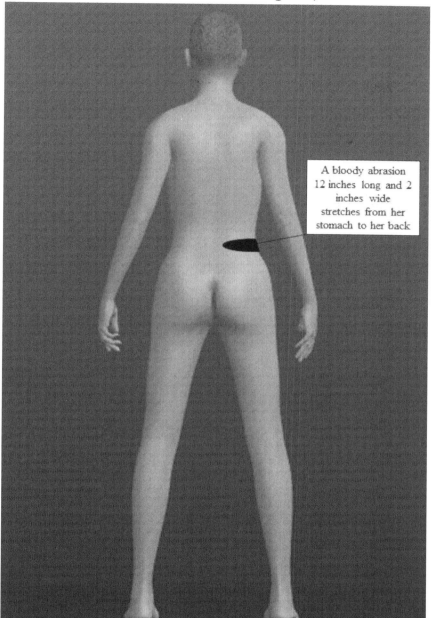

A bloody abrasion 12 inches long and 2 inches wide stretches from her stomach to her back

Zina (Zinaida Kolmogorov)

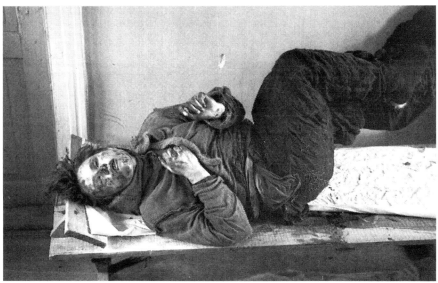

Zina (Zinaida Kolmogorov)

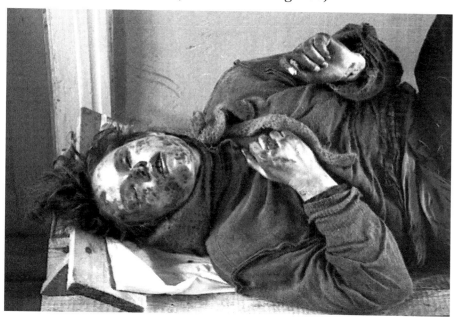

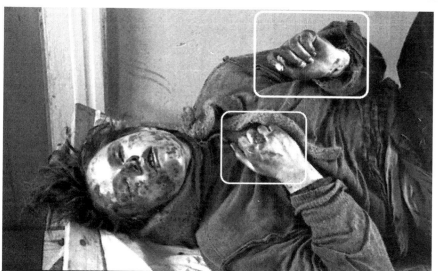

Zina in the morgue. Notice on her right hand the crescent-shaped injuries look like they're from fingernails. The bottom of her left wrist has abrasions that look like they're from restraints.

Rustem (Rustem Slobodin)

DOB: 11 JAN 1936 (23 years old)
Occupation: Engineer in Plant 817 Nuclear Facility

Body Located: In the forest between the tent and the Cedar area
Body Position: On his stomach
Cadaver Spots: Bluish red color on his back
Frostbite: On all fingers
Color Overall: Bluish red

Height: Not noted
Hair: Brown, curly, 3 inches long

Clothing:
A 'Star' brand watch stopped at 8:45
Black cotton sweater
Long sleeved, red and black plaid button up shirt. Left shirt pocket pinned
      closed with a safety pin. Inside the pocket is: Rustem's passport,
      310 Rubles, and a pen.
Two insoles in between the sweater and button up shirt
Natural color fleece sweatshirt
Blue long sleeve t-shirt
Black ski pants. In the pockets were: a box of matches containing
      43 matches, a pocketknife attached to a long string, a comb, a pen,
      a pencil, and a pair of socks
Blue satin sweatpants with a letter from his union dated Jan 20th, 1959 in
the back pocket.
Gray fleece pants
Blue underpants
Four pairs of socks (two white, one grey, and one brown)
A black boot on his right foot. His left boot was found in the tent.

External Injuries
Two bloody scratches on his forehead
An indented, bloody abrasion with bruising on his forehead
Bloody abrasion and bruising around his right eye
Bruising on and around both ears

External Injuries (Continued)
Bruise on his left temple
A large bloody abrasion surrounded by many smaller abrasions
        on his left cheek
Right side of his face is swollen with many bloody abrasions
Bloody abrasion on nose
Blood under his nose
Both lips are bruised and swollen
Bloody abrasions on the left side of his neck
Skin torn off and bloody in two places on his right forearm
Large bruise under his left forearm
Knuckles on both hands are bruised and bloody with many abrasions.
Bruises on his lower left leg near the ankle

Internal Injuries
Skull fracture on his left temple
Bleeding on his brain from the skull fracture
Blood around his right kidney
        This is often caused by a hit or kick to the area
Bloody foam in the lungs. This is pulmonary edema. It's often caused by
        strangulation or intense external pressure on the chest while alive.
Blood in the chest cavity. This is hemothorax. It's often caused
        by intense external pressure on the chest while alive.

Sexually Assaulted: No

Alcohol: None detected

Last meal: 6- 8 hours before death

Microscopic Examination: Not noted

Radiation Test: N/A not tested

Official Cause of Death: Freezing. Violent- an accident

Rustem (Rustem Slobodin)

Two bloody scratches side by side

Abrasion, bruising and skin indented (like from a restraint)

Abrasion above eye and eye is bruised and swollen

Abrasions all over his face

Right side of face swollen

Abrasion on nose and blood under his nose

Both lips are bruised and swollen

Skin is torn off and missing in these two spots

Abrasions, bruises, and bloody knuckles

Internal:
Blood around the right kidney. This is often caused by a hit or kick to the area

Internal:
Blood in the chest cavity and bloody foam in the lungs. These conditions are often caused by strangulation and/or intense external pressure on the chest

Internal:
There is a skull fracture on his left temple and bleeding on his brain

Bruising on and around both ears.

A large abrasion with many small abrasions and bruising

Many abrasions on the side of his neck

Bruise

Abrasions, bruises, and bloody knuckles

Abrasions and Bruises

(Copyright: Launton Anderson)

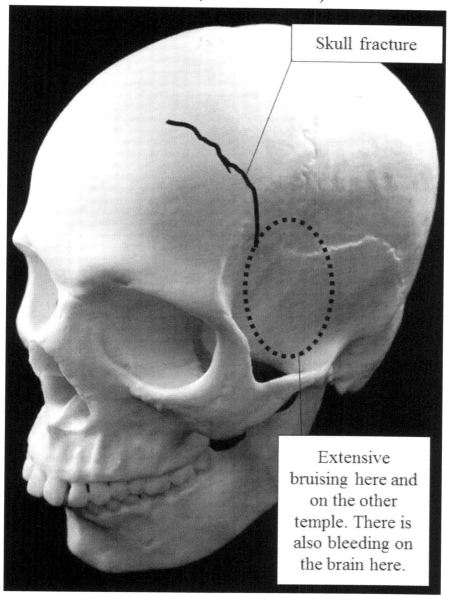

Skull fracture

Extensive bruising here and on the other temple. There is also bleeding on the brain here.

(Copyright: Launton Anderson)

Rustem (Rustem Slobodin)

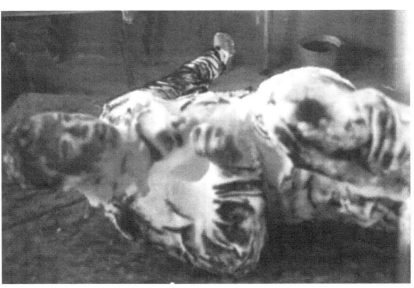

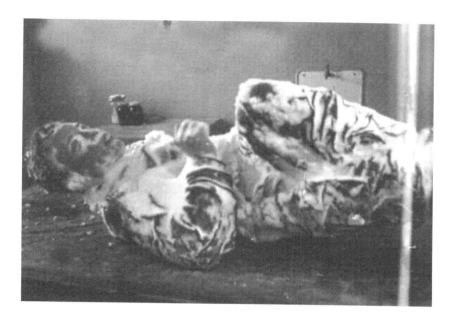

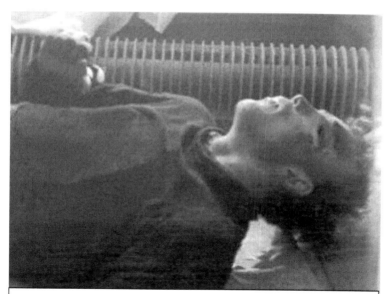

The bruise from his skull fracture extends up and down this side of his face.

Igor (Igor Dyatlov)

DOB: 13 JAN 1936 (23 years old)
Occupation: Student majoring in Radio Engineering

Body Located: In the forest between the tent and the Cedar area
Body Position: On his back
Cadaver Spots: Bluish red on his back
Frostbite: On all fingers
Color Overall: Bluish red

Height: 5 ft. 7 inches
Hair: Light brown, 2 ½ inches long

Clothing
A 'Star' brand watch stopped at 5:31
Blue fur lined sleeveless vest. Yuri Yudin gave this vest to Alexander
      before the hike
Blue sweater
Long sleeved, red and grey checkered button up shirt with 4 aspirin
      in a pocket
Blue sleeveless t shirt
Brown fleece ski pants
Bluish green sweatpants
Black satin pants
A white sock and a brown sock on his right foot
A brown sock on his left foot

External Injuries
Bloody abrasion on the left side of his forehead near his eyebrow
Bloody abrasions on both upper eyelids
Bloody abrasion on his nose with blood under his nose
Two 'U' shaped injuries with bleeding and bruises. There is one on each
      side of his face. Each of these also have small double abrasions
      around them. These injuries are similar to those found on
      George's leg and Yuri's arm.
Bruised and bloody lips
Several bloody abrasions on his right forearm
Bloody abrasion on the back of his left hand

Igor (Igor Dyatlov)

External injuries (Continued)
Bloody cut on his left palm across all of his fingers
Knuckles bruised and bloody on both hands
Bruises on both knees
A cut and bruise on the front of his right leg just above the ankle
Indented bloody abrasions with bruising on the front and back
       of both ankles.

Internal Injuries
Bloody foam in the lungs. This is pulmonary edema. It's often caused by
       strangulation or intense external pressure on the chest while alive.

Sexually Assaulted: No

Alcohol: None detected

Last meal: 6- 8 hours before death

Microscopic Examination: Not noted

Radiation Test: N/A not tested

Official Cause of Death: Freezing. Violent- an accident

Igor (Igor Dyatlov)

Abrasions on both upper eyelids

Abrasion

Strange 'U' shaped injuries with bleeding and bruising. Each 'U' includes small double abrasions. These injuries are on both sides of his face. They match similar injuries found on George's leg and Yuri's arm

Abrasion on his nose with scratches and blood under his nose

Many abrasions on his face

Bruised and Bloody lips

Several abrasions on his forearm

Abrasions, bruises, and bloody knuckles

Abrasion

Internal: Bloody foam in the lungs. This can be caused by strangulation and/or intense, external pressure on the chest

Abrasions, bruises, and bloody knuckles

Cut on the palm across four fingers

Bruise

Bruise

Cut and bruise

Abrasion, bleeding, and bruising with skin indented (such as from a restraint)

Abrasion, bleeding, and bruising with skin indented (such as from a restraint)

(Copyright: Launton Anderson)

120

Igor (Igor Dyatlov)

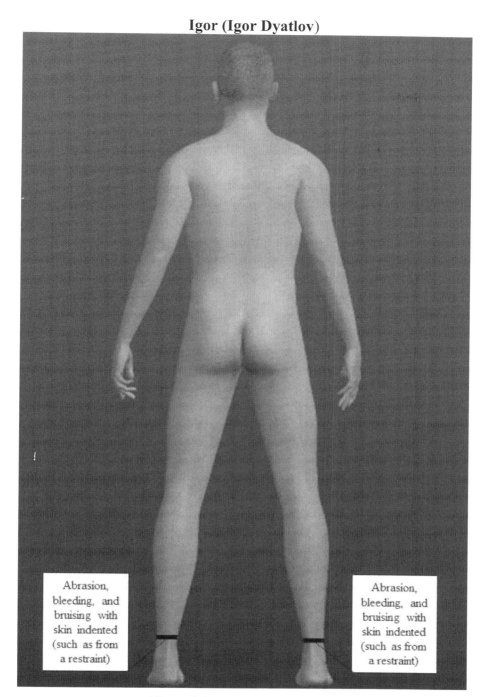

Abrasion, bleeding, and bruising with skin indented (such as from a restraint)

Abrasion, bleeding, and bruising with skin indented (such as from a restraint)

(Copyright: Launton Anderson)

Igor (Igor Dyatlov)

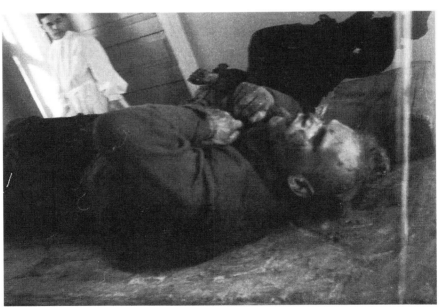

Igor (Igor Dyatlov)

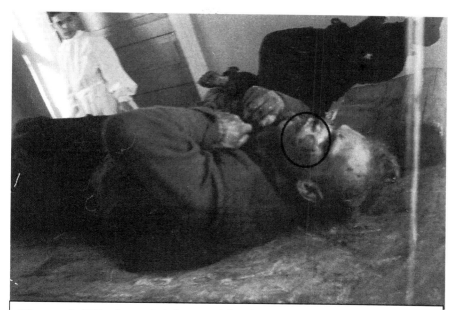

Unusual 'U' shaped injury with abrasions around it. There's another one on the other side of his face. The butt of a gun would cause this type of injury.

These injuries are similar to the ones found on George's leg and Yuri's arm.

George (Yuri (Georgy) Krivonischenko)

DOB: 7 Feb 1935 (24 years old)
Occupation: Engineer in Plant 817 Nuclear Facility. Recently promoted
to supervisor.

Body Located: In the Cedar area
Body Position: On his back
Cadaver Spots: Purple on his back
Frostbite: On both arms, both legs, all fingers and all toes
Color Overall: Described as 'cyanotic grey' which is defined as a bluish
grey usually associated with lack of oxygen

Height: 5 ft. 5 inches
Hair: Dark, curly hair 4 inches long

Clothing
Blue, red, and black plaid button up shirt. In the right pocket is a coil of
copper wire and a pink ribbon. A small secret inner pocket is sewn
into the inside of the left pocket. Both of these are empty.
White t shirt
White pants torn and burnt. The left pants leg is cut off up to the knee
Blue underpants
One torn and burned white sock on the left foot.

External Injuries
Bruise on his forehead
Two bloody abrasions on his left temple
Left eye swollen and bruised
Bloody abrasion on his nose
Damage to the tip of his nose (from an animal feeding on his body)
Both ears are bruised and swollen
Bruises on both cheeks
Both lips are swollen
A piece of skin torn off his finger was found in his mouth.
        The piece of skin was 1 inch long and 1/5 of an inch wide
Bloody abrasion near his right armpit
Two bloody abrasions on the right side of his stomach
Bloody cuts, bruises, and abrasions on both sides of his right hand

George (Yuri (Georgy) Krivonischenko)

External Injuries (Continued)

Skin is torn off the third finger of his right hand. This piece of skin
was found in his mouth.

Knuckles on both hands are bruised, cut, and bloody

Bloody abrasion across his left wrist

Bloody cut across his left palm

Back of left hand is swollen and bloody with skin torn off. This injury
measures 3 inches long by 1 inch wide

All fingers on his left hand are charred with 3rd degree burns

Two bloody abrasions and bruises on the upper half of his right leg

Two bloody abrasions and bruises on his right shin

Large bloody abrasion and bruise on left thigh stretches around to buttock

Two large bloody abrasion with bruises and several small bloody
abrasions with bruises between his left thigh and genitals

Three 'U' shaped injuries with bleeding and bruises on his upper left leg.
Each of these also have small double abrasions around them.
These injuries are similar to the injuries on Igor's face and
Yuri's arm

Bloody abrasion on his left knee

Bloody abrasion under his left knee

Three bloody abrasions on his left shin

Left shin swollen

Bruise on the left calf

Entire outer left leg, ankle and foot charred from a 3rd degree burn

Internal Injuries

Bleeding on his brain from his right temple to the back of his head
This is caused by a blow to the head

Bloody foam in the lungs. This is pulmonary edema. It's often caused by
strangulation or intense external pressure on the chest while alive.

(No sign of sexual assault. No alcohol in his system. Last meal was 6- 8
hours before death. No microscopic exam or radiation test perfomed.)

Official Cause of Death: Freezing. Violent- an accident

George (Yuri (Georgy) Krivonischenko)

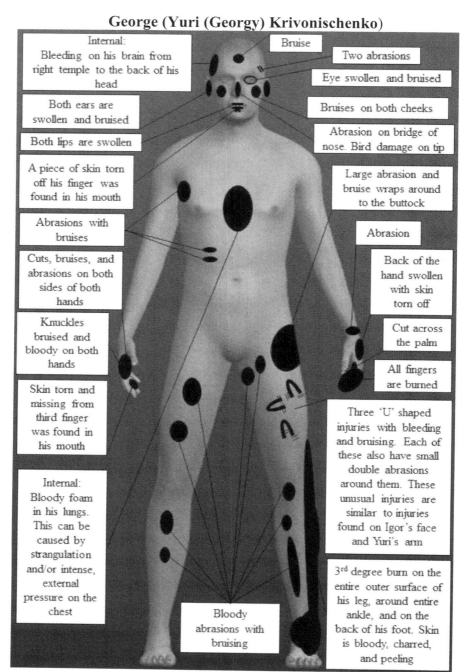

Internal: Bleeding on his brain from right temple to the back of his head

Bruise

Two abrasions

Eye swollen and bruised

Both ears are swollen and bruised

Bruises on both cheeks

Both lips are swollen

Abrasion on bridge of nose. Bird damage on tip

A piece of skin torn off his finger was found in his mouth

Large abrasion and bruise wraps around to the buttock

Abrasions with bruises

Abrasion

Cuts, bruises, and abrasions on both sides of both hands

Back of the hand swollen with skin torn off

Knuckles bruised and bloody on both hands

Cut across the palm

All fingers are burned

Skin torn and missing from third finger was found in his mouth

Three 'U' shaped injuries with bleeding and bruising. Each of these also have small double abrasions around them. These unusual injuries are similar to injuries found on Igor's face and Yuri's arm

Internal: Bloody foam in his lungs. This can be caused by strangulation and/or intense, external pressure on the chest

3rd degree burn on the entire outer surface of his leg, around entire ankle, and on the back of his foot. Skin is bloody, charred, and peeling

Bloody abrasions with bruising

(Copyright: Launton Anderson)

126

George (Yuri (Georgy) Krivonischenko)

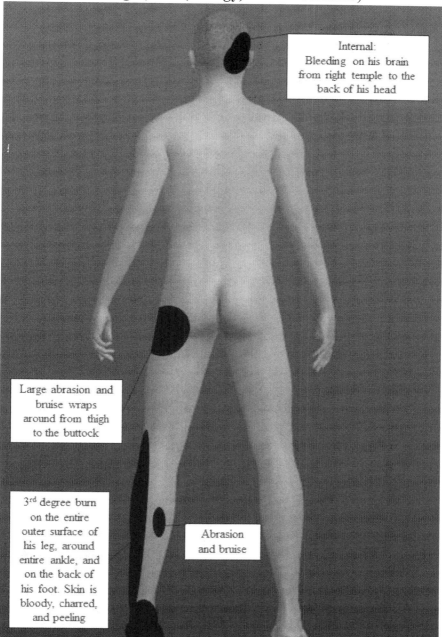

Internal:
Bleeding on his brain from right temple to the back of his head

Large abrasion and bruise wraps around from thigh to the buttock

3rd degree burn on the entire outer surface of his leg, around entire ankle, and on the back of his foot. Skin is bloody, charred, and peeling

Abrasion and bruise

(Copyright: Launton Anderson)

127

George (Yuri (Georgy) Krivonischenko)

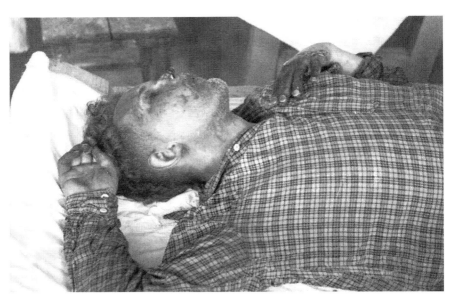

George (Yuri (Georgy) Krivonischenko)

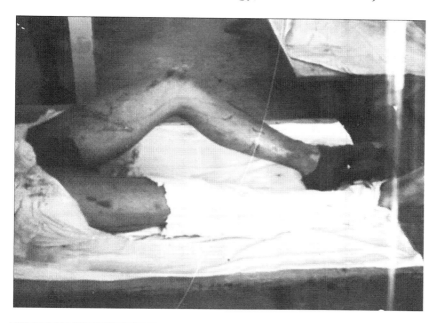

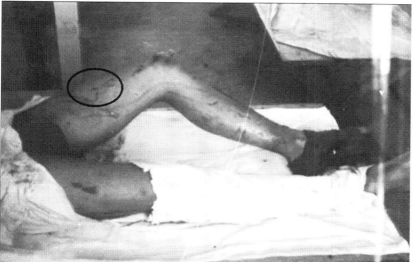

Circled are two of the strange 'U' shaped injuries. The butt of a gun would cause these type of injuries. These injuries are similar to the ones found on Igor's face and Yuri's arm.

Yuri (Yuri Doroshenko)

DOB: 29 JAN 1938 (21 years old)
Occupation: Student majoring in Radio Engineering

Body Located: In the Cedar area
Body Position: On his stomach
Cadaver Spots: Purple on his back
Frostbite: Both arms and legs and all fingers and toes
Color Overall: Brownish. Countours of his face are smooth and swollen

Height: 5 ft. 9 inches
Hair: Dark, 2 ½ inches long

Clothing
Short sleeved, blue and red checkered button up shirt
Sleeveless green t shirt
Blue satin swimming trunks
Blue knit pants torn down the middle and on both thighs
Left foot- Two brown socks with tears on the heels and one white sock
        with a burn on the toe area
Right foot- One white sock (a match to the white sock on the left foot)

External Injuries
Hair burned on right side of head and all the way to the back of the head
Both ears bruised and swollen
Dried blood under his nose
Upper lip cut, swollen, and bloody
Dried foamy discharge from mouth to cheek on right side of face
Three linear bloody abrasions on outer right shoulder
Two indented bloody abrasions with bruises on upper right chest directly
        above right armpit
Bloody abrasion on upper left chest
Four bloody abrasions in linear stripes on and below inner left elbow
'U' shaped injury with bleeding on inner left forearm (this is similar to
        the 'U' shaped injuries on Igor's face and George's leg)
Both hands swollen with many cuts and abrasions on the front and back
Right hand second finger is cut and bloody
Bruises on both shins

Yuri (Yuri Doroshenko)

Internal Injuries
Bloody foam in the lungs. This is pulmonary edema. It's often caused by strangulation or intense external pressure on the chest while alive.
A quart of blood in the chest cavity. This is hemothorax. It's often caused by intense external pressure on the chest.

Sexually Assaulted: No

Alcohol: None detected

Last meal: 6- 8 hours before death

Microscopic Examination: Not noted

Radiation Test: N/A not tested

Official Cause of Death: Freezing. Violent- an accident

Yuri (Yuri Doroshenko)

Hair burned

Both ears bruised and swollen

Dried foamy discharge from mouth to cheek

Dried Blood under nose

Two indented, bloody abrasions with bruises (such as from a restraint)

Upper lip cut, swollen, and bloody

Abrasion

Three linear abrasions

Five linear abrasions on and below the elbow

Many small abrasions on lower forearm

Unusual 'U' shaped injury with bleeding. This is similar to the injuries on Igor's face and George's leg

Hand swollen

Many abrasions on front and back of hand.

Bloody cut on second finger

Many abrasions on front and back of hand.

Internal: Bloody foam in his lungs. This can be caused by strangulation and/or intense external pressure on the chest. This is also the source of the dried foam on his face.

Hand swollen

Bruise

Bruise

(Copyright: Launton Anderson)

132

Yuri (Yuri Doroshenko)

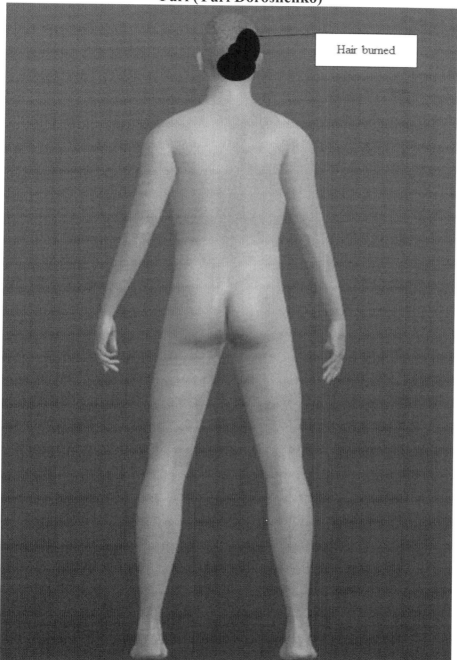

Hair burned

(Copyright: Launton Anderson)

133

Yuri (Yuri Doroshenko)

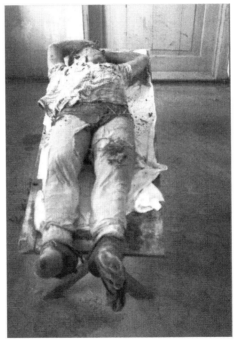

Yuri (Yuri Doroshenko)

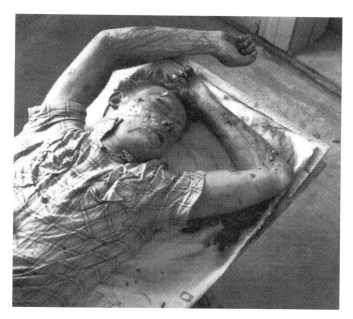

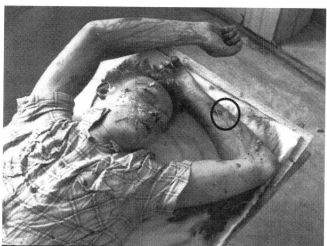

Circled is the unusual 'U' shaped injury similar to the ones found on Igor's face and George's leg. The butt of a gun would cause this type of injury.

Alexander (Alexander Kolevatov)

DOB: 16 NOV 1934 (24 years old)
Occupation: Student majoring in Physics and Technology. Formerly worked in Moscow for three years as a senior lab assistant researching nuclear material. Prior to that, he obtained a degree in Metallurgy.

Body Location: Near the snow den
Body Position: On his right side in running water. Body was originally deposited on snow and ended up in the stream below as the snow melted. Body was immersed in running water for approximately 2 weeks.
Cadaver Spots: Crimson on his back and right side
Frostbite: Not noted
Color Overall: Greenish grey with a purplish hue

Height: 5 ft. 7 inches
Hair: Brown, 4 inches long

Clothing

Black ski coat unzipped and all the buttons unbuttoned. Upper left sleeve has a large burn 10 inches long and 5 inches wide. The right elbow has a tear 3 inches long.

Brown fleece sweater

Grey sweater

Long sleeved blue, red, and black checkered button up shirt with two front pockets. In the right pocket is a small key on a safety pin. In the left pocket is a small piece of paper that was once part of the packaging for 'codeine with soda'.

Grey fleece shirt

Canvas overalls with a box of matches in the right pocket

Blue ski pants with a handkerchief in one of the pockets

Grey fleece pants

Dark blue underpants

A white sock and three brown socks are on his left foot. Also, around his left foot was a loose gauze bandage that had slipped down from his knee. This gauze was from a possible knee injury that may have occurred earlier in the hike.

A white sock was on his left foot. It matched the white sock on the other foot.

Alexander (Alexander Kolevatov)

External Injuries

Skin missing from around the eyes and brow area. The bone is exposed.

A large amount of bruising on the right side of his face from his ear to his jaw and wrapping around to the back of his head and the base of his neck

Open wound with exposed bone at the base of his skull on the back of his head

Right cheek has an open wound with exposed bone

Broken nose

Nostrils pinched closed (like with a clothespin)

Bruise on his left knee (possibly from an earlier injury since there was gauze found also)

Internal Injuries

Blood in the chest cavity- Pulmonary edema

Bloody foam in his lungs- Hemothorax

Both of the above conditions are often caused by strangulation and/or intense, external pressure on the chest while alive.

Crushed thyroid cartilage. This is the 'Adam's apple' area of the neck. This area is often injured during strangling.

Sexually Assaulted: No

Alcohol: Not Noted

Last Meal: Not noted

Microscopic Examination: No hemorrhages (prior bleeding) in wounds.

Radiation Test: The waistband of his grey sweater and the bottom part of his blue ski pants were tested. Beta particles double the normal range were detected on both. These numbers dropped by half after being immersed in running water for 3 hours. Note: Alexander was found in running water and estimated to have been in the water for up to 2 weeks. There has been no value assigned to how high the beta particle count was originally.

Official Cause of Death: Freezing. Violent- an accident

Alexander (Alexander Kolevatov)

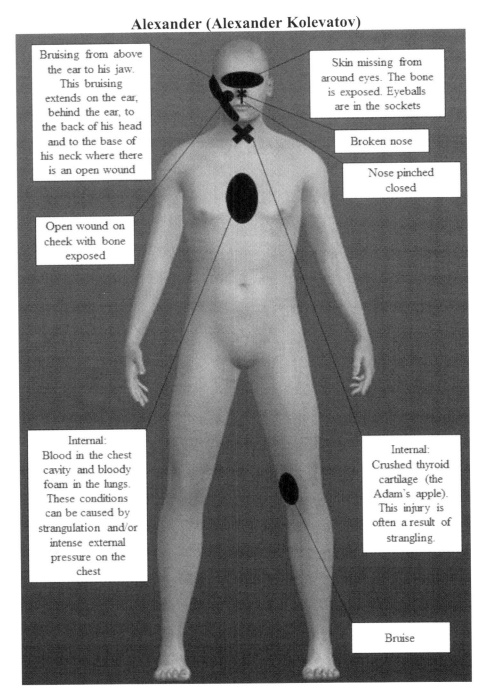

Bruising from above the ear to his jaw. This bruising extends on the ear, behind the ear, to the back of his head and to the base of his neck where there is an open wound

Skin missing from around eyes. The bone is exposed. Eyeballs are in the sockets

Broken nose

Nose pinched closed

Open wound on cheek with bone exposed

Internal:
Blood in the chest cavity and bloody foam in the lungs. These conditions can be caused by strangulation and/or intense external pressure on the chest

Internal:
Crushed thyroid cartilage (the Adam's apple). This injury is often a result of strangling.

Bruise

(Copyright: Launton Anderson)

138

Alexander (Alexander Kolevatov)

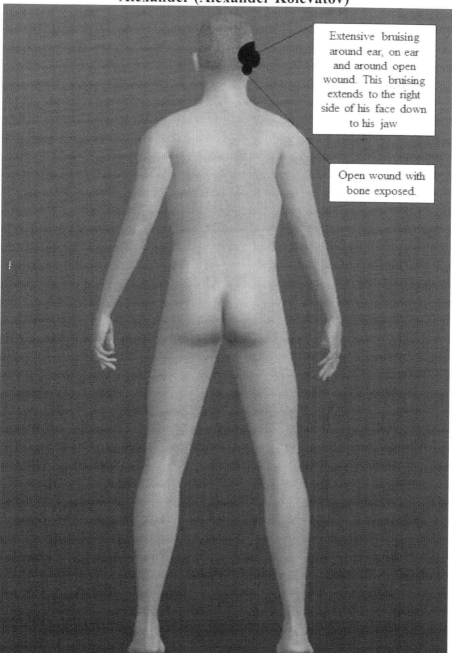

Extensive bruising around ear, on ear and around open wound. This bruising extends to the right side of his face down to his jaw

Open wound with bone exposed.

(Copyright: Launton Anderson)

Alexander (Alexander Kolevatov)

Alexander (Alexander Kolevatov)

Note: There are no pictures of Alexander in the morgue

Nicholas (Nikolay Thibault-Brignoles)

DOB: 8 JUL 1935 (24 years old)
Occupation: Civil Engineering Foreman

Body Location: Near the snow den
Body Position: On his back in running water. Body was originally deposited on snow and ended up in the stream below as the snow melted. Body was immersed in running water for approximately 2 weeks.
Cadaver Spots: Lilac greenish color located on his back
Frostbite: Not noted
Overall Color: Greenish

Height: 5 ft. 7 inches
Hair: Black hair, 4 inches long

Clothing
A sports watch stopped at 8:14
A 'Victory' brand watch stopped at 8:39
Green wool cap with three round holes in front. The cap is tied tightly
    under his chin
Khaki canvas fur hat tied tightly under his chin
Green sheepskin fur lined coat. In the left pocket is a pair of wool grey
    Gloves. In the right pocket are coins adding up to 32 Kopeks,
    two folded pieces of paper, and a comb.
Grey wool sweater inside out
Blue t shirt with a hole at the bottom
Wool winter pants with a leather belt and a metal belt buckle. In one
    pocket was a white button and a metal chain from a wall clock.
Blue sweatpants
Black underpants
Almost new grey felt boots
A pair of white wool hand-knitted socks
A pair of crumpled brown socks used as insoles

External Injuries
Bruise in front of and under the right shoulder- This is an unusual injury
    that's often caused by the arm being forcefully twisted up behind
    the back. Such as if he were being restrained by someone.

External Injuries (Continued)
Open wound on upper left side of mouth exposing the teeth and gums

Internal Injuries
Skull fracture- Right temporal area bone fracture 3 ½ inch by 3 inch
    by 1 inch deep. This fracture then extends 7 inches to the base of
    the skull. The bone is pushed into the cranial cavity with bone
    splinters throughout.
Extensive bleeding on the brain due to skull fracture and bone fragments
Bloody foam in the lungs. This is pulmonary edema. It's often caused by
    strangulation or intense external pressure on the chest while alive.
Dry heart- The blood flow to the heart was abruptly cut off causing
    damage to the heart itself. A dry heart is the sudden deprivation
    of circulating blood.

Sexually Assaulted: No

Alcohol: Not noted

Last Meal: Not noted

Microscopic Examination: The exposed wound was examined.
Hemorrhages (prior bleeding) were found in this area meaning the injury
occurred while he was alive.

Radiation Test: The bottom part of his wool winter pants were tested.
All numbers were within normal range. However, the beta particle
numbers drop to half after being immersed in running water for 3 hours.
Nicholas' body was found in running water and had been immersed for
approximately two weeks. There has been no value assigned to how high
the beta particle count was originally

Official Cause of Death: Crushed fracture in the region of the crest and
base of the skull with a profuse hemorrhage to the brain membranes and
on the brain. Violent.

Nicholas (Nikolay Thibault-Brignoles)

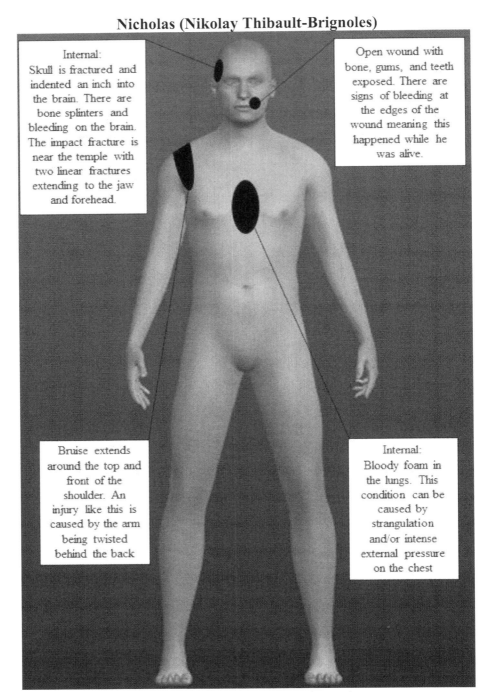

Internal: Skull is fractured and indented an inch into the brain. There are bone splinters and bleeding on the brain. The impact fracture is near the temple with two linear fractures extending to the jaw and forehead.

Open wound with bone, gums, and teeth exposed. There are signs of bleeding at the edges of the wound meaning this happened while he was alive.

Bruise extends around the top and front of the shoulder. An injury like this is caused by the arm being twisted behind the back

Internal: Bloody foam in the lungs. This condition can be caused by strangulation and/or intense external pressure on the chest

(Copyright: Launton Anderson)

144

Nicholas (Nikolay Thibault-Brignoles)

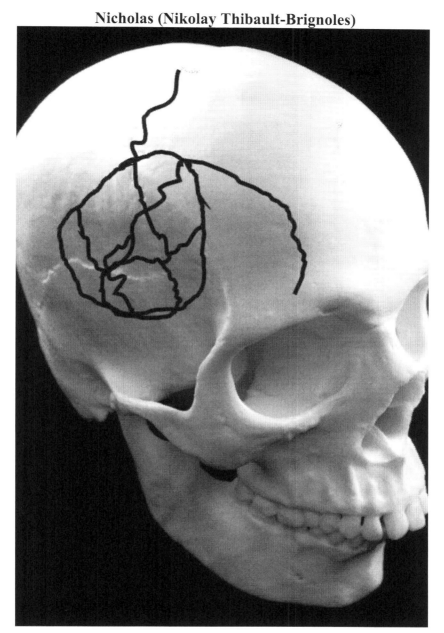

(Copyright: Launton Anderson)

Nicholas (Nikolay Thibault-Brignoles)

Nicholas (Nikolay Thibault-Brignoles)

Note: There are no pictures of Nicholas in the morgue

Simon (Semyon (Alexander) Zolotarev)

DOB: 2 FEB 1921 (37 years old)
Occupation: Sports instructor, former soldier in WW2

Body Location: Near the snow den
Body Position: On his right side in running water. Body was originally deposited on snow and ended up in the stream below as the snow melted. Body was immersed in running water for approximately 2 weeks.
Cadaver Spots: Lilac colored on his back and on the right side of his chest
Frostbite: Not noted
Overall Color: Greenish Grey

Height: 5 ft. 6 inches
Hair: Black, 4 inches long
Tattoos: Back of right hand near thumb: 'Gena'
Back of right forearm: A picture of a beet along with the letters '+C'
Back of left forearm: The letters 'G.S.DAERMMUAZUAYA',
    a five pointed star with the letter 'C', the letters 'G+S+P=D'
    and '1921'

Clothing
A wrist compass on the left wrist
A black cap trimmed with black fur with earflaps
A red wool cap with three light strips
Brown and blue checkered scarf
Green cold weather mask with elastic straps
Black sheepskin fur lined vest
Brown jacket
Black cotton sweater
Blue long sleeved t shirt
Red sleeveless t shirt
Khaki canvas overalls. In the right pocket is an onion and 18 Kopeks.
    In the inner front pocket is a comb and a ball of yarn. A rolled up
    newspaper is in the back pocket.
Blue flannel pants.
Blue flannel pants with suspenders. In one of the pocket is 44 Kopeks,
    and pieces of newspaper.

148

Simon (Semyon (Alexander) Zolotarev)

Clothing (Continued)
Grey cotton shorts
Blue underpants
Thick black quilted boots
A brown sock on the right foot
A wool sock and a cotton sock on the left foot

External Injuries
Wound with exposed bone on the left forehead area
Wound with exposed bone on the left eyebrow area
Exposed bone and skin missing from around both eyes
Both eyeballs are missing. The orbs are completely gone.
Both eyebrows are missing
Left half of mustache is missing
Nose pinched closed (an example would be like with a clothespin)

Internal Injuries
Five broken ribs on the right ribcage. Rib numbers 2, 3, 4, 5, and 6 are
each broken in two places.
Bloody foam in the lungs. This is pulmonary edema. It's often caused by
strangulation or intense external pressure on the chest while alive.
A quart of blood in the chest cavity. This is hemothorax. It's often caused
by intense external pressure on the chest while alive.

Sexually Assaulted: No

Alcohol: Not noted

Last Meal: Not noted

Microscopic: The exposed wounds and his ribs were examined.
Hemorrhages (prior bleeding) were found in the open wounds (the eye
sockets) and ribs meaning that these injuries occurred while he was alive.

Simon (Semyon (Alexander) Zolotarev)

Radiation Test: His black sheepskin fur lined vest was tested.
All numbers were within normal range. However, beta particle numbers drop to half after being immersed in running water for three hours. Simon's body was found in running water and had been immersed for approximately two weeks. There has been no value assigned to how high the beta particle count was originally.

Official Cause of Death: Multiple rib fractures and internal bleeding into the pleural cavity. Violent

Here's a graphic explaining Simon's tattoos:

Back of right hand near thumb: 'Gena'

Back of right forearm: (a picture of a beet) along with '+C'

Back of left forearm: The letters 'G.S.DAERMMUAZUAYA'
(a five pointed star) with the letter 'C'
the letters 'G+S+P=D'
and '1921'

Simon's tattoo in the original Russian letters

Back of right hand near thumb: Гена

Back of right forearm: (a picture of a beet) along with '+C'

Back of left forearm: Г.С. ДАЕРММУАЗУАЯ

(a five pointed star) with the letter 'C'

Г+С+П=Д

and '1921'

(Copyright Launton Anderson)

Simon (Semyon (Alexander) Zolotarev)

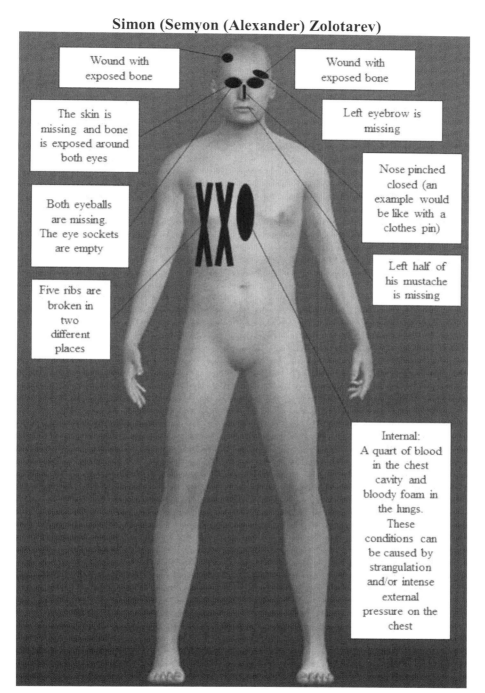

(Copyright: Launton Anderson)

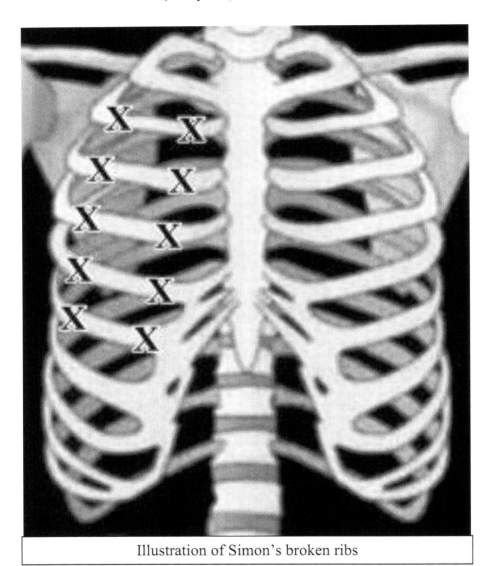

Illustration of Simon's broken ribs

(Copyright Launton Anderson)

Simon (Semyon (Alexander) Zolotarev)

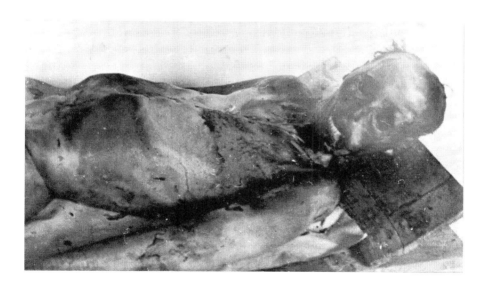

Simon (Semyon (Alexander) Zolotarev)

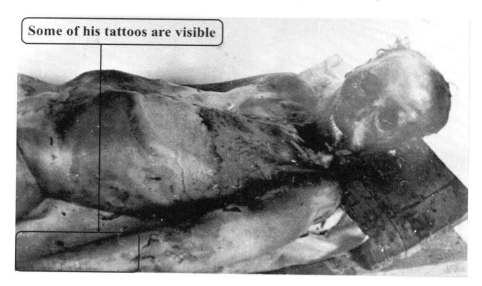

Some of his tattoos are visible

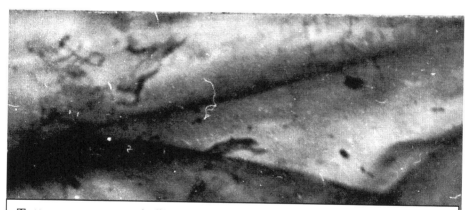

Tattoo area cropped, flipped, and enlarged.

Simon (Semyon (Alexander) Zolotarev)

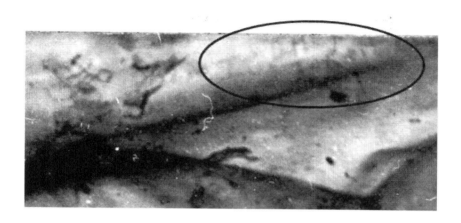

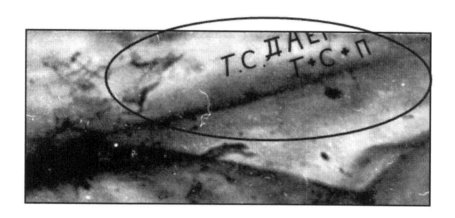

Luda (Lyudmila Dubinina)

DOB: 12 May 1938 (20 years old)
Occupation: Student majoring in Engineering and Economics

Located: Near the snow den
Body Position: On stomach in running water. Body was originally deposited on snow and ended up in the stream below as the snow melted. Body was immersed in running water for approximately 2 weeks.
Cadaver Spots: Cyanotic grey on her back
Frostbite: None noted but hands and feet were described as 'pale grey with purple hues'
Color Overall: Yellowish brown

Height: 5 ft. 4 inches
Hair: Blond hair, 20 inches long, braided in one braid woven with blue ribbon

Clothing:
Knitted hat
Grey-brown wool sweater
Beige wool sweater
Plaid button up shirt
Yellow short sleeved t shirt
White bra buttoned with three buttons
Dark cotton pants with an elastic belt. The pants are ragged, torn, and have burns. These were probably removed from either Yuri or George's body after they died.
Black cotton tights with a tear in the crotch and around the waistband
Shorts fastened with a belt and buttons
The shin and foot of her left leg is wrapped in a torn grey jacket. This was probably removed from either Yuri or George's body after they died.
Stockings on both legs held by elastic bands. The left stocking had fallen around her ankle
A matching pair of grey socks
A matching pair of torn blue socks
A tattered brown sock on the left foot

Luda (Lyudmila Dubinina)

External Injuries
Wound with bone exposed on top left side of her head
Nose pinched closed (an example would be like with a clothespin)
Skin missing from area around the eyes to include the brow,
      nose, and left cheek. Bone is exposed in this area.
Both eyeballs are missing. The orbs are completely gone.
Skin missing from upper lip. Jawbone is exposed
Tongue is missing
Bruise on upper part of left leg

Internal Injuries
Tongue is missing
Diaphragm of mouth missing. This is called the mylohyoid muscle. It
      connects the bottom of the mouth to the hyoid bone in the neck.
Hyoid bone is mobile. The hyoid bone is a delicate bone at the top of the
      neck just below the jawline. A mobile or broken hyoid bone is a
      sign of strangulation.
Hyoid bone exposed. This is because the mylohyoid muscle and tongue
      are missing. The autopsy report offers no further explanation of
      the area such as if the edges around the hyoid were ragged or
      clean cut.
Crushed thyroid cartilage. This is the 'Adam's apple' area of the neck.
      This area is often injured during strangling.
Bloody foam in the lungs. This is pulmonary edema. It's often caused by
      strangulation or intense external pressure on the chest while alive.
1 ½ quarts of blood in the chest cavity. This is hemothorax. It's often
      caused by intense external pressure on the chest while alive.
Four broken ribs on the right side of her ribcage. Rib numbers 2, 3, 4,
      and 5 are each broken in two places.
Six broken ribs on the left side of her ribcage. Rib numbers 2, 3, 4, 5, 6,
      and 7 are broken
Blood on sternum. The sternum is the middle of the ribcage
Fractured ribs caused hemorrhaging
Her heart was pierced by one of the broken ribs causing a 1 inch hole in
the right ventricle

Luda (Lyudmila Dubinina)

Sexually Assaulted: No

Alcohol: Not noted

Last Meal: Not noted

Microscopic Examination: The exposed wounds, hyoid bone, heart, and ribs were examined. There were no hemorrhages (prior bleeding) in the hyoid bone. However, there were hemorrhages in the open wounds (the eye sockets), heart, and ribs meaning that these injuries occurred while she was alive.

Radiation Test: The jacket that was wrapped around her leg, the torn black pants, and both the grey and the brown sweaters were tested.

Luda was wearing the brown sweater on top of the grey sweater. It's unknown if Luda was originally wearing either sweater or if she obtained one or both of them from someone who had already died. It is unknown who originally owned the sweaters.

The brown sweater was positive for beta particles in excess of double the normal range. This number dropped in half after the sweater was immersed in running water for 3 hours. Luda's body was found in running water and had been immersed for approximately 2 weeks. There has been no value assigned to how high the beta particle count originally.

Official Cause of Death: Extensive hemorrhage, multiple bilateral fracture of the ribs pierced the heart, and internal bleeding into the thoracic cavity. Violent.

Luda (Lyudmila Dubinina)

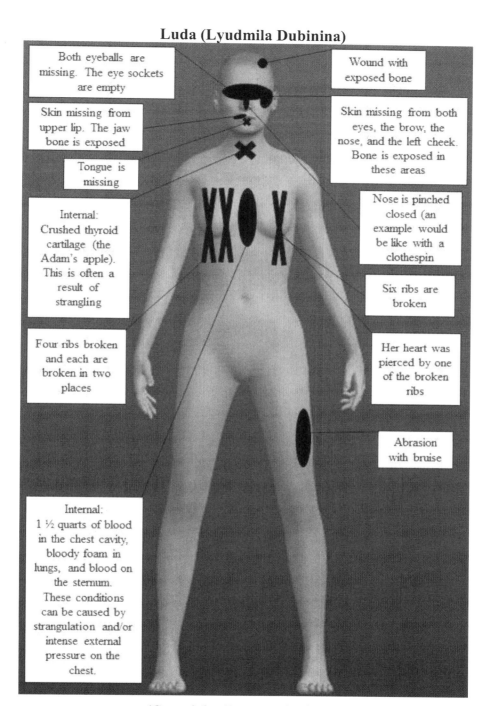

Both eyeballs are missing. The eye sockets are empty

Wound with exposed bone

Skin missing from upper lip. The jaw bone is exposed

Skin missing from both eyes, the brow, the nose, and the left cheek. Bone is exposed in these areas

Tongue is missing

Nose is pinched closed (an example would be like with a clothespin

Internal: Crushed thyroid cartilage (the Adam's apple). This is often a result of strangling

Six ribs are broken

Four ribs broken and each are broken in two places

Her heart was pierced by one of the broken ribs

Abrasion with bruise

Internal: 1 ½ quarts of blood in the chest cavity, bloody foam in lungs, and blood on the sternum. These conditions can be caused by strangulation and/or intense external pressure on the chest.

(Copyright: Launton Anderson)

159

Luda (Lyudmila Dubinina)

Luda rib injuries

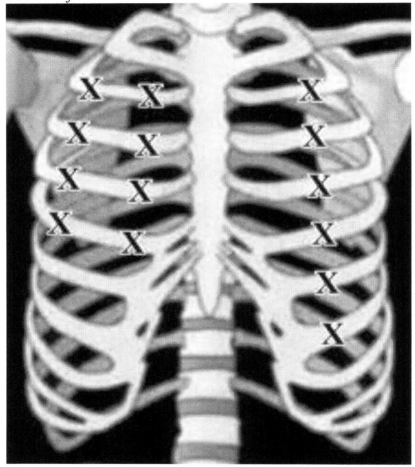

(Copyright: Launton Anderson)

Luda (Lyudmila Dubinina)

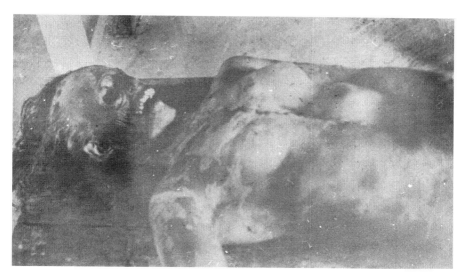

As we look over their injuries, we can see that they were numerous and several are unusual and unexplained. In particular are the 'U' shaped injuries on Igor, George, and Yuri. The coroner noted the injuries, but did not offer any explanation. They do resemble an intentional injury. The butt of a gun, the edge of a ski pole, or some other unknown instrument could have caused these injuries.

Some injuries were found only on one person. George, for instance, was the only one with burns. However, his burns were horrific. There were 3rd degree burns up and down his left leg and on his entire left hand. He was found in the Cedar area where we know there was a campfire, but that type of burn is not quick. 3rd degree burns means the fire burnt all the way through the skin and down to the muscle leaving the area charred. This is indicative of the fire being intentionally used to harm him rather than an accident. If it was accidental, he would have thrown himself in the snow to extinguish the flames. This type of burn would have taken a long time with sustained contact for it to char and burn through the skin and down to the muscle.

In addition to the major injuries, we have the microscopic reports that show that the open wounds on Nicholas, and the missing eyes on Luda and Simon were inflicted while they were alive. These wounds had hemorrhaging meaning they bled while the person was alive. A wound inflicted on a dead body would result in a negative microscopic reports meaning there was no bleeding from the injury because the person was already deceased. So, someone cut out their eyes while they were alive.

In addition to the microscopic reports- and the horrific findings that their eyes were removed while alive- we have the radiation report. In it, the officials tested the clothes, bodies, and internal organs of Luda, Simon, George, and Alexander. Not only did they test these four hikers, but they also tested a control subject who was from the local area and had died in an accident. The control subject provided the normal ranges of radiation for the officials to compare to the tested objects.

Everything was within normal limits for radiation except for Luda's outer sweater and the bottom of Alexander's pants and his sweater waistband. The radiation on these objects were more than double the normal limits. In addition, after these objects were immersed in running water for three hours, the radiation numbers dropped to half. Since Luda and Alexander were found in running water, we have no idea what the original radiation numbers are.

We also have no idea if radiation was found on any other objects such as the tent, other clothing, or even the other five hikers- Igor, Zina,

162

Rustem, George, and Yuri. If there was radiation testing on anything else, that report has never been released.

Like many other things in this mystery, the radiation is another incomplete part of the puzzle. We know some things tested positive for radiation, but not all things were tested. And we don't know how those items became radioactive or where the radiation came from.

Another item of interest from the autopsies is what was or wasn't in the hiker's pockets. Some pockets were unbuttoned and empty, while other's had small items such as a key or coins.

The tent area had many small objects such as coins and combs that would belong in their pockets. This paints the picture of someone ordering the hikers to remove the items from their pockets once they outside the tent. This piece fits with the fact that clothes and a coat were found outside the tent also. It also fits with Rustem having one shoe on and one shoe off. If they were abruptly ordered from the tent, then the intruder did not let them finish dressing and ordered them to drop anything in their hands.

The tent area and the area around the bodies was not collected nor tested for blood or any other evidence. In fact, the official criminal investigation was shut down in June 1959- a month after the last autopsies were completed.

Not only was the official investigation closed, but entire region where the tragedy occurred was closed for hundreds of miles in all directions. And it remained closed for three years. Only government officials were allowed access.

While this action is prudent to prevent further tragedies, the timing of it is too coincidental. There are nine dead experienced hikers, positive radiation, autopsies with major injuries that could not be self-inflicted, and no sign of avalanche or other natural event.

The investigation was closed with the official explanation being the hiker's inexperience caused their own deaths.

Basically that they panicked when they heard a loud noise, ran away from the tent for an hour, and then died when they couldn't find their way back. Yet, we have eyes that were removed while they were alive.

The autopsies and other unexplained clues are in direct conflict with the 'panicked and died' theory. These clues paint a more sinister picture.

Chapter 6

Unusual Clues

"The side of the cedar facing the tent was cleared of branches up to 5km (16 ft.). These branches were not used. Some fell on the ground and others got suspended on the lower branches. By clearing the branches, it looked like people had made something like a window at the top of the cedar so they could watch the tent."

~Vladimirovich Atmanaki~
(Searcher and friend)

This entire case is a study in contradictions, from the injuries, to where the bodies were found, to the tent, there is no clear answer as to what happened.

To add to the confusion, is the fact that there are disputes even among the officials involved in the original investigation. Whose knife was where, and how many set of footprints are just a few of the examples.

With every accident/crime scene there are clues left behind. These clues help put together the story of what happened. Whether these clues are items, previous conversations, early actions, photos, or eye witnesses, they all provide a piece to complete the story.

In this case, there are no eye witnesses. The closest we have is Yuri Yudin, who was the last person to see the hikers alive. We have his recollections and memories to help put some pieces together.

We also have the first impressions of the original searchers. What things looked like when they were found. What condition the tent was in, how the bodies were positioned, who was where and how far were they from each other. The searchers add valuable information.

Most important, and often overlooked, is the memories and photos from the hikers themselves. We have their last diary entries, we know where their last campsite was, and we have rolls of film from their cameras. The hikers speak through all of these things. Some things are normal everyday things, but when we carefully study their words and photos we can see some things and spot some patterns. Unusual clues begin to emerge. In this chapter we'll review some of the photos in earlier chapters as well as parts of the diaries. We'll also review the injuries and other items while we search for unusual clues.

For instance. Alexander's birthday is November 16th, yet the hikers celebrated it on January 30th. Why? There's no explanation in the diary, just the fact that 'today is Alexander's birthday'. That means that Alexander told them that day was his birthday. There's really no other way for them to know. His passport had his November birthday listed. And it's not like they all carded each other. He must have stated it was his birthday.

Did he just want to add some more fun? Yuri Doroshenko's real birthday was celebrated the day before and Simon's was February 2nd, did Alexander just want to squish another birthday in there during the hike? Or more ominously, was he celebrating on the 30th knowing full well that 'something' was going to happen in a few days? Was he celebrating 'something' personal for himself and wanted to extend that celebration to his fellow hikers by making up a pretend birth date?

These are things we don't know the answer to, but we can place in our list of 'unusual things' and hope it helps to make up more answers to the puzzle.

To continue our exploration of unusual things- clues- left behind by the hikers, we'll start chronologically.

On January 24th, the group was in the train station. George began singing and begging for money. He was quickly arrested and taken away. This could have been an incident that happened just for comedy reasons. However, George was one of the three members of the group carrying a 'Finnish knife'. These were long, sharp knives and were illegal for a citizen to own in the Soviet Union at the time.

Luda, George (with knife circled), Nicholas, and Rustem

These knives weren't completely banned. Official authorities were allowed to carry them. But regular citizens needed permission and a permit to carry such knives. The other two members of the group that were known to carry knives were Nicholas and Alexander. Of the three who had knives, Alexander was the only one with a permit to carry such a knife

So, going back to the train station, if George's knife was on his belt then he would have been in serious trouble once he was arrested for disrupting the peace. But, we don't know if his knife was on his belt or in his backpack.

So, what makes this story unusual? The fact that in those days, methods of communication were very limited. Police stations had dedicated phone lines that could make unmonitored calls to anywhere in the country. One theory is that George was secretly on the hike in some sort of an official capacity. He got arrested on purpose, verified his 'official' status at the police station, and made a phone call to touch base with his higher ups. This was during the cold war. The Soviet Union and the United States were in a nuclear race with each hoping to become more powerful than the other. And each was paying huge sums of money for the other country's classified nuclear information.

George worked in the Kyshtym nuclear facility and worked on the clean-up after the disaster. He was in a sensitive position and held a security clearance. The leap to having nuclear knowledge is not too far. But was he a spy? We don't know for sure, but we do know he had access to information that was very valuable to other countries.

Before we move away from this subject, we need to address what or how someone would pass on nuclear secrets.

Beta radiation acts as a signature in nuclear production. Each nuclear facility has its own signature. If someone had pieces of clothing covered in radiation dust, these articles could be passed onto an interested party. The radiation dust would be analyzed and information gleaned from the beta particles themselves.

The trick would be passing these articles on to the other party. It's not something you would want to do in the middle of the city. Not only is the city full of people, but there may be people assigned to occasionally monitor the nuclear facility workers activities.

So, a meeting far away from civilization would be one way to guarantee secrecy. As long as both parties knew where and when to meet.

In the case of the Dyatlov group, they were behind schedule and off course from their proposed itinerary. To set such a meeting up, there would have had to have been constant flow of communication. Or, without communication, then someone would have had to follow the group.

But, it's a large leap to accuse someone of spying based on a frivolous moment in a train station. We need to continue to look at the totality of the situation.

Another strange incident happened in the train station and that was an encounter with an angry man accusing the group of stealing his money and vodka. To keep in line with the spy theory, we could say that this was a signal of 'message received' in response to the clandestine police station phone call.

We'll keep those incidents in mind as we continue to explore the other unusual clues.

Moving onto the next few days, the group stayed in the logging town overnight and enjoyed music, movies, and hospitality with the loggers. Here is where we have some interesting activities captured on film.

These two pictures were taken by two different cameras. In the top one, Luda is kneeling and picking something up. In the bottom one she's holding the unknown item in her hand.

These two pictures were taken on two different camera and just so happened to be a few seconds apart. What we're looking at is the actions of Yuri and Luda. They're both in the far left of the group picture.

These pictures are interesting because in the first picture, Luda is kneeling down to pick something up, yet is staring directly into the camera as if to take attention away from the fact that she's picking something up. Meanwhile, Yuri looks like he's trying to hold her back to keep her from picking up the object. The black object is under the soldier's leg and it appears as though this object dropped out of his coat or pocket.

In the second photo, she has this black object in her hand. The snow on her knee is from her kneeling position in the previous picture.

What is this object? In the first picture it looks almost flat, while in the second picture it appears to have more bulk.

There is nothing written about this event in any diary, so it may be inconsequential to the mystery, however, it may be very important just because nothing was written about it.

So, let's for a moment consider that Luda picked up something that belonged to the soldier. Perhaps she meant it as a joke. Perhaps it was something important that she shouldn't have had access to. And perhaps she took it with her on the hike intending to return it once the hike ended.

If this object was important, and Luda took it with her, then maybe an individual or group followed the hikers into the wilderness.

And by secretly following the hikers, whether for this reason or another, is one sure way for someone to catch up to the hikers and cause them harm. In fact, back to the spy theory, following the group is a more likely way to meet, rather than setting a definite date/time to meet in the wilderness.

As we move down the timeline, the group travels from the logging village to the uninhabited mining town. This is where Yuri Yudin departs the group and returns home. This is where the group was last seen alive by Yuri Yudin and Velikyavichusk, the sleigh driver.

In the afternoon of that same day, January 28th, the other nine hikers left the abandoned village and set off on their trek. Later that evening, after what was the first day's hike, Zina made and interesting statement in her diary: *'Sasha Kolevatov (Alexander) tested his device, then quit.'* What device was this? Alexander was studying physics at UPI. He worked with nuclear development in Moscow after obtaining a degree in metallurgy. He left Moscow and was a student at UPI studying for a second degree in Physics. So, in the case of Alexander's device, it could be related to metallurgy, physic, radiation, or something else altogether.

Zina's entry is short and to the point. Alexander tested his device and put it away. Zina doesn't add any more details, so the device itself was probably not concerning. Alexander apparently had it out for Zina to see, so he wasn't being secretive about it. So, what was it? A device to test for radio signals? A Geiger counter to test for radiation? A portable radio? The group was denied their request to carry a radio, so this would be unlikely that Alexander brought one because it would nullify the category 3 rating of their hike. This wouldn't matter so much for the Alumni of the group- Nicholas, George, and Rustem. It would matter to the students, though. And Alexander was a student and a member of the hiking club along with Zina, Luda, Yuri, and Igor. Simon was on this category 3 to obtain more experience for his instructor duty, so it would have mattered to him. Not to mention that Igor, had received the official denial, so he wouldn't have allowed the use of a portable radio. So, more than likely this device wasn't a portable radio. Another thing to note is that this device wasn't found in the tent, nor was it found near any of the bodies. There's no mention of anything other than flashlights, cameras, clothes, food and other hiking related things in the final inventory or by witnesses. There's no further mention of the device in any diary, nor does it show up in any photo. It remains one of the many unanswered questions in this mystery.

The next day was as normal as could be for a wilderness hike. There's a very short- and seemingly reluctant- entry in the group diary from Nicholas:

The Group Diary
1.29.59
Second day of our hike. We made our way from the Lozva river to the Auspiya river. We walked along a Mansi trail. The weather is −13C. The wind is weak. We often find ice on the Lozva river. That's all.
~Nicholas~

But, there are a few interesting statements in Zina's diary:

Zina's Diary
29.1.59
Today is Yurka's (Yuri Doroshenko) birthday. *We go first to Lozva then we turn to Auspiya. Surroundings are beautiful. Along the Auspiya Mansi have passed. A trail is visible, grooves, a path is visible. We often see Mansi signs on the trail. I wonder what they write about? Now the Mansi trail goes South.*

173

Now we sit the three of us: Rustem, Yuri and I Waiting for the rest. For the night stopped near the ski tracks. We are burning firewood with Yuri. We talked about the past. Such a playboy.

There are a few things of note here. First of all, Zina briefly mentions Yuri's birthday. It's a short statement, but she acknowledged it. Later she and Rustem and Yuri sat around the campfire together. We'll go into more detail about the 'Yuri Birthday' statement soon. For now we'll explore the 'sitting around the fire statement'.

This is of interest, because it shows that the group didn't do everything together 24/7. There were times they splintered off into separate groups. Luda mentions it in the group diary on January 28th:

*'Someone comes up with an idea that we need a special notebook for ideas that we might come up with. **Conspiring, we started going into the tent two people at a time.**'*

Yes, it's a small thing- going into the tent two at a time, yet it also helps us to realize that this group- although they moved as a single unit when skiing, they also formed and re-formed small groups. Whether this was to conspire for their idea notebook, or to gather wood, they did indeed become groups of two or three rather than a single group of nine.

So, back to the 29th and Zina's statement that she, Yuri, and Rustem were sitting around the campfire discussing the past and waiting for the others. This implies that the others were further away and not within earshot of the conversation. The other six could have been in one large group or further broken down into groups of two or three. Some gathering firewood and some scouting around the area. Some would seek privacy away from the others to attend to personal matters.

At some point, Alexander would have tested his device again. If it was important enough to carry- and remember they all had to carry everything on their backs- then the device was important enough to be used more than once.

Another point to remember is that there were always two people 'on duty' at the campsite. These two were tasked with staying awake to keep an eye on the campsite as well as keeping an eye on the stove that burned throughout the night providing heat.

Moving onto the 30th, the diary entries gives us a strange mix of details.

First we'll look at Zina's:

Zina's diary
30.1.59
We go on Auspiya. Cold. Mansi trail ended. Pine forest. There was sun in the morning, now is cold. All day long we walked along Auspiya. Will spend the night on a Mansi trail. **Nicholas didn't get to be a watchman so me and Rustem will stay on duty today. Burned mittens and Yuri's second quilted jacket. He cursed a lot. Today, probably, we will build a storage.**

Rustem modeling Yuri's burned jacket. In the background are trees and scenery that match the diary descriptions for the 30th noting that they were in the forest and the weather was cold but pleasant.

While short, there's a lot of information packed in that entry. First, we see that Zina and Rustem are on duty today due to some unforeseen

175

situation that prevents Nicholas from being on duty. Zina- nor anyone else- mentions what changed to keep Nicholas from being on duty. If it was an injury, then it wasn't specified. Perhaps he had another duty that outranked the night watchman duty.

So, here, for the 30th, we know that Zina and Rustem are on duty. An interesting note is that Zina and Rustem were found (along with Igor) in the forest before the cedar area. This entry on the 30th is the last entry in Zina's diary.

Moving onto Zina's next statement. We learn that somehow, Yuri ended up with burned mittens and a burned quilted jacket. Presumably there are extra quilted jackets. These are used as jackets as well as liners under their coats during cold weather.

Since there is no further explanation for the burned items, we can only deduce that this burn happened sometime during the day on the 30th. Maybe it was from the campfire while they prepared breakfast. It also doesn't explain who burned the items or if someone was wearing them at the time.

It was a common practice to share items among members of the group. So, someone else could have been wearing the items. Either way, it was mentioned in passing with no further explanation.

In this picture, we see Rustem modeling Yuri's burned coat. In the background are trees and scenery that match the diary descriptions for the 30th noting that they were in the forest and the weather was cold but pleasant.

The next sentence in Zina's diary is about building the storage site. She says 'we will probably build a storage today'. This implies that she wrote in the diary while hiking and before the hike ended for the day. The group assumption was that they were going to build a storage site, yet we know that didn't happen on the 30th, because Igor talks about building a storage site in the group diary entry for the 31st.

So, somehow the day ended with no storage site built- and no further update from Zina.

In fact, that was her last entry aside from one more final word: Rempel. There is no other context, just this single word. Rempel is the name of the hunter who helped Igor with directions and advice in Vijay. This is the village they stayed in before they rode in the back of the truck to the 41st Quarter which was the logger's village. We'll go into more details about Rempel soon.

Back to the 30th. Zina's diary entries have told us that she and Rustem are on duty again due to some unforeseen circumstance preventing Nicholas from being on duty. We learn that she thought they would build a storage site on that day, but we know that they did not. And, somehow Yuri's mittens and coat were burned. The assumption is that Yuri burned them somehow while lighting a campfire, but there is no explanation to determine that for sure.

Now, still staying on the date of the 30th, we'll take a look at the Unknown diary:

In the morning it was 17 ° now it is getting colder. **"Volunteers"** **Alexander and Nicholas are repeating their duties as a punishment for slowing the group yesterday** *took a long time to start a fire. In the evening it was decided that we will leave the tent exactly 8 minutes after waking up. Therefore, all have been awake and waiting for the command. But it is useless. Around 9:30 in the morning we began the passive preparation. Nicholas is joking about something in the morning. Everyone is reluctant to get up.*

And the weather! In contrast to the rest of the warm days —today is a sunny cold day. The sun appears playful.

Today as yesterday were are following the path of Mansi. Sometimes Mansi writings appear on trees. In general, all sorts of obscure mysterious characters. There is slogan for our campaign, "In a country of mysterious signs." If we knew these letters, it would be possible, without any doubt, to go down the path, confident that it would lead us to the right place. Here the trail takes us to the shores of the river. We lose track. In the future, the trail follows the left bank of Auspii River, but the team of deer crossed the river and we are going through the woods. At the first opportunity we will turn back to the river. As it is easier to follow it.

At approximately 2 pm we stop for a lunch. Dried meat, guest crackers, sugar, garlic, coffee, stocked in the morning - that's our lunch.

Good mood.

A couple more hours - and we will stop at 5 pm for the night. We have been looking for a place, then we returned about 200 meters back. Charming place. Deadwood, high pines, in short, everything you need for a good night.

Part 2.

Luda quickly got tired and sat down by the fire. **Nicholas changed his clothes. He began to write a diary.** *The law is that until all the work is done, do not approach the fire. And so they had a long argument, of*

177

who will sew the tent. Finally Nicholas gave up and took a needle. Luda remained seated. And we sewed the hole (and there were so many that there was enough work for all except two attendants and Luda). Guys are terribly outraged.

Today is the birthday of Alexander. Congratulations. We give him a tangerine, which he immediately divided into 8 pieces (Luda went into a tent and did not come out until the end of the dinner). *So another day of our trek went well.*

Whoever wrote this diary, wrote it throughout the day and into the evening. In fact, they even broke it up into parts 1 and 2. The writing is descriptive and explanatory. They've included the temperature, what food they ate for lunch, and details about their evening. They even give a mini lesson about the Mansi trail and signs. It's a shame we can't give credit to whichever of the hikers wrote this diary.

Through process of elimination we can exclude Zina, Luda, and Rustem as the authors, because their diaries were found in the tent. Since this diary mentions Nicholas and Alexander, we can exclude them too

So, that leaves Igor, Yuri, Simon, and George as the possible authors of the Unknown diary. We can't compare handwriting samples because the original diary has never been seen. All the entries exist as a typewritten file. There have been no photos released of the original diary.

This is very typical of the official file for this case. Many of the original objects- such as the hiker's spoof newspaper- have never been seen. They only exist through descriptions from witness testimonies and official reports.

In fact, only half of the whole original case file has been released. The other half is either missing or is kept secret. It has never been available to researchers.

As we look through the entry of the Unknown diary, there are many things of note. First is the statement that '"Volunteers" Alexander and Nicholas are repeating their duties as a punishment for slowing the group yesterday'. Yet, in Zina's diary she says that she and Rustem are on duty because Nicholas can't do it. There's no explanation for this contradiction between these two entries. Perhaps Zina and Rustem were on duty during the day and then Alexander and Nicholas for the evening.

There is also no explanation for how Alexander and Nicholas slowed the group down. But apparently it was enough of a hindrance to assign them extra duties the next day. Did Alexander and Nicholas stop too often? Stop and carry on conversations between themselves?

Ski hiking, like the group was doing, requires the group progress in a single file line. Delays happen if people straggle behind or if they stop frequently. There is no further explanation of the 'Nicholas and Alexander' event, but the fact that two hikers slowed the group- and seemed to do it on purpose- is notable.

The next item of interest in this entry is: *'Nicholas changed his clothes, and began to write in a diary'*. This is interesting and implies that Nicholas had a diary, even though it wasn't ever found (or has not been released to researchers and is still in the file somewhere).

However, Nicholas did write in the group diary twice and both entries are short and reluctant.

His first entry was made on January 26th and is simply: *'I can't. although I tried.'* That's it, five words and then his signature. His next entry in the group diary is on January 29th. It's a bit longer, but still the second shortest entry in the diary (with his 26th entry being the shortest). This entry reads: *'Second day of our trip. We made our way from Lozvy river to river Auspii. We walked along a Mansi (native Siberian tribe in the Urals) trail. The weather is -13C. The wind is weak. We often find ice on the Lozvy river. That is it.'*

So, Nicholas was a reluctant diary writer, yet this entry on January 30th in the Unknown diary states that Nicholas quickly finished changing and sat down to write in a diary. In fact, he was in such a hurry that he didn't complete all his chores. He and Luda argued about this until Nicholas stopped writing to help with chores which in the case was to sew the tent.

What diary was Nicholas writing in? His own? If so, then that diary has never been found. Or it's still in the official file and has never been released for viewing or research.

Another idea is that Nicholas is writing in the group diary. That may very well be the case because the group diary entry for that same date is not signed. Yet, it's very similar to the Unknown diary entry. It's a long entry and very descriptive. In fact, it's a two part entry also. It would be unusual that Nicholas, who had the two shortest group diary entries, would suddenly write one of the longest entries. This in and of itself is not too strange, but it is something to consider since the whole group died a few days later. And since we're considering all odd and unusual clues, we'll add this oddity to the list.

The next unusual statement in this diary entry is: *'Today is the birthday of Alexander. Congratulations. We give him a tangerine, which he immediately divided into 8 pieces (Luda went into a tent and did not come out until the end of the dinner).'*

Ok. So, Zina didn't mention this at all, yet she mentioned Yuri's birthday in her diary entry from the day before. Perhaps Zina wrote her diary entry prior to the birthday celebration? But, if the birthday was announced, it seems that Zina would have at least mentioned it. She's the one who includes personal tidbits about the group. She mentioned Alexander testing his device, Yuri's burned clothes, Yuri's birthday, conversations around the bonfire, etc. Lots of people things. Yet, here, she makes no mention of Alexander's birthday.

To celebrate, they divided a tangerine into 8 pieces. That would account for everyone except Luda who remained in the tent for the evening. So, it seems that Zina was part of the celebration. She must have written her diary entry earlier in the day and then didn't get her diary out that evening.

All of these little facts tell a story, but most important is the fact that it wasn't Alexander's birthday at all. His real birthday is November 16th. Why did he tell the group that January 30th was his birthday? What significance did this date carry?

The next day (January 31st) is the last entry in any diary. And the following day (February 1st) would be the last day of their lives. Why celebrate his false birthday on January 30th? That's something we will never know, but is definitely an unusual fact in this case.

In fact, Alexander has quite a few unusual tidbits going on, from his device check, to him and Nicholas holding up the group, to celebrating a false birthday. He also, according to his sister, brought along extra sweaters because he said the university didn't provide enough. The university did provide each hiker two sweaters. In fact, the university provided several items of clothing to include underwear and socks as well as one set of skis and one set of ski poles per person.

So, Alexander brought extra sweaters on the trip. He good naturedly shared them with his fellow hikers. And coincidentally, later during the radiation tests, two sweaters tested positive for radiation. One that Luda was wearing and one that Alexander was wearing.

What was the real story behind Alexander bringing extra sweaters? We'll never know. But how coincidental is it that Alexander brought extra sweaters and two sweaters tested positive for radiation?

Speaking of Luda's sweater. We'll also never know if it was indeed her sweater or if it was borrowed. She was one of the least dressed when she was found. We know that some of Yuri and George's clothes were removed. Some of those items were found on Luda. Other items were found in the Cedar area cut in half. There were also some found on the ground between the Cedar area and the snow den. And finally, some were found in the snow den itself.

A thought to consider is: Did Alexander lend Luda one of his sweaters? We know they traded and wore each other's clothing. Before Yuri Yudin left the group, he gave his winter vest to Alexander. When Igor was found he was wearing that same winter vest.

We know that clothes swapping and lending was quite prevalent during hikes. Everyone wanted to complete the hike and everyone wanted their hiking group members to be as comfortable as possible to do it.

So, the question remains. What did Alexander do with the extra sweaters? What was his real reasoning for bringing them? Was it merely that he did want to help the group out by bringing extra clothes? Or did he have an ulterior motive? Were the sweaters contaminated with radioactive particles on purpose?

A quick note here on radioactive materials. We must remember that these events happened during the cold war between the Soviet Union and the United States. Radioactive particles are unique and can be traced to their origin. They act as fingerprints in fact. Each nuclear facility creates a unique radioactivity. During the cold war, the US and the Soviet Union were in a race to outdo each other in the nuclear field. Not only were nuclear achievement highly kept secrets, the materials themselves were classified along with the process to create such materials.

The radioactive signature contained on a piece of clothing (such as a sweater) would be a prize secret to either nation wanting to know the other nations nuclear capability in a particular facility.

We'll delve more into the radioactivity report as we discuss the discovery of the bodies. For now, we'll continue with the diary entries from January 30th.

In addition to Zina's diary entry, and the Unknown diary entry, there was one more entry for January 30th. This is from the group diary. As previously mentioned, this entry is unsigned.

The Group Diary
30 January 1959
Diary is written in the cold on the go.
Today is a third cold night on the bank of Auspiya river. We are getting used to it. The stove does a great job. **Some of us (Thibeaux (Nicholas) and Krivonischenko (George)) think we need to build steam**

heat in the tent. *The curtains in the tent are quite justified. We get up at 8:30am. After breakfast we walk along the Auspiya river, but the ice again doesn't allow us to move forward. We went on the bank on a sledge-deer trail. In the middle of the road the saw Mansi shed. Yes, Mansi, Mansi, Mansi. This word comes up more and more often in our conversations. Mansi are people of the North. Small Hanti-Mansijskiy nation located in Salehard with 8 thousand population. Very interesting and unique people that inhabit the North Polar Urals, close to the Tyumen region. They have a written language, and leave characteristic signs on forest trees.*

Weather: temperature in the morning - 17 C
day - 13 C
night - 26 C.

The wind is strong, south-west, snow begins to fall, heavy clouds, drop in temperature. The temperature is normal for Northern Urals.

This is a story about the forest. Mansi signs tell about animals they saw, resting stops and other things. It is particularly interesting to solve its meaning for the tourists as well as historians.

Deer trail turns into a trodden path, and then ends. To go without a trail is very hard, snow is 120 cm (4 feet) deep. The forest gradually thins and trees get smaller. Lots of dwarf birches and pines. You can feel the altitude. It is impossible to walk on the river. It is not completely frozen, there is ice and water under the snow. We have to go back on the bank of the river. ***The day is over and we have to find a place for bivouac. That's the stop for the night.*** *Strong west wind. It blows the snows off the cedar and pine trees, creating the impression of a snow fall.*

As usual we quickly start a fire and pitch the tent on some fir branches. We are warmed by the fire and go to sleep.
(Unsigned)

This entry is descriptive, unhurried, and informative. The writer explains the area, temperatures, and Mansi signs. All in all it gives a lot of information, but it doesn't match anything at all written in the other two diaries.

As previously mentioned, Zina's diary talks about Yuri's burnt clothes. The Unknown diary says that Nicholas and Luda got into an argument and then group celebrated Alexander's birthday while Luda remained in the tent. This group diary entry, however, does not mention any of that. Even though this entry is long and goes from waking up in

182

the morning until going to bed in the evening. It doesn't mention burnt clothes, arguments, or birthdays.

One interesting thing about this entry is the sentence '*Some of us (Thibeaux (Nicholas) and Krivonischenko (George)) think we need to build steam heat in the tent.*' The reference to 'us' could mean that either Nicholas or George is the writer (and including themselves in 'us'). Or the reference to 'us' could mean 'them' someone outside of the writer. This could be a potential clue to who wrote the diary entry. This diary entry is important due to the fact that it encompasses the day, yet is a complete mismatch to the other two diaries.

Next is: '*The day is over and we have to find a place for bivouac. That's the stop for the night*'. That's an interesting sentence with the use of 'bivouac' and then the explanation for it. Bivouac is a French term and a common Army term. Nicholas is French and Simon served in the Army. Again, this could be a clue to who the writer was or perhaps the writer just wanted to use a unique term.

Finally, is the last sentence: '*As usual we quickly start a fire and pitch the tent on some fir branches. We are warmed by the fire and go to sleep.*' No mention of burnt clothes, arguments, sewing, tangerines, or birthdays. Just 'we set up camp, lit a fire, and went to bed'.

If we were to read the three diary entries separately from each other and with no context, we would think that each entry was talking about a different day. Yet, they are all dated January 30th.

If we take a step back and look at what we know: In the Unknown diary, it is stated that '*Nicholas wrote in a diary*'. It's been previously mentioned that there was no diary found for Nicholas and we know that he was a reluctant writer in the group diary. His entries are the two shortest. Did he suddenly decide to write an elaborately descriptive entry in the group diary that night? And then not sign it? Why? Why that night. In and of itself, it's not that unusual, but given the fact that the entire group died a few days later, this inconsistency bears some review.

So, we have one diary entry about Nicholas writing in a diary and Alexander's birthday. We have a second diary talking about Yuri's burned clothes. And then we have yet a third diary saying it was a normal night and everyone went to bed. All three entries complete, yet completely different from each other. What if one of the three was falsified?

Zina's diary was recovered and all the entries are in her handwriting. The group diary and the Unknown diary were also recovered, but the only available evidence to see of those diaries are the

183

typewritten transcripts. Those two diaries have never been photographed or released to the public. So, we have no way to compare handwriting or to know who wrote them. While most of the group diary entries are signed, some are not. And the Unknown diary is yet to be linked to a single hiker.

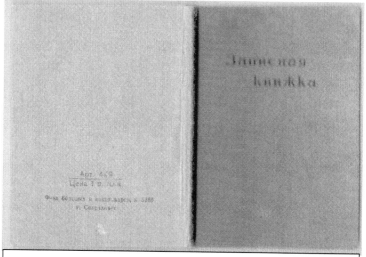

The front and back cover of Zina's Diary

The very last page of Zina's diary with the single name 'Rempel'

In addition to not knowing who the Unknown diary belongs to, we also have the mystery of what happened to Simon and Alexander's diaries. Both were known to have them. And, yet neither was ever found. If Nicholas and George had diaries, then theirs weren't found either.

From January 30th we move onto the final diary entry of the group diary. That of January 31st. This entry was, fittingly perhaps, written by Igor.

31 January 1959

Today the weather is a bit worse wind (west), snow (probably from the pines) because the sky is perfectly clear.

Came out relatively early (around 10 am). Took the same Mansi sled trail. **Till now we walk along a Mansi trail, which was crossed by a deer hunter not long ago.**

Yesterday we apparently came across his resting stop. Deer didn't go much further. The hunter didn't follow the beaten trail and we are now in his steps.

Today was surprisingly good accommodations for the tent, air is warm and dry, despite the low temperature of -18C to -24C. Walking is especially hard today. Visibility is very low. We can't see the trail and sometimes we have to advance gropingly. **All we can do is 1.52 km (1 mile) per hour.**

We are forced to find new methods of clearing the path for the skis. The first member leaves his backpack on the ground and walks forward, then returns and rests for 10-15 minutes with the group. Thus we have a non-stop paving of the trail. It is especially hard for the second to move down the new trail with full gear on the back. We gradually leave the Auspiya valley, the rise is continuous, but quite smooth. Fir trees are replaced by wispy birch-wood. We came out of the tree line. Wind is western, warm, penetrating. The speed of the wind is similar to the air draft created by a taking off airplane. Firn, open spaces. **I can't even start thinking of setting up a storage. It's close to 4. We have to start looking for a place to pitch the tent.** *We are going south in Auspiya river valley. This apparently is the place covered with the deepest snow. Wind is not strong, snow cover is 1,22 m. Tired and exhausted we started the preparations for the night. Not enough firewood. Frail damp firs.* **We started fire with logs, too tired to dig a fire pit. We had supper right in the tent. It's warm. It is hard to imagine such a comfort somewhere on the ridge, with a piercing wind, hundreds kilometers away from human settlements.**

~Igor~

This heartfelt entry is especially moving considering it contains the last words from the group. There are a few things I'd like to explore in this entry. The first is that Igor is talking about following a deer hunter. The group has seen his tracks and his camp. In fact, they spent the day following his footsteps. To this day, we don't know who this deer hunter is. Or even if there was more than one. Despite countless official interviews with the locals as well as the Mansi, no one has ever come forward to say they were this deer hunter.

This is important because the Dyatlov group could have crossed paths or met the hunter sometime during the course of the following day. Since there are no further diary entries, we don't know if the Dyatlov group ever actually met up with the hunter. Dyatlov's group was close enough to follow the tracks and see the previous campsites. So, it's not too much of a leap to think that these two groups crossed paths soon after.

If investigators were to ever re-open this case, one of the first priorities should be to identify who this hunter was.

Another note about the hunter is that Rempel was a hunter. He's the man who talked to Igor in Vijay. His name 'Rempel' is also the last word in Zina's diary. The fact that this man is a hunter, talked to Igor in the village and was a name written in the back of Zina's diary are an awful lot of coincidences for one person.

The next item we'll discuss in this entry is the statement *'All we can do is 1.5 kmh (1 mile per hour)'*.

The Cedar area is one mile from where the tent was situated. To get to the Cedar area from the tent, one must walk through the woods and climb a 15 foot cliff.

On their very last night, the group exited the tent for an unknown reason. Some were barefoot and some were wearing only socks.

Now back to the diary entry. If the group traveled 1mph on skis. Then how long would it have taken them to walk a mile through 4ft deep snow barefoot? And that doesn't include climbing the cliff near the end of the mile walk. I surmise it would have taken them at least an hour, but probably longer.

This length of time- and the fact that some of them were very poorly dressed- runs completely counter to a scenario of the group scrambling from the tent, running off into the darkness, and quickly becoming lost.

Even if we explore the idea that they got spooked for some reason and fled from their tent in a panic, it's very difficult to imagine that they then willingly continued to walk away from the tent for more than an hour. Even if the danger in the tent was so extreme as to convince them to not turn back, they still could have stopped somewhere in the woods prior to the cedar area to start a fire, warm up, and re-group.

To deliberately walk an hour or more in -30° weather, wearing short sleeve shirts and socks, is a stretch of the imagination. A much more likely scenario is that they were forced.

Next is Igor's comment that he can't even begin to *think about setting up a storage*. Zina's diary entry from the day before mentions that they were going to set up a storage the next day. Here, on what is the next day, Igor is saying that he can't even think of setting one up. Since we know they did build a storage area and their belongings were in there, then that means they built the storage area before they set up their tent for the final time.

Let's visit the scenario of building the storage area for a moment. We know there was a pair of skis left there marking the spot. Whose skis were they? Remember that each hiker had one set of skis and one set of poles. There were no extras. Yet, a pair of skis was left at the storage area. And to sidetrack a little, we also know that a ski pole was cut up and left behind in the tent. These things- the skis and the ski pole- are absolutely vital to each hiker. They're the only way to continue the hike, and most importantly, they're the only way to get home. The skis at the storage site can be retrieved, but a cut-up ski pole cannot be repaired to a usable condition. Thus, it would be useless to use to continue the hike. So, again, we must ask: whose skis were left at the storage area? And why?

One idea is that the group split up, leaving some behind to build the storage area. This would have served a few purposes, one being that the group building the storage area could do so while the rest of the group moved forward to build the campsite. Thus accomplishing two major tasks at once. And then someone building the storage area left their skis there to mark the spot. Who would have done that and why? My thought is that someone volunteered their skis and offered to stay behind with the tent while the group completed the ascent of Mt. Kholat.

When the smaller group finished building the storage area, they left the upright skis there and then followed the ski tracks left behind by the rest of the group. The tent and storage area were only about 1/3 of a mile apart. According to the 1 mph estimate, it would have taken the storage building group about 20- 30 minutes to walk to the campsite.

They would have been slowed by the person without skis, but that person could have walked behind in the ski tracks of another hiker thus making the trek a little easier.

So, who may have volunteered for this? Who remained behind to build the storage area?

My thoughts are that Simon and Nicholas volunteered to stay behind to build the storage area. They were the warmest dressed when their bodies were found and they were, in fact, still in their winter hiking clothes. They were both wearing their warm winter coats and boots. Their bodies were also found together near the snow den (along with Luda and Alexander).

Whoever- or whatever- forced the other six hikers from the campsite area did so after those hikers had changed clothes for the evening. The fact that Simon and Nicholas were completely dressed leads me to believe that they were not at the tent when the other six were forced from the campsite.

We'll explore some more of those clues as we get into the discussion about the tent and the way the bodies were found. For now, we'll finish up the diary entries.

Now, we'll take a look at the last paragraph in this entry. Igor describes it as being too cold and uncomfortable to stay outside long. He states that they did not have enough good wood to start a campfire and that they ate their meal right in the tent.

A note about their food. They brought cured meat that could be eaten warm or cold. This meat has been described as bacon, brisket, and ham. On this final night of the final diary entry, the group ate their meal in the warm tent without using a campfire to cook.

The stove in the tent is not for cooking, it is only a heater. It was an invented device created by Igor to provide heat for the winter. The stove itself is shaped like a muffler, with one end that opens to insert wood. The back end is closed except for the pipe that exhausts smoke and fumes from the tent.

There is much discussion over whether the stove was actually assembled or not. The searchers description of the stove is only that they found it in the tent. They didn't find any burned wood in the tent or in the stove, so the stove had not been utilized that last day. However, a few pieces of unburnt wood were found in the tent. These are assumed to be fuel for the stove for that evening.

And finally, we have Igor's last sentence: '*It is hard to imagine such a comfort somewhere on the ridge, with a piercing wind, hundreds kilometers away from human settlements.*' On the night he wrote this they were camped in a wooded forest area. We know they moved camp one final time and set-up on the cold ridge for what would be their final night.

The tent was found on a mountain slope. The slope itself measured about 30°. The group dug out a flat area, laid skis down for flooring, and then set the tent up on top of that. As with many details in this case, there are disagreements about how many sets of skis were found under the tent. The fact that the tent and all of its contents were disassembled and placed in a big heap doesn't help with any clear idea of where the skis or anything else was initially located.

We do know that a set of skis was left at the storage area. This was an unusual occurrence and would have hindered the group's progress and rendered one individual unable to complete the ascent the next day. That person could have volunteered to stay behind to watch the campsite while the others hiked the ascent.

However, due to the fact that the tent and all contents were heaped together with no formal inventory, we'll never know how many skis were found with the tent. What if there were nine or more? That would indicate that one or more people had joined up with the group.

This clue has unfortunately been lost. For now, all we can do is speculate whether someone had chosen to leave their skis at the storage site or whether more people had joined the group.

Another oddity about the tent area is that there was clothing, a coat, a pick axe, hats, gloves, change and several small items found outside the tent. These other items are not described except to say they were 'small' such as items that would be found in pockets. A scene like that suggests that the Dyatlov group were forced to drop whatever was in their hands and remove the contents of their pockets.

Did the Dyatlov group encounter another group out there in the wilderness? Did they end up crossing paths with the hunter previously mentioned in the diaries? Were they forced out of their tent by armed intruders?

In a harsh, unforgiving environment, people are quick to help others in need. Where losing a tent or coat will lead to death, strangers will help others quickly and willingly.

Did an unknown group or individual cross paths with the Dyatlov group? The strangers could have easily become part of the group by saying they need help with shelter, food, or clothing.

Or perhaps the Dyatlov group was followed. Someone could have followed the Dyatlov group for a few days, caught up to them, used some excuse to join their group and then abducted them by gunpoint.

Back then, one common style of execution in the USSR was to have a person disrobe and simply leave them out in the freezing weather to die. With temperatures that drop to -40°, the person freezes to death quite quickly. It's a very hands off and cost efficient execution and the executioner does little except to drop someone somewhere with few clothes no shelter.

So, let's say these intruders were looking for something or someone in particular. They force the Dyatlov group out of the tent and have them empty their pockets. They then force the group to drop whatever they're holding and start walking downslope towards the tree line. To maintain control of the group, the strangers force the group to link arms and walk side-by-side.

When searchers found the tent and the footprints they noticed that the footprints were side-by-side like the group had walked away next to each other. This type of walking was opposite of the single file hiking that was typical during a winter hike. Another detail noticed by the searchers is that one or two sets of footprints led away from the group for a short distance and then eventually returned to the group.

It's also noted that some of the footprints look like they had been stepped in more than once. The visual that comes about from these descriptions is a large group- either shoulder-to-shoulder or with arms linked- walking side-by-side down the slope. The outer persons occasionally veer away and return to the group while another one or two people lead the group or follow close behind.

Unfortunately there are very few pictures of the footprints. One picture shows a chaotic grouping of the footprints, handprints, and unidentified marks while other pictures show the footprints going down the slope side-by-side.

There are several footprints that look like bare feet. One print in the snow appears to be a handprint suggesting someone fell down along the way.

Today, a clue such as this would be measured, evaluated, and photographed from every angle. The prints would be compared to the hikers' feet and hands.

While they weren't measured or evaluated, the footprints add an important piece to the overall mystery. If nothing else, they verify that some of the hikers were indeed barefoot. And despite that fact, they did indeed continue to walk up to a mile away from the tent.

What drove them to do that is one of the keys to this mystery.

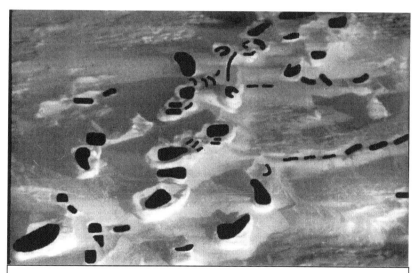

Top picture: The grouping of footprints, handprints, and other marks found near the tent.
Bottom picture: Identical to top picture with the prints highlighted.

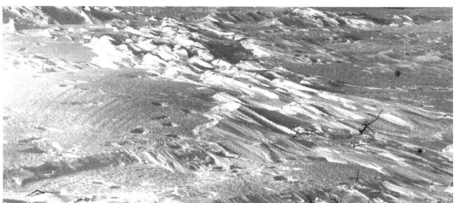

Both of these pictures show the footprints going downslope (from left to right in each picture)

The small items scattered around the tent could have been from a variety of things. One idea is that the hikers were forced to empty most of their pockets. Since some still had change in their pockets and there was a large amount of money left in the tent, the motive was not to steal money. Nor was it food or shelter. There was plenty of food left behind in the tent and the tent itself was slashed and destroyed. Money and food left behind eliminates a burglar or escaped convict.

I've brought up an intruder a few times and while we'll continue to discuss other theories, I'd like to point out that one of the biggest mysteries of this tragedy is why the hikers left their tent.

We know where they were found and we know what injuries they had, but we don't know why they left their warm tent in the first place.

These nine hikers were experienced outdoors people. All of them had done grueling hikes before. As we search through and explore this mystery we must address them leaving their tent partially dressed to walk towards a certain death.

Going through the possible scenarios at the tent itself, we can identify the few facts that we know. We know that food, money, warm clothes, and tools were left behind. We know a set of skis were at the storage site and many skis were at the tent site (unfortunately we don't know the exact number left at the tent site). We know a ski pole was cut up for some reason. We know there were no burn marks in or outside the tent. We know delicate items such as crackers were not crushed. We know the tent was sliced from the inside.

Through these known facts we can begin a process of elimination. Nothing crushed the tent. Any event that involved crushing the tent would have also crushed the food, crackers, tins, and other items. This rules out an avalanche, animal stampede, or ice slide. Not to mention there were no animal tracks nor any indication of an avalanche.

Common theories include 'they cut their way out of the tent'. We have no indication that they cut their way out, we only know the tent was cut up. But let's explore the scenario that they did cut their way out.

Scenario: Something causes a panic. Everyone needs to evacuate the tent immediately. The ones who have knives cut at the tent wall. As they slice, their knives penetrate and they and the others tear their way out.

That would be the scenario of a panicked situation forcing the hikers to cut their way out. Yet, as we look at the tent we can see that there are many, many small cuts. An emergency situation would create one, two, or even three long tears in the tent wall. No one is going to have the time or the inclination to make small cuts here and there. They are going to cut, penetrate, and tear their way out.

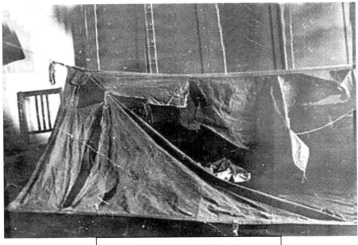

Left half of tent

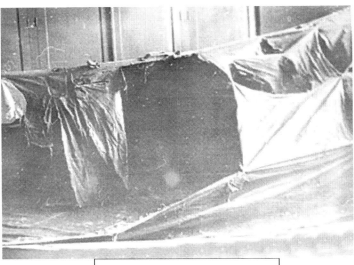

Right half of tent

As we can see in the above photos, the tent is shredded with cuts. There are many more than necessary to escape in an emergency situation. And, as we know, the hikers were experienced. Even if they were to cut their tent, they know it must be reparable and usable for them to survive.

Also, another argument against them cutting their tent is just one side is cut. Why would they cut only one side? There are no cuts on the other long side, nor are there any cuts near the door. A frantic emergency exit would mean they're trying to get out any way they can. And again, no items were crushed in the tent and no items were scattered and out of place. The piles of clothes stayed together, piles of shoes stayed together and the pile of blankets stayed together.

Despite the unknowns in this case, the 'knowns' point away from a panicked issue happening in the tent. We don't know why they left their tent, but we do know it wasn't in a panic.

Along with that we don't know why they cut up their tent. But, what if they didn't do it? If someone did force them out with the intention of killing them, then it's a logical leap to think that same person would destroy the hikers' tent to prevent them from having shelter. A dire situation like that out in the bitter weather would and thus freezing to death.

A working flashlight was found on top of the tent. It was switched 'off', but turned on when the searchers tried it. Again, this would not have happened in any chaotic panicked situation. It does, however, make sense that someone else- someone outside the Dyatlov group- dropped the flashlight there after they destroyed the tent.

Another sign of the hikers being killed by a human event rather than some sort of natural event is the fact that the body positions point to them being tied or restrained at some point.

It's very common for a person to curl up into a ball to try to stay warm in freezing weather. However, all the hikers' bodies were prone and laying on their stomach or back. Now we know there are exceptions to every rule, however what's the likelihood of all nine hikers being in positons where they're more or less straight from head to toe rather than any of them being curled up as is common with hypothermia.

Now, we know that the clothes were cut off of Yuri and George, so their bodies were moved after they died. These two were found lying prone. Yuri was on his stomach, while George was on his back.

Luda, Nicholas, Simon, and Alexander were found in a stream after the snow began to melt. Nicholas, Simon, and Alexander were lying side by side and in the prone position. This would be a very unusual way for them to die if their deaths happened naturally.

Zina, Rustem, and Igor were all found in the forest before the Cedar area. All of them were found in the prone position.

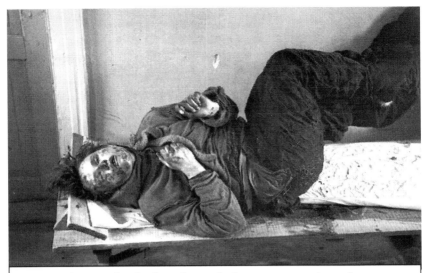

Notice how Zina's hands and feet appear that they were restrained as she died. She also has injuries on her wrists as if from a restraint and fingernail injuries on her hand as though she tried to pull her hands out of a restraint. Zina also has bloody abrasions on her eyelids and forehead as if she was blindfolded.

Rustem's ankles are together. It looks like his hands were tied and he got one free. His pose is very similar to Zina's.

Igor's position is very unusual. It looks like he died with his hands and ankles bound. His back is arched and his arm is wrapped around a branch. Like Zina and Rustem, he has bloody abrasions on his eyelids and forehead as if he was blindfolded.

None of the nine hikers were found curled up in a ball as you would expect if they froze to death naturally.

Zina, Rustem, and Igor have abrasions on their foreheads and eyelids as if they had been blindfolded. These injuries were bloody and thus happened while they were alive.

All three are in positions that look as if they died while restrained. Each of the three were found with their ankles together as though they had been tied up. Igor's hands are clenched together in front of his chest as though his wrists were bound. Zina has fingernail injuries on her wrists that look like she was struggling to free herself. And Rustem looks like he got one of his hands free before being knocked down again.

But where are the bindings that tied them up? Remember the windings found in the cedar area and in the snow den area? Perhaps those are what's left over from the bindings. Whoever restrained the hikers removed the bindings because it could have identified them or more practically, they needed the bindings for something else. When you're out hiking in the cold weather and have to carry everything on your back, supplies are scarce and you keep what you can with you.

Many of the hikers had similar injuries even though they were found in different areas. On the next few pages we'll look at the similarities of their many injuries. In addition to the similarities, I'll also note the injury, the hiker, and where the hiker was found. For example: I'll use 'Forest' for the area between the tent and Cedar. I'll use 'Cedar' for the Cedar area. And I'll use 'Snow Den' for the snow den area.

(Note about the term 'bloody': this was used by the coroner to denote the injuries that had happened while the hikers were alive.

Bloody abrasions on eyelids (sign of a blindfold):
Zina (Forest)
Rustem (Forest)
Igor (Forest).

Bloody abrasions with an indent (possibly caused by a restraint):
Rustem on his forehead (Forest)
Igor around his ankles (Forest)
Yuri around his chest (Cedar)
George around his wrist. He also had a piece of his finger in his mouth as if he was trying to bite through a restraint and bit his own hand in the process (Cedar)

Knife cut on palm:
Igor on his left palm (Forest)
George on his left palm (Cedar)

Bruised, bloody knuckles (boxer's knuckles as if from a fight):
Zina (Forest)
Rustem (Forest)
Igor (Forest)
George (Cedar)

Strange 'U' shaped injuries (could be from the butt of a gun)
One on each side of Igor's face (Forest)
Three on George's left leg (Cedar)
One on Yuri's left arm (Cedar)

Burns
Yuri's hair (Cedar)
George's outer left leg, left foot, and his left hand (Cedar)

Black Eye:
Rustem (Forest)
George (Cedar)

Arm Twist Shoulder Bruise:
Nicholas

So far, there has been no overlap between the injuries of those found in the forest, cedar, and snow den areas. As we continue the list of injuries, we'll find more in common between all three groups.

Skull Fracture:
Rustem (Forest)
Nicholas (Snow Den)

Bleeding on the brain:
Rustem from his skull fracture (Forest)
Nicholas from his skull fracture (Snow Den)
George (Cedar)- bleeding was under his right temple and all the way to the back of his head. Although he didn't have a skull fracture, he did have bruised and swollen ears, a bruised and swollen eye, bruised cheeks, and swollen lips. All of these injuries indicate blows to the head resulting in bleeding on the brain.

Unusual bruises:
While many of the bruise injuries are unusual, there are two that really stand out.
Zina (Forest)- had a narrow 12 inch long bloody bruise that extended around her waist from her stomach to her back. This looks to be a result of being hit with a long thin rod or branch. It could also be the result of a restraint.
George (Cedar)- had a large bruise on his upper left leg that extended from his thigh to his buttock. This is also the leg that had 3rd degree burns from top to bottom.

Body Positions:
The only hikers whose positions were not compromised by clothing removal or water are Zina, Rustem, and Igor (all found in the forest area).
In theory, those three hikers should have been found in the positions they died in. Of those three, only Igor was not moved after death. Zina and Rustem both have cadaver spots on their backs. Meaning when they died, their blood pooled into spots on their backs because they were originally laying on their backs. However, when they were found, both Zina and Rustem were on their stomachs. Someone moved them

after they died. This supports the theory of someone removing restraints and/or someone checking to see if they were really dead.

Wearing someone else's clothes:

Igor was wearing Alexander's vest (Igor- Forest, Alexander- Snow Den). Alexander was wearing a winter coat, so it's improbable that Igor removed this vest from under Alexander's coat and then re-dressed Alexander. More than likely, Igor was wearing the vest when he left the tent. Although Alexander could have given it to Igor once they were all out in the freezing cold.

Luda was wearing torn and burnt dark cotton pants over her tights. The burns lined up with the burns on George's legs making them more than likely his. (Luda- Snow Den, George- Cedar). She was also wearing a torn grey jacket that was wrapped around her left shin and foot. This is another item that more than likely belonged to George or Yuri (Cedar). A note here is that these were half clothes. The other halves were found in the area between the Cedar and snow den or on the snow den itself. It's unclear why the clothes were torn in half. One thought is that they were trying to leave a trail or use pieces for a torch. Luda was wearing two sweaters. It's unknown if she was wearing these originally or if she removed one from Yuri or George.

Alexander's coat had a burn on the upper left arm (Snow Den). George's left leg and hand were burned. This could possibly be George's coat due to the burn marks, but it could very well be the one Alexander was wearing originally. The burn marks do not line up with George's burns and Alexander could have burned it getting near the fire.

Other oddities about the clothing are that Nicholas had a pair of gloves in his coat pocket (Snow den), George had a little secret pocket sewn into the inside of his shirt pocket- both were empty (Cedar). Rustem had matches in his ski pants pocket (Forest).

The fact that Nicholas had a pair of gloves in his coat pocket and was not wearing them is suspicious and is another indicator of being restrained. In fact, none of the hikers had gloves on and gloves were found in the tent and scattered outside the tent.

Blood in the chest cavity- Hemothorax

Hemothorax is when blood collects between the chest wall and lungs. This area where blood can pool is known as the pleural cavity. It's caused by an injury to the chest such as broken ribs. It can also be caused by intense external pressure on the chest.

Rustem (Forest)
Alexander (Snow Den)
Nicholas (Snow Den)
Simon (Snow Den)
Luda (Snow Den)

All four in the snow den suffered hemothorax along with Rustem from the forest area. A common torture method is to lay the victim on their back and have someone sit or kneel on their chest. Like the execution-by-freezing mentioned earlier, this method of torture is easy, quick, and doesn't require any tools. The victim suffers extreme pain and can't breathe. This causes damage in the chest area and results in bleeding in the chest cavity.

Bloody foam in the lungs- Pulmonary edema
Everyone except Zina (Forest).

Pulmonary edema is a condition caused by excess fluid in the lungs. This fluid collects in the numerous air sacs in the lungs, making it difficult to breathe. This can be caused by trauma to the chest wall. If a person has a severe pulmonary edema, he might have a pink frothy sputum from the lungs. In rare cases, this sputum will come out of the person's mouth and/or nose.

This is exactly what happened to Yuri. When he was found he was described as having a frothy substance from his mouth to his cheek. If someone leaned on him, sat on him, or ropes were tied around his chest, all those situations could have caused a pulmonary edema. Strangulation is another situation that can cause this condition.

Luda and Simon both suffered extreme chest injuries, so that was likely the cause of their pulmonary edema. Alexander had signs of being strangled, so that probably caused his. We've already mentioned Yuri having the frothy sputum on his face. George suffered a lot of torture like injuries, so his pulmonary edema could have been a result of someone kneeling on his chest or strangulation. Nicholas, Rustem, and Igor could have had the torture applied to them as well.

Broken ribs:
Simon had five broken ribs on his right rib cage. Each of these ribs were broken in two places. A person kneeling on his chest would have caused this type of break (Snow Den)

Luda had four broken ribs on her right rib cage. Each of these ribs were broken in two places. She also had six broken ribs on her left rib cage. Like with Simon, a person kneeling on her chest would have caused this type of break (Snow Den).

As we continue the injuries list, note that the most extreme torture-like injuries were inflicted on some or all of the four found in the snow den.

Nostrils pinched closed such as with a clothespin:
Alexander (Snow Den)
Simon (Snow Den)
Luda (Snow Den)
There's no clue as to what pinched their nostrils shut, but these three were found with their noses pinched closed. Whatever device caused this was removed. This is also a common form of torture to restrict a victim's breathing.

Thyroid cartilage (Adam's Apple) crush injury:
This is a common area to be crushed/injured during strangulation:
Alexander (Snow Den)
Luda (Snow Den)

Broken Nose:
Alexander (Snow Den)

Missing Tongue
Luda (Snow Den). There are many theories as to what happened to Luda's tongue. Her tongue and the entire inside bottom of her mouth was missing. The coroner did not give any explanation except to say that her hyoid bone was visible. The tongue attaches to the hyoid bone in the throat. This means the tongue and entire bottom part of her mouth was cut or pulled out somehow. One theory is that wild animals ate her tongue as the weather warmed up.

Luda was found with her mouth closed while Alexander (who had his tongue) was found with his mouth open (Snow den). Nicholas (who also had his tongue) had a hole in his face right next to his mouth (Snow den). This is not to say that an animal didn't eat her tongue, but there were no other signs of animal damage to Luda. There were no bite marks or anything to indicate how an animal ate Luda's tongue out of her closed mouth.

Luda's hyoid bone was microscopically inspected and they found no sign of bleeding meaning the tongue and mouth aperture were removed after her death. Or, because she was found with her face in running water, the blood could have washed away.

Another missing detail is how the rest of the inside of her mouth looked. Were the cuts clean or ragged? Details like this would help solve the mystery of what happened to Luda's tongue, but the coroner completely neglected to give any further details except to say it was missing.

Tongue removal is a torture method. Luda's stomach contained a reddish-brown, slimy mass that may have been blood. If so, then she swallowed blood when her tongue was removed. Again, there are far too few clues to determine what happened to Luda and her tongue and if she was alive when it was removed.

Positive Radiation Test:
Alexander's grey sweater and blue ski pants (Snow Den)
Luda's brown sweater (Snow Den)
The clothes that tested positive on Alexander were the inner clothes and not his outerwear. Luda's sweater that tested positive was her outer sweater. The radiation test also included earth from where they were found and another body from the nearby town. All items tested within normal ranges except for Alexander's sweater and pants and Luda's sweater. These items were more than twice the normal range. After they were immersed in running water the numbers dropped in half. However, Luda and Alexander were found in running water and had been there for up to two weeks. There's no indication how high the radiation was originally. And there's no explanation for the radiation in the original investigation.

Missing skin around the eyes:
Alexander (Snow Den)
Simon (Snow Den)
Luda (Snow Den)

Missing Eyeballs- Completely removed from the sockets:
Simon (Snow Den)
Luda (Snow Den)

The eye sockets of both Simon and Luda were microscopically examined. Signs of bleeding were found meaning their eyeballs were removed while they were alive.

Even if we were to ignore every other injury, this fact- that their eyeballs were removed while they were alive- is enough to point to a situation that was not a natural event. It was murder.

Another troubling injury is Luda and Simon's crushed ribs. A current theory is that the ribs were crushed during a fall. This can be discounted for a few reasons. One is that when you fall down you throw your arms and legs out to break the fall. No one had broken arms, legs, wrists or ankles. If a fall was high enough to caused crushed ribs, then it was certainly high enough to break other bones, yet no one had fractures or breaks in their extremities.

One other reason against a fall is where did they fall from? These two were found in the snow den area of a field near a stream. There is now where to fall from. If we posit the theory that they fell from the Cedar then why were they moved to this area? And again, why no other fractures?

It's also been suggested that the weight of the snow caused their broken ribs. The microscopic test showed us that these injuries were sustained while they were alive and thus not incurred after they died and were buried in the snow.

The falling from a great height theory dissolves under scrutiny. The crushed ribs were not an injury from a fall, they were an injury from someone kneeling on their chests.

Who would kill these nine hikers? Why then and why there? There are too many details missing to determine why these nine individual were killed. Simon's diary is missing, we don't know what equipment Alexander was testing. We don't know why the group was behind schedule. We don't know what Alexander and Nicholas were doing to slow down the group. We don't even know whose clothes were whose or what anyone had in their backpacks because the backpacks were dumped into a big pile with the tent items and all rolled up together and flown out of the area.

So, we're left with lots of gaps, but we do have a few details from the hikers themselves. We have their diaries and we have their pictures.

We've already addressed the conflicting information in the entries. There's the entry about celebrating Alexander's birthday even though it was not the right day or month. There's the different entries about the storage area. We have Igor's final words about being warm and comfortable and we have Zina's final word, which is a name: Rempel.

We know little about Rempel except that he was a hunter. He did give a statement to investigators saying that he didn't know what happened to the hikers. He did recount talking to Igor in Vijay before the group left. He also said there was bad weather during the time the hikers disappeared. It was snowing and windy at the time. He also suggested that the high winds blew the hikers out of their tent and caused their injuries.

Now, like everything else, there are many gaps in his testimony. He may be telling the truth. However, we'll never truly know how much he did or didn't know. The group diary talks about following a hunter's tracks. We don't know if that was Rempel, or someone wanting to do harm, or someone just innocently going about their business. There is just too little information to determine that.

A big thing missing is motive. Motives for murder include burglary, sexual assault, revenge, witness elimination, and a myriad of other reasons. We've already ruled out burglary because all the valuables were left behind. We can rule out sexual assault because there was no sign of it during the autopsies and the coroner did make a point of stating that fact. One thing we do have is the strange little behaviors leading up to their deaths.

George got arrested for singing. He was taken to the police station. During that time in communist Russia, the only secure phone lines were in the military and the police stations. George could have made a secure call from the police station. Perhaps as a signal to someone that all was well.

The group encountered a drunk at the next station. He could have been part of this and was giving a sign that all was well.

We have Luda picking up a strange package in a photo. Was it hers? The officers? Some lighthearted prank or joke? Did she keep it and take it with her on the hike intending to return it when the group returned? And if she kept it was it important enough to someone else for that someone to follow them into the wilderness to retrieve the item. Was it an important classified item that fell into the wrong hands and the hikers were killed because of it?

What device was Alexander testing? Why did he lie about his birthday? What were he and Nicholas doing to hold the group up?

What did George have in his hidden pocket? Was it always empty or did something important get removed during their last night alive.

Why was Simon holding a pen and notebook when his body was found? His hands were frostbitten and there's no way he was writing something when he died. Someone put that notebook and pen in his hand either as he died or after he died. Why? Was it a message that got lost when his body ended up in the water?

Why did Simon have a camera around his neck? Or was it just a camera case with something else inside.

Why did Nicholas have a full pair of gloves in his pocket? He- and everyone else- were out in the freezing weather. Why not put his gloves on? This is another sign of them being restrained or under duress.

What did Alexander do with all those extra sweaters? Since the entire contents of the tent were dumped together we'll never know which sweaters were the ones Alexander brought.

Luda's sweater tested positive for radiation. Was it originally one of Alexanders? Why just Luda and Alexander for the positive radiation test? If someone was following Alexander, and knew he had these items, why not just deal with Alexander? Why take out the whole group?

I believe part of that answer is that whoever came across the group didn't know exactly who he was looking for, he just knew he was looking for a male with radioactive material. The torture could have been a way to gain more information and to see who really knew what.

The fact that there was torture involved points to a situation where the murderer doesn't know who he's looking for at first. He just knew he'd been sent to find someone.

There were portable Geiger counters back then. If one was used and then perhaps it detected radiation in the campsite and on the hikers. If everyone denied knowledge of radiation, then the intruder resorted to torture and execution to find out the truth. Of course, this is all theory, but it does explain the torture-like wounds and deaths.

As mentioned earlier we have the hiker's last words through their diaries. Now, let's take a look at their very last photos.

Along with the negatives and photos contained in the official government file was an envelope containing loose pictures of the hikers. While we don't know which roll of film these pictures belong to, we can surmise the last photos through process of elimination along with the items that were photographed. Two of these photos are known to be the very last photos of the hikers.

These two photos were found loose in the official file and are not assigned to any particular role of film. They show the hikers preparing the tent site and are thought to be the last photos of the hikers alive.

The top photo is thought to be one of the last of the hikers taken while setting up the tent for the last time. Notice the ski pole circled in the foreground.
The bottom photo is of the collapsed tent with the same ski pole circled in the background.

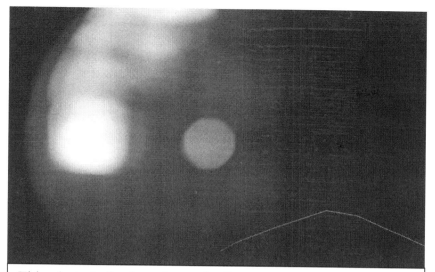

This photo is the last picture in George's camera.

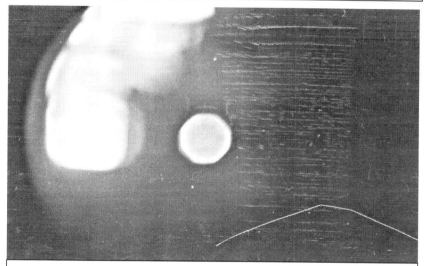

This is the same picture after it has been lightened to show details. The middle spot is a light fixture on a ceiling and the light 'trail' is a reflection on the lens. This picture is the result of someone accidentally snapping a picture while removing the film from the camera after the camera had been moved to the search headquarters.

The following picture is the last picture taken by a camera found in the tent. This camera is believed to belong to Nicholas.
Who is this?

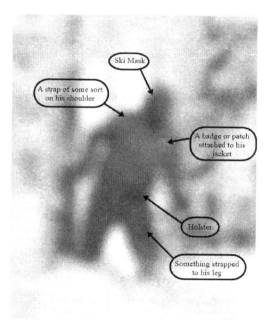

211

A photo of the group for comparison.

Mystery man appears bigger and huskier than any of the hikers. He's also wearing a pouch or kit around his waist and has something strapped to his leg. There is also a badge or patch on his jacket. None of the hikers have this type of appearance even at a distance.

The last photo in one of the rolls of film is of a mystery man. The man is in the distance. He has a distinct appearance and does not resemble any of the nine hikers of the Dyatlov group.

The group photo on the opposite page shows that none of the hikers are built like the mystery man. The hikers are all shorter and more slender. They did not wear ski masks, nor did any of them wear a belt around their waist or a weapon attached to their leg.

At first glance it's easy to dismiss this last photo as a picture of one of the hikers. But as we look closer we can see details that don't line up with what any of them are wearing. We can see that this person is heavier than anyone in the group. This person is wearing a ski mask. They have something that looks like epaulets on their shoulders. They have a badge or patch on the left side of their chest. They're wearing a pouch or holster around their waist. And they have tools hanging from their belt as well as a gun or knife strapped to their leg.

No hiker was ever dressed like this. As we look over all the hiker's pictures there is not one where anyone has a tool pouch around their waist, tools strapped to their belt and leg, epaulets, and something that looks like a badge or medal pinned to their chest.

As we explore the mystery man photo we can see details of items that none of the other hikers wore. As an experiment, I dressed up a GI Joe in similar garb.

I added a holster to his belt and strapped a knife to his leg. However, the mystery man in the original photo could be wearing tools such as a shovel, pick axe, hammer, machete, or innumerable other items.

For the sake of this comparison I added similar items to GI Joe. One of the most apparent items in the mystery man photo is the ski mask which I did add to GI Joe. GI Joe doesn't have epaulets (straps on his shoulders), however I was able to make the v neck and add gloves as our mystery man was apparently wearing gloves.

I took a black and white picture of GI Joe and then purposely blurred the photo to resemble the original photo. The similarities are uncanny. A side-by-side comparison emphasizes the items the mystery man is carrying with him.

GI Joe with ski mask, holster
and knife strapped to leg
(Copyright: Launton Anderson)

Mystery Man

Who was this mystery man? Did the group see him before he was caught on camera? Did they even know he was there? He may have approached the group and asked for help and joined the group that way. Or he could have been following them and surprised them by showing up at their campsite on that final night. Either way, he was probably armed.

To get the Dyatlov group out of the tent while they were partially clothed would have taken an armed group of intruders. A single individual could have gotten their attention and gotten them to move. But after desperation and cold set in, the Dyatlov group would have overpowered a single individual.

I believe this mystery man was part of a group of at least three armed individuals. They took the Dyatlov group by surprise and forced them out of the tent.

Forcing the Dyatlov group away from their own campsite would have accomplished a few things. One is it would have removed them from a familiar setting. Another is it would have eliminated them from utilizing any potential weapons.

Once the Dyatlov group was removed from the tent, the intruders had the advantage of complete control over the group. More than likely, the intruders had a campsite set up near the Cedar area. It makes sense since this is the direction the group traveled once out of the tent.

In fact, the intruders would not have risked their own lives just to move the Dyatlov group. The intruders would have wanted to be near shelter and warmth and would not have directed the group towards the empty wilderness. They would have directed them toward their own area. The Cedar area provided an ideal spot for a shelter. In fact, this is how George and Yuri's bodies were found. The searchers were, at that time, looking for a good spot to set up another shelter. They found the Cedar area to be a perfect spot for this. And then they found the bodies.

The intruders knew they were going to kidnap the Dyatlov group. And they knew they were going to kill them. This is why the group was forced away from the tent. And this is why there was no sign of panic in the tent. The Dyatlov group was taken by surprise and ordered out of the tent. They had no choice but to comply. Their injuries show that some did fight back. Some were even tortured. But ultimately, all nine lost their lives.

Chapter 7

Theories

*"If they were really killed by a natural force,
then there would be no secret,
and we would not be talking about this
more than 50 years later."*

~Yuri Yudin~

Over the years there have been many theories and speculations about this case. Some were ruled out immediately by the original investigators and some are still being scrutinized. While the case has been officially closed since 1959, the mystery remains. Here we'll examine the more prominent theories and discuss what could have or could not have caused this tragedy.

Avalanche

The slope where the tent was is at a 30° angle. This is enough of an angle for an avalanche even though they are scarce in that area.

The first searchers and the ones who found the tent ruled out an avalanche almost immediately. There were simply no signs of one. No displaced snow, no downed trees, and no debris.

In addition to there not being any sign of an avalanche outside the tent, there was no sign of avalanche damage within the tent. Nothing was crushed. There were tins of food that were still whole. A cup of cocoa remained upright. Crackers and other delicate items were undamaged.

A related theory is that they heard an avalanche, panicked, sliced their way out of the tent and ran down the mountain getting lost in the process.

Even if they did hear something that frightened them into exiting the tent, we must remember that they were found ½ mile to a mile away. That means they walked or ran for almost an hour in the snow while partially dressed. At some point someone would have turned around and realized there was no danger. And that would have happened within minutes. At that point they would have seen that there was no avalanche and immediately returned to their shelter.

As with the very earliest officials who investigated this mystery, we can safely rule out 'avalanche' and 'hearing an avalanche' as the reason the hikers left their tent.

Unusual loud sound/flashes of light

Like the avalanche theory, it's highly unlikely that a loud sound or flashes of light would have led the hikers to destroy their tent and walk/run a mile away without proper clothing in the elements. It was -30° that night and the snow was over four foot deep. Loud sounds/bright lights would have made them come out of the tent to see what was going on, but they wouldn't have left their shelter and risked their lives by leaving everything behind.

Military Activity

We can't rule out the military in this case, simply because we aren't privy to the military activities in the area at that time.

However, whatever military activity the group may have inadvertently seen, does not equate to them leaving the tent in a panic. All the tangible clues point away from a self-induced chaotic exit from the tent.

If the military was involved, and killed the group because the group 'saw something they weren't supposed to see' then we'll have no way of knowing that for sure. If the group saw a top secret activity, then it seems to reason that the military would detain them. Or, if it was serious enough, they might even make them disappear.

The military would have weapons available for a quick execution style death and the hikers would have been quickly shot. The military would have no need to hide the fact or cover-up the deaths.

We can't completely rule out the military, but we can say that this case doesn't fit with a military style situation.

Fireballs

This theory frequently falls under the 'military intervention' theory with the fireballs being the reason the group left the tent in a panic.

Another student hiking group reported seeing fireballs on February 17th, 1959. This would have been well after the Dyatlov group died. That, however, does not eliminate the fact that the Dyatlov group may have seen fireballs on their last night.

But, like the 'heard an avalanche' and 'unusual loud sounds/flashes of light' theories, the hikers would not have destroyed their own tent and fled upon seeing something like this. They would have behaved as the other groups did: watched, noted it in their diary, wonder about it, and then continue with the hike.

High Winds

Rempel and other witnesses close to the area reported that there was snow and high winds during the beginning of February. High winds and weather could have affected the speed of the hike. But high winds did not blow them into the places their bodies were found. Nor did it blow them out of their tent as some theories have postulated.

This does not make physical sense and there would be no way for a wind to blow nine adults out of their tent, yet leave small delicate items in the tent.

Weather may have hastened their deaths, but high wind was not the cause of the tragedy.

Murder/Suicide

This theory states that one of the group members killed the rest of the group and then himself/herself.

We can eliminate this possibility by exploring the hiker's injuries and the way they died.

Luda and Simon both had broken ribs that could not have been self-induced, so we can rule both of them out as the offending member.

Nicholas and Rustem died by violent head injuries caused by something external to themselves, so they did not do this.

Alexander was strangled and someone cut the clothes off of George and Yuri after they died, so none of those three could have done it.

Zina was found in a different position that what she died in so we can rule her out.

That leaves Igor. A murder/suicide means that Igor went crazy and crushed Simon and Luda's chests and pulled their eyes out while they were alive, burned George, strangled Alexander, killed Yuri and Zina, and hit Nicholas and Rustem in the head hard enough to kill them.

Then Igor laid on his back and wrapped his arms around a branch and froze to death. While he could have likely killed himself that way, there's a very little chance that he could have single handedly controlled the group and killed off the other members.

More than that, there was nothing for him to gain, nor any motive for this behavior.

It's highly unlikely that Igor was the cause of this tragedy.

Infrasound/Karmen Vortex Street

Infrasound is a low-frequency sound that is too low for normal human hearing. However, even though it's such a low sound, humans can still sense it. This situation causes feelings of dread, anxiety, and panic. Infrasound, along with Karmen Vortex Street, has been used as a theory of what drove the hikers out of the tent.

Karmen vortex street is the phenomena that happens when high wind encounters a stable body. An example is how wind can make a car antenna vibrate or high wires 'sing' and make sounds. This force can be disruptive both physically and emotionally when encountered by humans.

The infrasound/karmen vortex street theory states that this phenomena happened that night to the hikers. They set up their campsite in a location that was ideal for these conditions. And when the phenomena occurred it drove the hikers into a panic where they destroyed their tent and ran down the mountain ultimately leading to their deaths.

Despite the fact that this particular area has not had any evidence of being susceptible to neither infrasound nor karmen vortex street, we must examine the possibility.

In controlled experiments, infrasound affects 20% of the subjects of the experiment. This means that 80% are not affected at all or have very few effects.

Karmen vortex street is a known condition to exist in certain favorable situations.

So, if in the possibility of a 'perfect storm' of these events happening on that night, it would have affected 20% of the hikers. That would mean it affected two of the hikers at the most.

If two hikers were suddenly panicked and tried to flee the tent by cutting the side open, the other seven would have stopped them. Even if the phenomena affected a few more people, the others would have been able to stop them.

Even if the panicked individuals ran out of the tent partially dressed, the others would have dressed prior to pursuing them. All nine hikers would not have left the tent partially dressed and walked for over an hour on purpose.

Most importantly, is again, the fact that there was nothing in the tent to suggest a group panic. Nothing was crushed and items were not in a chaotic jumble.

While it's important to understand infrasound/karmen vortex street, this is not what caused all nine member to exit the tent.

Drugs

The drugs theory is very similar to the infrasound/karmen vortex street theory.

Only this theory is based upon the group taking some sort of psychedelic drug. There are several reasons against this theory. One is there was no sign of drugs in the tent or in their systems. Two is that a drug is going to affect everyone differently. They're not all going to have the same panic inducing vision. And three, they were in a survival situation. There's no reason or evidence that drugs were part of their hike.

Escaped Prisoners

Interestingly enough, two escaped prisoners were caught during the search. These two readily gave themselves up and denied any involvement with the Dyatlov group. It's highly unlikely an escaped convict caused the group's death. A convict would be interested in the food, money, and shelter. The shelter was destroyed and the food and money were left behind. The Dyatlov tragedy was not caused by escaped prisoners.

Mansi

The early investigation ruled out the Mansi. The area the Dyatlov group was in was not of any importance to the Mansi. There had never been any violent encounters with the Mansi. Although indigenous to the area, the Mansi were not the cause of the Dyatlov tragedy.

Murder

If we take into consideration all the variables that the other theories don't explore such as the radiation report, the microbiology report, the torture-like injuries, and the signs of restraint, then we're left with the fact that a human being murdered the hikers. We know when and how it happened, but we don't know why or who did it.

We can build a scenario on what we do know. Let's take a moment to consider such a scenario with the caveat that this is all supposition.

George is in on this. He makes contact with someone via phone call at the police station.

Nicholas is in on this. Probably more for cover and to act as a look out.

Alexander is the main player. He already has a degree and he worked in Moscow in a classified facility. Yet, for some reason, he is moved from that facility to go to UPI to pursue another degree.

Back in those days, very little happened without the approval of the government. With his security clearance, Alexander would have been tracked regularly. He would not have been able to make a unilateral decision to quit a classified job and return to school- not without the approval of the government.

So, we'll say that Alexander is a spy with the blessing of the USSR. We don't know who he's passing secrets to, but to be historically accurate we must surmise that it's the US or Germany. Either way, he's passing secrets onto this other country, but the USSR knows and is setting up what secrets he does or doesn't pass on. In other words, the 'other country' thinks he's passing secrets when indeed they're all only fake.

The other country finds out that the secrets are fake. Back in this day and time the secrets were more than likely nuclear related since the nuclear arms race was going strong. For the sake of brevity, let's say the 'other country' is the US.

So, the US finds out Alexander's secrets are fake. They send out an assassination team. The US sets up a meeting with Alexander for Alexander to pass on radioactive garments. In this case, he's going to pass on a sweater.

So, he brings extra sweaters on the hike. They're all radioactive, but he only needs one to pass along. This can be easily accomplished by befriending someone in the forest during a long hike. They don't want this meeting to happen in a busy city, they want it to happen in the isolated wilderness.

So, Alexander thinks he's passing a sweater along. The plan is that someone will approach the group and claim he's lost some clothing. Hiking groups always help each other, especially in deadly environments, so Alexander will pass one of the contaminated sweaters to this stranger. The deal is done. This is what Alexander thinks is going to happen.

To keep his cover, Alexander uses a false birthday to the group. He also has a 'device' which is actually a radio wave device that sends out a radio signal so his point of contact can find him easily. Alexander tells the group it's some sort of scientific device to check air quality or something. The group buys this explanation. After all, none of them are studying his degree (physics) and why would they question a scientific device.

Alexander's point of contact is going to follow them and meet up with them in the wilderness. This is quite an easy and believable scenario. It's probably happened before.

Alexander and Nicholas hold the group up by lagging behind to talk about the situation. Nicholas will help to find the point of contact and he'll help with the group buy-in to help out the point of contact.

George has passed the message on that the hike is under way.

That plan is what Alexander thinks is going to happen.

However, the US has realized it's been given false information from one of Alexander's previous meetings with them. On their end, they set-up the meeting in the wilderness, but with the understanding that Alexander will be killed for his duplicity and to also send a message to the Russians.

The assassination team follows along with the group. On the day they cross paths, one of the hikers accidentally takes a picture of them. Hence the 'Mystery Man' photo.

The killer group surprises the Dyatlov group. The killer group forces everyone out of the tent, has them empty their pockets to figure out who's who and who's carrying what. The killers then force them downslope and towards the killer's own camp.

This is also the day that Nicholas and Simon are on duty. When the killer group approaches the Dyatlov group, Nicholas and Simon are not at camp. They're setting up the storage site. As the killer group forces the Dyatlov group out of the tent, Simon and Nicholas are away and still warmly dressed

Once in the woods, the killer group has decided that Zina, Rustem, and Igor are not the ones they're looking for. They tie those three up, blindfold them, and leave them to die in the elements. The killer group forces the other six up towards to the Cedar area.

One factor that helped determine who to keep and who to abandon is that the killer group utilized a Geiger counter. Zina, Rustem, and Igor tested negative, so it was easier to tie them up and leave them to die rather than deal with them as part of the bigger group.

Once in the Cedar area, everyone else was tied up with George and Yuri tied up to the Cedar tree. The killers light a campfire for their own warmth, for light, and to utilize as a torture device.

To force them to talk, the killers tortured George and Yuri. Yuri did not know anything and died from his injuries.

George was tortured and burned and died from his injuries. The blood found on the Cedar tree is left from the effects of this torture. Alexander and Luda remain tied up in the Cedar area.

Back to the group left behind to freeze to death. Zina, Rustem, and Igor struggle and finally get themselves free. Someone from the killer group hears them and the killers leave the group at the Cedar to take care of the group in the woods.

By this time Zina, Rustem, and Igor were making their way back to the tent. The killers caught Rustem first, they fought and the killers bashed Rustem on the head with the butt of a gun. This knocked him out and ultimately killed him.

Then, they caught up to Igor, fought with him, and hit him with the butt of a gun. They wrestled him to the ground and tied him up so he couldn't get free again. Then they went after Zina. She fought with them. They hit her hard on the waist with a baton to bring her down. They tie her up and leave her.

Rustem, Igor, and Zina remain restrained and freeze to death.

When the killers get back to the Cedar, Alexander agrees to tell them everything they want to know. They take Alexander away to their campsite. They leave Luda tied up to die in the Cedar area.

Meanwhile, Simon and Nicholas return to the tent. No one is there. They see the footprints going downslope and the campfire in the Cedar area. They make their way there.

Once there, they find Luda. She's dressed very lightly in a button-up shirt and stockings. Even with a fire, she's in danger of freezing to death. They do everything they can to save her. They cut clothes off Yuri and George and wrap them around Luda.

They take broken limbs and wrap clothing around the top for makeshift torches which they're going to use to search for the others. That's when the killers return to the Cedar area. They fight with Simon and Nicholas and bash Nicholas' head with a gun butt.

They extinguish the campfire in the Cedar area. They force Simon, Nicholas, and Luda towards their camp which is located near the snow den. The killers have made the snow den for their own purposes rather than for the hikers. However, it's a convenient spot to drop them all and tie them up.

The clothes that were cut off Yuri and George and wrapped around Luda fall off along the way from the Cedar to the snow den area.

The makeshift torches are dropped and fall apart leaving more clothes and sticks behind. Other trees and branches that were found cut, were actually cut by the killers for their own use in their own campsite.

Nicholas passes out and dies from his head wound. Alexander talks, but the killers are interested in Simon, too, since he served in the war he might know secrets also.

They torture Simon by kneeling on his chest and cutting out his eyes. He dies from his injuries. Luda's outer sweater, which was given to her by Alexander or removed from Yuri or George, gives a positive sign for radiation via the Geiger counter.

The killers torture her the same way they tortured Simon. She dies from her injuries.

Once they're finished with Alexander they strangle him. They leave Luda, Nicholas, Simon, and Alexander lying next to each other a few feet from the snow den. To taunt the authorities, they pose Simon with a notebook and pen in his hands. We'll never know if anything was written in the notebook because ultimately the notebook and Simon ended up in water.

The killers go back to the Cedar area where they collect the bindings that they used to tie up Yuri and George. They go back to the tent, stopping to collect the bindings from Rustem, Igor, and Zina along the way.

They get to the hiker's tent and it's sagging in the middle. One of the killers cut a ski pole to prop the tent up while they're inside. Inside the tent, they go through diaries and keep the ones they want. They collect and keep Alexander's device and any other items of interest to them. They collect flashlights, but leave the money, passports, food, and clothing.

They cut the tent up to destroy it.

Outside the tent, they shine a flashlight around looking for anything of significance on the ground. They leave the flashlight on top of the destroyed tent (probably by accident).

They use the other flashlight to make their way downslope and towards their camp. The flashlight burns out along the way, so they toss it aside.

At their campsite, they stay for another day or so then pack up and leave. Thus leaving behind a mystery.

There were probably a total of three to five killers. Enough to contain the Dyatlov group of nine, but not enough to draw attention to a large encampment. The killers also didn't want to use guns to shoot any of the hikers because gunfire would draw attention. Knives could have

226

been used for killing, but the blood would draw predators. So, they used the most efficient means possible: the freezing weather.

Even though they took their bindings and tools and tent away, they did leave behind a few things such as the two military style windings found later. There are probably more clues that were revealed once the snow thawed, but the USSR authorities shut down the area before any civilians could discover these things.

Some of these undiscovered clues could have been signs of an intruder's campsite. As noted earlier, the Cedar area was discovered because searchers thought it would be a good place to set up camp.

If the intruders had set a campsite up there, then they would have been able to see the Dyatlov tent. The big Cedar tree itself had its branches cut off one side. It was said that it looked like someone cleared the branches to get a good view of the Dyatlov campsite.

The cut tree tops, branches, and wood would also explain the presence of another campsite. No matter the theory of how the hikers got to the Cedar area, it's not likely that they cleared 20 some trees, cut wood, and scattered clothing between the Cedar area and the snow den. The hikers did not have gloves and only had one knife among them.

And, speaking of the snow den, we know that as the winter went on, snow drifted to bury the snow den. Yet, there are signs that it was originally dug out and then branches laid on top for flooring. If the hiker's did it, what did they use to dig out the snow? Their hands were bare. They would not have spent their energy digging into the snow with their bare hands.

So, there are clues that point to the fact that another camp was there. The intruders were the ones who cut the branches and the tree tops. They dug out the snow den and possibly utilized it for a tent. We know that tents were built on branches to help with insulation. That snow den could have been a spot for a tent.

Of all the theories out there, this one answers the most questions. It accounts for the unusual details of the case such as the destroyed tent, the strange torture-like injuries, the Dyatlov group being spread out in different places, the lack of panic in the tent, and the items scattered around the tent.

The use of Alexander in this theory is merely an example. His strange actions during the hike warrant further investigation if possible. However, any of the others could just as well have been the target.

Conclusion

The evidence in this tragedy points to the group being murdered. Who murdered them is a question that may unfortunately never be answered. Perhaps the answer lies in the remaining official file that has yet to be released. Perhaps the authorities know who killed them and why, yet prefer to keep that answer a state secret.

Together, the Dyatlov group had a combined 55 years of outdoor survival experience. They were a group of well-liked, personable, and athletic young people. If they would have lived, there's no doubt they all would have led successful lives. While this mystery may never be fully resolved, we can safely say that this tragedy wasn't due to an amateur hiking group run amok. They were a group of professionals.

As we read their words and see their pictures we can feel their joy and excitement. We get a sense of their teamwork and protectiveness. Not only do their words tell us that, but their past experiences have proven it.

While the questions remain of who and why, we do know that the hikers did their best under extreme circumstances. They stayed together, they helped each other, and they did their best to survive.

In this book we've explored the unusual clues. We've examined maps, autopsies, photos, and diaries. We then took each piece of this puzzle and put it together to create a narrative. This narrative shows how each clue fits into the bigger picture. And as we evaluate the bigger picture we find the key to this tragedy. They were killed.

We may never know who killed them or why. But the murderer is not the focus. In contrast to the hikers' bravery, he's a coward. He hid his agenda, surprised the group, and took advantage of the isolated situation. He's merely a speck of dust in the overall picture. Whoever he is will always be overshadowed by the Dyatlov group.

Igor, Zina, Rustem, George, Yuri, Luda, Nicholas, Alexander, and Simon are bigger than any single piece of this mystery. Their names and their courage live on. Their actions were brave in the face of adversity.

May their names and legacy live on forever.

Top Row: Igor, Nicholas, and Zina
Middle Row: Yuri, George, and Alexander
Bottom Row: Simon, Luda, and Rustem
May they rest in peace.

Appendix

Please note: All official documents are translated 'as is'. Due to this, the reports do have syntax errors, odd symbols, and words that are out of order or did not properly translate. This is an artifact of the language translation. To keep with the spirit of the reports, I have left the translation as is. These reports are in a constant state of inspection and translation therefore are subject to change. They are accurate at the time of publication, however the author is not responsible for any errors they may contain.

The Group Diary

January 23, 1959
Now we are sitting in the room 531, or rather of course do not sit, but rather frantically shoving into backpacks any oatmeal, cans, canned meat. Zavchoz (head of provision distribution) stands and makes sure everything is included. Where are my felt boots? Y.K (Yuri Krivonischenko) Can we play mandolin on the train? Of course! We forgot the salt! 3kg (kilograms) Igor! Where are you? Where is Doroshenko? Why did he take 20 packs? Give me 15 kopecks. Spring balance, spring balance. Where is spring balance? Can't fit it. Damn. Who has the knife? Yura drove it to the station. Slave Khalizov has arrived. Hallo, Hallo! Luda is counting the money. The room is an artistic mess. And here we are on the train. We sang all the songs that we know, learned new ones, everyone goes to sleep at 3 (am). I wonder what awaits us in this trip? What will be new? The boys solemnly swore not to smoke the entire trip. I wonder how much they have will power, if they can get by without cigarettes? Everyone is sleeping and Ural taiga is spread in all directions.
Zoya Kolmogorova

January 24
(7am) We arrived in Serov (town). We traveled with a group of Blinov. They have... things for hunting and other accessories. At the station, we were met with "hospitality". They didn't allow us into the building. The policeman stares at us suspiciously. There is no crime or violation, as under communism. Yuri Krivonischenko started to sing a song and a cop grabbed him and took him away. The sergeant explained that the rules of Section 3 prohibited all activity that would disturb the peace of passengers. It is perhaps the only train station where the songs are forbidden. Finally, everything is settled with the law.

Going to Ivdel from Serov at 6:30 pm. We were welcomed warmly in the school near the railway station. Zavchos (who takes care of physical property), who is also a janitor, heated water for us, gave us everything she could to help us during our track. We are free all day. I wanted to go to the city, visit nature museum or take a trip to a factory, but too much time is taken by the distribution of equipment and training.
12:00 pm In the interval between 1st and 2nd shifts in school we organized a meeting with the students. Small room is cramped with all the kids that are curious. Zolotarev: "Kids, now we'll tell you... Tourism is, makes it possible to..." Everyone is sitting, quiet, worried. Z. Kolmogorova: Tra- ta- ta- ta. What's your name? Where were you before?

And she went on and on. There was no end of questions toward Zina. We had to explain every detail to the kids, from torches to setting up tents. We spent 2 hours lecturing and kids did not want to let us go. They sang songs to each other. At the station, we saw the whole school. In the end, when we were leaving, the kids yelled and cried, asking Zina to remain with them. They promised to listen to her and study well.

On a train station, some young alcoholic accused us of stealing his wallet from a pocket. For the second time the police are on the scene. Debate- talk about love thanks to provocation by Z. Kolmogorova. Songs, revision, Dubinina under the seat, garlic bread without water and we arrived in Ivdel around 12 am. Large waiting room. Total freedom of action. Took turns all night to keep stuff safe. Bus to Vijay leaves early in the morning.

Yura Yudin

25 January 1959.

We got up at half past five, quickly gathered and left for the city of Ivdel with the first bus. After an hour of waiting, we managed to grab a bus (such as GAZ-51). The twenty-five-seater bus was forced to accommodate a full twenty-five plus twenty backpacks packed to capacity and as many pairs of skis. We were full up to the ceiling. First layer passengers sat on the seats, on a pile of skis, on backpacks. Second layer passengers sat on the backs of the seats, finding a place for legs on the shoulders of comrades. It was not so tight, however, as not to sing, so we did it almost all the way to Vizhay.

The trip was not uneventful. The bus made a small detour away from the highway, in the village of Shipichnoe, and we were given the chance to step out, which we did with pleasure. Four of the most agile went far ahead to the settlement of Talitsa to see the power station. Suddenly the heard: "The bus." We rush out the door, but, alas, it was too late. The bus passed by and we were forced to chance after it as fast as we can, hoping fate would be merciful and, perhaps, we would catch up with it (I am part of the "agile" four). However, the first hundred meters clearly demonstrated the advantages of a fifty horse power engine. Our heels flashed far behind the bus, and the gap widened. The prospect to walk about thirty kilometers on the highway with no breakfast and lunch already seemed quite real, when suddenly ... I mentioned that fate is merciful. The mercy came in the form of a girl going to Vizhay that hailed the bus and stopped the object of our persecution. A minute later we were already safely sitting on the second floor of the seats and traveling to Vizhay. We arrived in Vizhay about two pm. It turned out that we can continue our automobile journey in the next morning.

Warmly said goodbye to Blinov's group, who went further (to the west of Vizhay in the deep forest area). After dinner, which was held in a warm "friendly atmosphere," we moved to the "hotel", which was the usual hut with three windows. We went to the cinema, leaving "home" Doroshenko and Kolevatov. We watched the "Symphonie in Gold", came back in "musical mood". Now we are busy getting ready the equipment. Tonight, according to the local commandant, we will leave on.

Kolevatov.

January 26

We slept in a so- called hotel. Two people per bed. Sasha K. (Alexander Kolevatov) and Krivoy (Yuri Krivonischenko) slept on the floor between beds. Woke up at 9 am. Everyone sleep well despite the fact we did not completely close the small window and room got a bit cold. Outside temperature is -17 C. We did not boil in the morning, wood is moist, in the evening it took us 6 hours to boil water. Went to lunch in the dining

232

room. Had some goulash and tea. Then they served tea Igor Dyatlov spoke with a smile: "If the tea is cold, then go out and drink it on the street, it will be hot". The original, though. Agreed to go to 41 by car. We left only at 13:10 (1:10 pm). Froze while riding on top of GAZ- 63. While traveling sang songs, discussed various topics, including love, friendship and problems of the cure for cancer. The 41st settlement they met us friendly, gave us a private room in the hostel. Talked with the local workers. I remembered particularly the red- bearded man. The Beard as his friends call him. Ognev, old friend, described by Lyuba Dubinina in her private diary. Cooked lunch, then ate and now resting. Half of the group is watching a movie, another is sitting on backpacks doing their things. Rustik (Rustem Slobodin) is playing his mandolin while talking with Nicky, and I am going to deal with adjusting the equipment.
Krivonischenko

01/26/59
I can't. although I tried.
Nick Thibault

1/27/59
The weather is good, the wind is blowing in the back. Guys agreed wit the locals and horse with drive us to Second Severniy settlement. From 41st settlement it will be about 24 km. We helped grandfather Slava to unload hay from a carriage and waited for the horse (she went to get more hay and wood). We waited until 4:00. Boys started rewriting some song. One guy san beautifully. We heard a number of illegal prison songs (Article 58 counter- revolutionary crimes). Ognev told Igor how to find the house in which we can spend the night. We bought four loaves of bread and went there at 4:00. Soft warm bread. Ate 2 pieces. Horse is slow. What a pleasure to go without backpacks. We covered 8 km in 2 hours. (River Ushma). It gets darker. All the delay due to a horse. Yuri Yudin is riding with us. He suddenly fell ill and he can't continue with the track. He wants to gather few local minerals for the University and return. Second Severniy (Northern) is an abandoned village of geologists with total of 2025 houses. Only one is suitable for living. In complete darkness we found a village and the house. We started a fire. Several people pierced their hands with old nails. Everything is good. Then the horse came. We were talking and throwing jokes till 3 o'clock in the morning.
Doroshenko

January 28
We were awaken by Yurka Kri and Sasha Kolevatov. Weather is perfect. It is only -8C outside. After breakfast, some of the guys headed by Yury Yudin, our well- known geologist, went to look for local minerals. They didn't find anything except pyrite and quartz veins in the rock. Spend some time with skis, fixed and adjusted the mounting. Yuri Yudin now goes back home. It is a pity, of course, that he leaves us. Especially for me and Zina, but nothing can be done about it.
We go up the river Lozva. We take turns to head the group for about 10 minutes. Depth of snow cover is significantly less than last year. Often we have to stop and scrape the wet, melting snow from skis. Yurka Kri is behind and makes sketches of the route. We pass few cliffs on the right bank of Lozva river. Overall the terrain becomes flatter. We stop at 5:30pm. Today we spend our first night in the tent. The guys are busy with the stove. With some thing completed and others not, we sit for a dinner. After dinner we sit around the campfire and sing beautiful songs. Zina even tries to learn how to play

233

mandolin under guidance of our musician Rustik (Rustem Slobodin). Then again and again we resume our discussions, mostly about love. Someone comes up with an idea that we need a special notebook for ideas that we might come up with. Once we are done we are making our way inside the tent. No body wants to sleep by the stove and we agree that Yurka Kri will sleep there. Yuri moves to the second compartment with terrible cursing and accusation that we betrayed him. We can't fall asleep for awhile and arguing about something.
Luda Dubinina

01.29.59
Second day of our trip. We made our way from Lozvy river to river Auspii. We walked along a Mansi (native Siberian tribe in the Urals) trail. The weather is -13C. The wind is weak. We often find ice on the Lozvy river. That is it.
Nick Thibault

30 January 1959
Diary is written in the cold on the go.
Today is a third cold night on the bank of Auspiya river. We are getting used to it. The stove does a great job. Some of us (Thibeaux and Krivonischenko) think we need to build steam heat in the ten. The curtains in the tent are quite justified. We get up at 8:30am. After breakfast we walk along the Auspiya river, but the ice again doesn't allow us to move forward. We went on the bank on a sledge-deer trail. In the middle of the road the saw Mansi shed. Yes, Mansi, Mansi, Mansi. This word comes up more and more often in our conversations. Mansi are people of the North. Small Hanti-Mansijskiy nation located in Salehard with 8 thousand population. Very interesting and unique people that inhabit the North Polar Urals, close to the Tyumen region. They have a written language, and leave characteristic signs on forest trees.
30.01.59 (continued)
Weather: temperature in the morning - 17 C
day - 13 C
night - 26 C.
The wind is strong, south-west, snow begins to fall, heavy clouds, drop in temperature. The temperature is normal for Northern Urals.
This is a story about the forest. Mansi signs tell about animals they saw, resting stops and other things. It is particularly interesting to solve its meaning for the tourists as well as historians.
Deer trail turns into a trodden path, and then ends. To go without a trail is very hard, snow is 120 cm (4 feet) deep. The forest gradually thins and trees get smaller. You can feel the altitude. Lots of dwarf birches and pines. It is impossible to walk on the river. It is not completely frozen, there is ice and water under the snow. We have to go back on the bank of the river. The day is over and we have to find a place for bivouac. That's the stop for the night. Strong west wind. It blows the snows off the cedar and pine trees, creating the impression of a snow fall.
As usual we quickly start a fire and pitch the tent on some fir branches. We are warmed by the fire and go to sleep.
Unsigned

31 January 1959

Today the weather is a bit worse wind (west), snow (probably from the pines) because the sky is perfectly clear.

Came out relatively early (around 10am). Took the same Mansi sled trail. Till now we walk along a Mansi trail, which was crossed by a deer hunter not long ago.

Yesterday we apparently came across his resting stop. Deer didn't go much further. The hunter didn't follow the beaten trail and we are now in his steps.

Today was surprisingly good accommodations for the tent, air is warm and dry, despite the low temperature of -18C to -24C. Walking is especially hard today. Visibility is very low. We can't see the trail and sometimes we have to advance gropingly. All we can do is 1.52 km (1 mile) per hour.

We are forced to find new methods of clearing the path for the skis. The first member leaves his backpack on the ground and walks forward, then returns and rests for 10-15 minutes with the group. Thus we have a non-stop paving of the trail. It is especially hard for the second to move down the new trail with full gear on the back. We gradually leave the Auspiya valley, the rise is continuous, but quite smooth. Fir trees are replaced by wispy birch-wood. We came out of the tree line. Wind is western, warm, penetrating. The speed of the wind is similar to the air draft created by a taking off airplane. Firm, open spaces. I can't even start thinking of setting up a storage. It's close to 4. We have to start looking for a place to pitch the tent. We are going south in Auspiya river valley. This apparently is the place covered with the deepest snow. Wind is not strong, snow cover is 1,22 m. Tired and exhausted we started the preparations for the night. Not enough firewood. Frail damp firs. We started fire with logs, too tired to dig a fire pit. We had supper right in the tent. It's warm. It is hard to imagine such a comfort somewhere on the ridge, with a piercing wind, hundreds kilometers away from human settlements.

Dyatlov (last record in the diary)

Unknown Diary

January 24, 1959

Last night, about 9-00 we boarded the train №43. At last. There is 10 of us. Slavik Bienko didn't come, they didn't let him. We are going with Blinov group. Fun. Songs. Around 8 am we arrived in Serov. We were not allowed to stay on the train station, the train to Ivdel is at 6-30 pm. We are looking for a room. We are trying to get into the club (to the right of the dining room of the station) and school, but fail. Finally he (? not sure about the identity) finds school number 41 (about 200 meters from the train station), where we were very well received.

January 30.

In the morning it was 17 ° now it is getting colder. "Volunteers" (S. Kolevatov and K. Tibo are repeating their duties as a punishment for slowing the group yesterday) took a long time to start a fire. In the evening it was decided that we will leave the tent exactly 8 minutes after waking up. Therefore, all have been awake and waiting for the command. But it is useless. Around 9:30 in the morning we began the passive preparation. Nick T. is joking about something in the morning. Everyone is reluctant to get up.

And the weather! In contrast to the rest of the warm days - today is a sunny cold day. The sun appears playful.

Today as yesterday were are following the path of Mansi. Sometimes Mansi writings appear on trees. In general, all sorts of obscure mysterious characters. There is slogan for our campaign, "In a country of mysterious signs." If we knew these letters, it would be possible, without any doubt, to go down the path, confident that it would lead us to the right place. Here the trail takes us to the shores of the river. We lose track. In the future, the trail follows the left bank of Auspii river, but the team of deer crossed the river and we are going through the woods. At the first opportunity we will turn back to the river. As it is easier to follow it. At approximately 2 pm we stop for a lunch. Dried meat, guest crackers, sugar, garlic, coffee, stocked in the morning - that's our lunch. Good mood.

A couple more hours - and we will stop at 5pm for the night. We have been looking for a place, then we returned about 200 meters back. Charming place. Deadwood, high pines, in short, everything you need for a good night.

Luda quickly got tired and sat down by the fire. Nick Thibault changed his clothes. He began to write a diary. The law is that until all the work is done, do not approach the fire. And so they had a long argument, of who will sew the tent. Finally K. Tibo gave up and took a needle. Lyuda remained seated. And we sewed the hole (and there were so many that there was enough work for all except two attendants and Lyuda. Guys are terribly outraged.

Today is the birthday of Sasha Kolevatov. Congratulations. We give him a tangerine, which he immediately divided into 8 pieces (Lyuda went into a tent and did not come out until the end of the dinner). So another day of our trek went well.

Zina's Diary

Z. Kolmogorova
north Ural
trek III category
difficulty
leader Dyatlov

24.2.59. (note: the figure of the month is corrected, visible simultaneously, one on top of the other in an unknown sequence, the numbers "1" and "2")

Here we are on a trek again. Now in Serov. The entire evening yesturday till 3 AM we sang songs. With us is sr. instructor of the Kaurov sport base Alexander Zolotaryov. He knows a lot of songs, it's just happy somehow that we are learning new songs. Especially some the Zumba and others. Today I feel little sad. But it's nothing. We are on duty with Rustik. We went and talked to the schoolchildren, then they all saw us off, even burst into tears, didn't want to let us go.

25.1.59 (note: the figure of the month is fixed, visible simultaneously, one on top of the other in an unknown sequence, the numbers "1" and "2") arrived in Ivdel at midnight, spent the night at the train station pitching a tent on the floor. Yes, we have already been spotted 2 times by the police. Once Yuri Kriv was taken to the police station. He wanted to raise money for candy. It was funny. Then on the train Serov-Ivdel reached Ivdel, spent the night at the station, in the morning got on a bus, drove to a hotel in Ivdel. Then we took the bus and drove off. We are 20 people, backpacks and skis. Had to pile up on

3 levels, but we sang songs all the way. Arrived in Vizhay. First we stopped at the same club where we were 2 years ago. Then we were taken to the hotel. The whole evening there was a discussion about love about friendship, about dances and other things, etc. I talked a lot about things which are completely unfamiliar to me and I scarcely do, but I tried, sincerely. But this is all nonsense. But again the words of Volt come to mind. How well did he say it. We went to see "Symphonie in Gold" so powerful! So great!

26.1.59

We slept in beds. We got up late, very late. Rustik and I are on duty. We went into the dining room. And then we waited for the car and drove off. Today the road is not so beautiful, there is less snow. We are driving off road now. Drove for a long time. I, as always, was approached by some countryman. We arrived at the 41st settlement. Workers are simply working here, not prisoners, but recruits. There are many smart ones. We were accommodated in the small room of the driver. Today is the last day of civilization. Rustic plays the mandolin very well, I really enjoy listening to him. Today I wore Yuri's mittens, but how I did not want to! I was told that is not good not to accept them, so I took them. We talk. Not much.

27. Today is the first day of our journey. The backpack is not much but somewhat heavy. Yes, Yura Yudin is leaving us today. His sciatic nerves inflamed again and he is leaving. Such a pity. We distributed his load in our backpacks. It turns out that on the last day we see some kind of civilization,stove, people, etc. Today we arranged out backpacks to go on horseback and we are waiting them to be ready, and we will go skiing. Everyone is singing, the workers living in barracks, did not go to work, they sing. We sit and write songs. Many workers are very talented, intelligent people. Especially "the beard", his beard is ginger, ginger, and his eyes are also ginger, and brown. The guys sing well. And Rustic plays the mandolin very well. Today was the last day me and Lyuda slept in beds. Tonight we are going to be in a tent, apparently. Now we are in the 41st quarter, today our goal is to reach the 2nd Nortern. They say, there is a hut there, but no one lives in it. Hurry to the road, to the skis ... How about we go? I'm lately somehow very deeply affected by music, guitar, mandolin and other. Yesterday saw 3 movies here "In people", "There is such a guy" and again "Symphonie in Gold". I want to see "Symphonie in Gold" even more times.

tolya
Talaya, a river, many huts
ya - river
sos - brook, together
paste/pache-rum - hello friend
nyor - stone, if there nyor is added to the peak - the peak is bare
oyka - man
yani hum - man big
mais - small
ekva - female
ekvat - alone
ayrish - a girl
From Burmantovo to Volen paul airplane
nyan - bread
emos -good

mol - bad
saka - good
(at)Sol - (not)truth
Solval - salt
Pud - pot
Vat - water
Vit - wind
Hul - fish
Neul - meat
sali - deer
Vazhenka - female
sohta - alpha male
sun - sled
sushep - look
yun - house
pyrya - scram (to the dog)
col - city
pisal - gun
topor - truck
kasay - knife
seranki mayen - give me the matches
atim - don't have
oli - have
Teynkvem - eat
ail - drink
eri - must
ergan - sing
Olna - money
tselkoviy - ruble
akvat - 1
kita - 2
hurum - 3
nila - 4
at - 5
hot - 6
sat - 7
vovel - 8
nevel - 9
pul - 10
tinalil - eat
yuvtilum - sell
sup - pants m
gacha - f
sapaki - slippers
yelsup - dress
neks - sable
kutya - dog
pis-pis - mouse
suy - pine

238

paul - village
vor - forest
vorhum - bear forest man
vas - duck.
kat - hands.
layal - legs.
pum - head.
punki - teeth.
palin - ears of
ayemun - large
saam - eyes
nyel - nose.
ayserm - cold
polem - freezing
kur - stove
paltin - heat
chuval - stove
osemsau - good bye
ruma
nan - you, tav - he
am - I
nanki - you
amki - me

Tyumen region
Berezovsky district
village Nyaksimvol
(sable slope)
Ognev Nikolay Grig.
Rudik Ivan Ivanovich

The whole day went, in front of the horse, behind the horse on the river Lozva. They often flew to ice, cleaned skis. They came already in the dark for a long time looking for a hut with windows and doors. 2nd North is an abandoned village, nobody lives here at all, and what beautiful places! It's just Chusovaya. The stones on the banks are some cliffs, limestone, white. Today we go a few km along the Lozva River, and then we pass to the Auspiya river.

(note: the arrow from "Today" is drawn down to "Auspiya River" and to the following date "28.2.58")

28.2.58 (note: she wrote the wrong the month and the year)

Uncle Slava is leaving today on his horse, and Yura Yudin is leaving too. He took a few samples. I saw this type for the first after the drilling. There is a lot of chalcopyrite and pyrite. Last night the boys made stupid jokes. In my opinion, if we don't pay attention to them, maybe they will be less rude. And so far, nothing. It's time to go out, but they are still digging and digging. I do not understand what's taking so long. The first 30

239

minutes are over. Of course, the backpack is somewhat heavy. But it's possible to go. The first day is always difficult.

left forward
Sasha Kolevatov tested his device, then quit.
Second stop.
It was much easier to go yesterday without backpacks
snow, snow, snow, snow
on the banks frozen river snow snow
Boundary stone.

Lunch was an hour at 4 pm
After lunch we did just one more hike and stopped to rest.

I mended the tent. We lay down to sleep. Igor was rude the whole evening, I just couldn't recognize him. I had to sleep on the wood near the stove.

29.1.59
Today is Yurka's (Yuri Doroshenko) birthday. We go first to Lozva then we turn to Auspiya. Surroundings are beautiful. Along the Auspiya Mansi have passed. A trail is visible, grooves, a path is visible. We often see Mansi signs on the trail. I wonder what they write about? Now the Mansi trail goes South.

(note: the turn is the sketch of the notch, the initials with the date Oct. 5, 1958, the drawing of the ax?)

Now we sit the three of us: Rustik, Yurka and I Waiting for the rest. For the night stopped near the ski tracks. We are burning firewood with Yurka. We talked about the past. Such a playboy.

30.2.59 We go on Auspiya
cold (ayserm). Mansi trail ended. Pine forest. There was sun in the morning, now is cold (ayserm). All day long we walked along Auspiya. Will spend the night on a Mansi trail. Kolya didn't get to be a watchman so me and Rustik will stay on duty today. Burned mittens and Yurkin's second quilted jacket. He cursed a lot. Today, probably, we will build a storage.

(note: The next three pages are blank, Next is the following:)

The brighter, the greater diaphragm number, if the diaphragm is lower, there will be less light on the film, the shutter speed is longer. Aperture - closed
(note: There are arrows pointing to the last two word: Aperture closed)

(note: This one name was on the second to last page):

Rempel.

Tent Discovery- Official Statement from Boris Slobtsov

April 15, 1959
The official testimony of Boris Slobtsov

The witness showed: I started to study tourism in 1956, i.e. from the time of admission to study at UPI, I am a member of the tourist section of the Institute. I was only in 5 campaigns of the participants of the camping trip of the Djatlov group, I know, but not all. The group included Zolotarev, whom I did not know. The rest of the participants knew and can say that these people were fully prepared to participate in the winter hike III category difficulties. As I know, this group was prepared satisfactorily for the campaign. One of the drawbacks is only that a copy of the route sheet by the group leader comrade. Dyatlov was not left in the city committee for physical culture and sports, although the deadline for the departure and return of this group to the committee was known according to the protocol of the route commission.

The fact that the group Dyatlova from the campaign did not return during the check-in period, the institute became aware about the middle of February, I do not remember the exact date. The search group first took off on February 20, 1959. The second group, including myself, flew to Ivdel on an airplane on February 22, 1959.

On the scene I flew by helicopter on February 23, 1959. I led the search team. The tent of the Djatlov group was discovered by our group on the afternoon of February 26, 1959. When they approached the tent, they found out: the entrance of the tent came from under the snow, and the rest of the tent was under snow. Around the tent in the snow stood ski poles and spare skis - 1 pair. The snow on the tent was 15-20 cm thick, it was clear that the snow was on the tent, it was hard.

Near the tent near the entrance to the snow An ice ax was stuck in the tent of the tent, in the snow lay a pocket flashlight, the Chinese, which, as it was subsequently established, belonged to Dyatlov. It was not clear that under the streetlight there was a snow of about 5-10 cm thick, there was no snow above the flashlight, it was snowed slightly on either side. I took the flashlight first and found that it was not turned on. When I turned on, the snow came on. I did not notice that day, but then I heard from other people involved in the search that there was a trail of urine in the snow near the tent.

In the immediate vicinity of the tent there were no traces. Approximately 15-20 m from the tent in the direction where corpses were subsequently discovered, traces of the person's feet coming from the tent were visible on the snow, and it was evident that the tracks were left by the feet of a man without shoes in boots. The tracks protruded above the surrounding surface of the snow, for near the tracks the snow was blown out by the wind.

From the tent in the direction of the wind, i.e. in the direction where there were traces of people's feet, at a distance of about 0.5-1 meter, they found several slippers from different pairs, and ski caps and other small objects were scattered. I do not remember and did not pay attention to how many people were traces, but it should be noted that the tracks were initially left intact, next to each other, and the distant tracks parted, but now they do not remember how they parted.

On February 26, 1959, we dug snow over the tent and made sure that there were no people, and the things that were in the tent did not touch. With me was the student Sharavin. From the tent things were taken on February 27 and 28, 1959. At the same time students Brusnitsyn and others were present.

When I looked under the tent on 26.2.59 I saw the tent itself was torn, there were food in the bucket at the entrance, there was a liquid in the jar-alcohol or vodka, there were food in bags in the legs, blankets were unfolded, under blankets spread out cotton woolen jackets, storm bags, and under them rasstalany were backpacks. At the entrance hung Slobodin's jacket, in whose breast pocket money was about 800 rubles. In the tent, apparently, a sheet was hung, which was torn and part of it protruded outward.

Question: What can you add to your testimony?

Answer: How and where corpses were found, I will not tell, because it is known from the testimony of others, but I can note that the cedar, under which the corpses of Doroshenko and Krivonischenko were found, I saw how Mansi Bakhtiarov found in the snow 8 rubles . money in bills of 5 and 3 rubles. in a folded form, but without me they found a coin in the same place at 5 cents, a cowboy whole, in a simple simple cotton sock, a piece of sweater, a handkerchief. Personally, I saw how under this cedar was found a cloth belt of dark color with tambourines at the ends. This item belongs to whom I did not know. The length of this object is about 80 cm, the width is about 10 cm, it looks like a belt or strap, with which the mansi pulls the load, but this object for use instead of the strap is not suitable, because it is not strong.

Question: Who and under what circumstances found the database of the group Dyatlov, what was there?

Answer: Now I do not exactly remember the date, but on February 28 or March 1, I, Brusnitsyn and Lebedev in the upper reaches of the Auspii River found a pool of the Djatlov group. With us there were 2 more Mansi people. Labaz was organized in the penultimate parking lot, where were left: a pair of spare skis, leggings, in the snow in the pit there were products, about 60 kg, Djatlov's boots and spare ski boots, in shoes found cotton frosted socks, apparently they were left wet. There was also the mandolin of Krivonischenko.

Slobtsov (signature)

Interrogated: Romanov (signature)

Tent Damage- Official Report

Systems of threads - warp and weft, interwoven perpendicular to each other.

The damage resulting from the rupture usually follows the line of least resistance, i.e. tear either filaments of a duck, or warp threads. Such damage is usually very smooth and has right angles.

The incision, under any conditions, always disrupts both those and other threads at different angles randomly. Cut only either the threads of the weft, or the warp threads is almost impossible. /cm. scheme number 2.

As a result of the foregoing, and when examining the edges of all the damages on the tent, one can conclude that three damages / conditionally marked Nos. 1, 2, 3 / have arisen as a result of exposure to some sharp weapon (knife), i.e. are cuts. Yet the rest of the damage is a rupture.

Damage No. 1 has a shape in the form of a broken straight line, its total length is 32 cm. Above it there is a small puncture of the tissue in 2 cm. The corners of the hole are torn. /cm. photo ?4.

Damages ?2 and ?3 have not an even arcuate shape. The approximate length of these lesions is 89 cm and 42 cm. from the right edge of damage number 2 and from both edges of damage No. 3 there are no cloth flaps and it is possible that they had their continuation further.

In order to determine from which side the indicated incisions were made (from the inside, from the tent or from the outside), a thorough microscopic examination of the edges of the incisions of the adjacent tissue sections was made (an increase from 0.6 to 56X).

As a result of the conducted studies it was found that from the inside of the tent in the areas of the cuts close to the edges, there are surface damages of the tissue in the form of minor punctures, incisions of the tissue yarns and very thin scratches. /cm. photo ? 5-13 /.

All scratches and punctures are rectilinear. Scratches are observed in the surface damage of the filaments: the filaments are either cut in half / cm. photo No. 10 /, or with them the dye is simply scratched off and not the colored parts are visible / see. photo ? 5, 6, 11 /.

In the corners of the punctures, on the inside of the tent (unlike the outer tent), there are, as it were, continuations of damage, which are expressed in the form of thin scratches. /cm. photo ? 8, 9 /.

The nature and shape of all these injuries indicate that they formed from the contact of the fabric of the inside of the tent with the blade of a blade of some weapon / knife /.

All of the above indicates that the existing incisions were made from the inside, from the tent.

CONCLUSION

In the tourist tent of the group Dyatlova on the right slant of the canopy forming the roof, three damages of approximately 32, 89, and 42 cm in length / conditionally designated No. 1, 2, 3 / arose as a result of exposure to some sharp weapon / knife, e. are cuts.

All these sections are marked on the inside of the tent.

Printing

EXPERT

243

Storage Site Discovery and Inventory- Official Report

March 2, 1959 Camp search party in the headwaters of the river. Auspiya. Attorney forensic Sverdlovsk region Ivanov prosecution in the presence of the head search party t. Maslennikova (Sverdlovsk Str. Factory, 32) and Slobtsova Nemtsov (Sverdlovsk, st. Lenin. 13-a, SW. 23) made in accordance with Art. 78 Code of Criminal Procedure this Protocol as follows:

on this date in the upper reaches of rivers Auspii, under the pass of the river Lozvy found a storage shed (storage products) group Dyatlov.

Labaz located in place overnight groups are well closed cooked wood, coated cardboard, spruce paws. In a warehouse stuck in snow skis, one pair to wear Lyzhin hung tattered gaiters,

When excavation is detected following a warehouse number of products:
1. Condensed milk 2.5 kg.
2. Meat canned banks 4 kg.
3. Sugar - 8 kg.
4. Butter - 4 kg.
5. Cooked sausage - 4 kg.
6. Sol -. 1.5 to
7. Kissel-compote - 3 kg.
8. Oatmeal and 7.5kg buckwheat.
9. Cocoa 200g
10. Coffee - 200 g
11. Tea - 200 gr.
12. Loin - 3 kg.
13. Milk powder - 1 kg.
14. Sugar - 3 kg.
15. Crackers - 7 kg and Noodles - 5 kg.
16. Also found:

mandolin, a pair of shoes 41 size, and worn therein socks, couple warm boot mounting set battery 2 mounted with the bulb for lighting

From the words Blinov warm boots belonged Dyatlov.

Since the products are not of interest to the investigation, they transferred the head of the party t. Maslennikov as an emergency reserve. All containers of a product, and mandolin, two pairs of shoes, socks and fastening withdrawn.

Protocol read, write correctly.

Maslennikov (signature)

Slobtsov (signature)

Discovery of the Cedar Area, Inventory of the Tent, and the Discovery of George, Yuri, Igor, and Zina- Official Report

Protocol inspection
scene February 27, 1959

Prosecutor Ivdel Sverdlovsk region., Ml. Tempalov adviser of justice in the presence of the head of the search party Evgeny Maslennikov Polikarpovich living in Sverdlovsk, ul. Factory 32, Apt. 84 witnesses and Yarovoy George Paton living in the city of Sverdlovsk, ul. M Sibiryaka number 57, Apt. 81 Slobtsova Nemtsov, living in the city of Sverdlovsk, ul Lenina. 13a, Apt. 23 Kurikova Stepan Nikolaevich living Ivdelsky district, pos. Suevatpaul drawn up this protocol detection corpses, discovered on the northeast slope of the height of "1079". To the northeast of the height "1079" and a half kilometers to the origins of the right source Lozvy river beginning in the saddle between the heights of "1079" and "880"

about cedar 2 - 2.5 meters broken off dry branches. The branches are broken off and the cedar. Under the cedar tree in the hole traces of the fire, as evidenced poluobgorevshie branches. Around the campfire discovered poluobgorevshy sock and shirt, cowboy shirt. The shirt money - 8 rubles. Polusgorevshy balaclava greenish color. To the north of the fire at a distance of one meter heads west, feet to the east in the number of corpses lie next two. Identified: Krivonischenko Yury face up, wearing a shirt, cowboy shirt, torn pants. Head thrown back, eyes closed, mouth closed, lips clenched, right arm thrown behind his head, left arm bent, the brush is raised above the breast. Right leg stretched out, the left - slightly bent at the knees. Right foot barefoot on the left wearing torn brown sock identical polusgorevshemu detected by the fire. On the back of the left hand skinned. Between the blood fingers. The index finger stripped. The skin on the left lower leg torn off, blood came. Other injuries by external examination is not established. Next to him with Krivonischenko, lies the corpse Zolotarev? (top is written in brackets: "error"), Alexander A.. The corpse lies belly down. Dressed in cowboy shirt, blue shorts, pants underneath blue - torn. The feet wool socks on top - torn knitted socks. Ear and nose blood, bloodied lips. On the left hand middle finger bloodied. The corpses are photographed at the crime scene.

In the same area in the south-west of the two bodies at a distance of 400 meters is found corpse, lying belly up, legs slightly bent at the knees, his hands pressed to his chest. The left arm at the elbow rests on a birch branch. Head strictly behind the trunk of a birch in five to seven centimeters. Dressed: bare head on the body - fur jacket under her sweater, a sweater colored cowboy shirt. On the feet wearing ski pants, long underwear underneath. On the right leg wool socks, cotton on the left. Injuries not detected by external examination of the corpse. On the face and under the chin frost. In the same area is strictly in a southwesterly direction on a slope height of "1079" at a distance of 500 (forwarded with the "58" or "56" - approx ed.). Meters away from the body (in recognition proved Dyatlov Igor A.) found a female corpse. Kolmogorov identified Zinaida Alekseevna. The corpse is in the snow, he was under a layer of solid firn snow. Nearby within a radius of ("in a radius" is inserted - approx ed.). At a distance of 70 meters there is a single tree. The corpse lay his head in the same direction as the previous corpses face to the ground on his right side. Arms bent under the body. Both legs half-

245

bent. Right tightened to the stomach (it seems that the man climbed up the hill). At the head of the pink woolen cap. On the body wearing a ski jacket, under her shirt and cowboy shirt. On the feet wearing ski pants underneath leggings and underwear. The feet woolen socks. The person in the blood. On the back around the waist abrasions, blood came. It can be assumed that according to body location Kolmogorov tried not to climb up the hill, and held in place. The corpse photographed.

Hereto attached documents and valuables that were brought our party participants and taken out of the tent of the missing group Dyatlov.
Attached to the minutes as follows:
1. Fotoapparat "Sharp" with a tripod and a broken filter. Camera ? 488797. Filmed frame 34.
2. The camera "Sharp" ? 486963. Filmed 27 frames. In case deep scratches. Interrupted. The belt
3. The camera "Sharp" ? 55149239. Filmed 27 frames.
4. Wrist Compass.
5. Railway and bus tickets
6. Field Bag
7. Fonarik electric
8. Two banks with iron threads, etc.
9. Money Notebook Slobodina
money and a letter in the trade union gortorgotdel.
10. Money in the amount of nine hundred seventy-five rubles
11. Blog Kolmogorova. Last date of entry January 30
12 RIP Commission
13. Letter Dyatlova name
14. The route book number 5, in the amount of three pieces.
15. Bank sealed. In her 10 films, the roll of film and money in the amount of seven hundred rubles
16 trip to Dyatlov name.
17. Maps, tracing paper and photocopies of 9 pieces.
18. Hike Project
19. (or "11" - approx ed.). A cover letter from the Trade Union of the Institute
12. Passport to Dyatlov name

Prosecutor Ivdel ml. Tempalov Counselor of Justice (signature)

Head of the search party E. Maslennikov - signature / Maslennikov /

Discovery of Rustem- Official Report

Interrogation of witness Axelrod M.A.
Minutes of the examination of the witness Axelrod Master of the Ural Plant Gidromashyn
On April 24, 1959, the forensic prosecutor of the Sverdlovsk region Ivanov
Interrogated as a witness, in compliance with Art. 162-168 Code of Criminal Procedure of the RSFSR
Last name, first name and patronymic of Axelrod Moses Abramovich

246

2. Year of birth 1932 3. Place of birth of the city of Velikie Luki
4. Nationality of the Jew
5. Party membership b / n.
6. Education In 1956, he graduated from the Ural Polytechnic Institute
7. Lesson: a) at present: art. master of the Ural plant Gidromashin.
   b) at the moment to which the testimony relates: ibid.
8) Conviction: not convicted.
9) Permanent residence: pp Sysert, st. Rosa Luxemburg, 6, apt. 2
10) Passport: -
11) What is the relationship with the accused: -
On the responsibility under the first part of Art. 92 of the Criminal Code for refusing to testify and under Art. 95 of the Criminal Code of the RSFSR for giving knowingly false testimony warned
Axelrod (signature)

In February-March 1958, I was the head of a tourist campaign of the third category of difficulty in the Subpolar Urals (area of the town of Narodnaya). Among the participants of the campaign was Igor Dyatlov. Before this campaign, we together with him were participants of the campaign of the III category of difficulty on the Sayan in the summer of 1956. My first acquaintance with Dyatlov dates back to 1954, by the time he entered his institute. At that time I was the chairman of the bureau of the tourist section of the institute. From the point of view of tourist experience, and simply human qualities, I did not know Dyatlova at the time, so our first acquaintance dates back to 1956 (meaning close acquaintance)

Our Sayan group consisted mainly of graduates of the institute and engineers, which is probably why the second-year Dyatlov kept himself somewhat closed, not meeting anyone especially closely. Dyatlov's great contribution to the organization of the campaign was two transceiver ultrashort-wave devices of his design, intended for communication between the rafts. I was the supply manager of the group, my duties included, among other things, the distribution of the load among the group members, and from this side I had a serious complaint about Dyatlov k.k. I entrusted him to weigh his radio household himself, and he cheated me on 3 kilograms. It turned out the day on the third. I emphasize that this is my only complaint against him and that it was in 1956. After Sayan I went to work in Siberia, from there I returned only in April 1957 and my next meeting with Dyatlov took place in the winter of 1958 in the winter campaign. I must say that Dyatlov struck me with his dissimilarity with Dyatlov, whom I knew in 1956. He was an open, selfless, kind comrade, serious about serious things, able to bring, where necessary, discharge with a dose of humor, etc.

In the group, he was greatly respected for the above qualities, for his physical endurance, for his tourist experience, for his readiness at any moment to do any work. Naturally, as a boss, I appreciated the most recent quality in him. Long days and nights, evenings spent around the fire caused Dyatlov and me to become friends. My friend was a man who, besides a serious attitude to tourism (what we agreed with him), was very serious about life in all its manifestations (books, studies, science - especially art)

After Dyatlov and other members of the group (Bartholomew, Khan, Chubarev, Khalizov) went on a campaign of the third category of difficulty, they received the right

247

to lead such campaigns. And already with our return to Sverdlovsk, the question arose of where to go these tourists next winter. This question was not finally resolved and I only learned about Dyatlov's final route from him around the month of November. In November or December, I do not remember exactly, I witnessed Dyatlov's arrival at the meeting of the city section with the draft of the campaign. The route commission has sent the project for consultation to Maslennikov. After the end of the section Dyatlov and Kolmogorov (she was also in this section) accompanied me to the building of the regional party school. We talked about many things, in particular about the campaign, I recommended Dyatlov to maintain iron discipline in the campaign in order to get out as early as possible. It is better to have time left, than to catch up with him. Both of them, Woodpeckers and Kolmogorov, quite seriously persuaded me to take part in their campaign. Judging by their mood, both did not doubt that the trip would go well, and they waited a lot for themselves. Perhaps it was no longer in December, but in January, because I now recall that this was our last meeting. I promised Dyatlov that I would visit him sometime around the 20th of February and find out all about their trip. Finishing this section, I want to note that Dyatlov's personal qualities must be attributed to his direct expression of many feelings, as delight, satisfaction, joy.

February 22, on Sunday, using my stay in (the word "hike" crossed out) Sverdlovsk, I went to the hostel number 10 of the UPI in the room to Dyatlov. When I asked whether Dyatlov, his neighbor Chigvintsev, had arrived, he answered that he had not, and that the search for the group had begun. There I first heard about the tragedy, I heard that the search began. On the 23rd, I worked the day at the plant completely, and at 24 at twelve o'clock I started calling Dlovsk in order to find out if there is anything about the Dyatlov group. Called Rubel. She told me that she flew to Ivdel Maslennikov. It became clear to me that the case was taking a very serious turn. At about a quarter to twelve I called the headquarters of the search at the U.P.I. Blinova, who knew me, approached the phone, she told me that in the morning a plane was flying to Ivdel and that it might be possible to fly with him. At half past three in the morning I was at the institute, and in the morning I began to insist before Slobodin about my departure to Ivdel motivating my demand with experience (I'm the only one in Sverdlovsk who has four winter hikes of the highest category of difficulty) and that Dyatlov went to the winter "three with me and therefore he must in some way be inherent in my "creative style", if I may say so choosing a path on micro-sites, choice of overnight stays, climbing paths, etc. Not wanting to take responsibility for my flight to the Slobodin mountains, I refused. The head of the educational and sports department of the UPI sports club, Milman PS, who phoned Pavel A. Repyev, helped me, introduced me and arranged for me to travel to GK. F.K. and C. on search and rescue.

Together with the students of U.P.I. - I flew to Ivdel in the evening of February 25, as radio operator operators, mountain climbers Sogrin and Tipikin, where I almost immediately went to the search headquarters meeting. I questioned the stay of the group of Slobtsov on the town of Otorten and suggested that we put back our small but maneuver introduced me and arranged a trip for me to G.K. F.K. and C. on search and rescue.

The rented group near the town of Otorten is the Northernmost point of the Dyatlov group route. After a lengthy discussion, the proposal was accepted. During ("orga" - crossed out, approx. Comp.) Of the headquarters meeting, the weak competence of its members, with the exception of Maslennikov, was striking in tourism in general and ("searching" - crossed out, approx. Comp.) particular. Members of the headquarters cannot be blamed for this, but in such circumstances, in my opinion, it was necessary to entrust the search for questions of searching with the tourists, leaving general headquarters and organization behind the headquarters. On February 26, despite the bad weather, my group (I was appointed leader) consisting of Axelrod, Sogrin, Tipikin, Yaburov, Chigvintsev was landed from a helicopter 8 kilometers east of Otorten at 4 o'clock in the afternoon. As time went by in the evening, I decided not to conduct searches on this day, but to stop for the night, which we did below the border of the forest in the valley of the Sulpa River. On the morning of February 27 at 8 o'clock the search team consisting of Axelrod, Sogrin and Tipikin we went on a search, leaving Chigvintsev and Yaburov in the camp to communicate with the plane (this was agreed in advance) with R.B.S. For 10 hours of searching with a fifteen-minute lunch break, we searched for about forty, forty-five kilometers, passing the entire valley of the western tributary of the Sulpa river along the border of the forest, examining all the passes between he tops of the mountains Otorten, 1024, 1039; 1041, making a traverse of the top of Otorten from the southwest to the northeast and separately climbing to Otorten with a detour of the eaves of the southern carriage of Otorten. A note dated 1956, left by tourists of Moscow State University, was removed from the top of the mountain. At about 1 pm the plane flying over us dropped the pennant with the order to carefully continue further searches with the message that all things and skies of the Dyatlov group were found 12-13 kilometers south of us on the slope of 1079. For me it became clear she died and offered to bare her head. It was clear that without the ski group could not go anywhere.

When departing from Ivdel, we had an agreement that on February 28, at 4 in the afternoon, a helicopter would arrive at our place. At about five o'clock on the evening of February 28, the group in full was transferred to Ivdel. We flew together with Ivdelsky District Prosecutor Tempalov. He told me that naked corpses of four people had been found: Dyatlova, Kolmogorova, Krivonischenko and Zolotarev (later identified as Doroshenko). We returned to the camp only in the seventh hour of the evening.

In Ivdel, to the question of Artyukov, what are our future plans, I personally and the whole group gave their time to the search headquarters and the next day, together with the regional criminal prosecutor-criminalist Ivanov L.N. Sogrin, Tipikin and I were landed by helicopter in the search area.

Dyatlova group. Three corpses - Kolmogorova, Dyatlova and Doroshenko, were already brought from the valley near the rock-remains on the pass. The group immediately took part in the search. It was clear to me that none of the dead had left the valley, a lot of time had passed, the corpses, of course, lie under the snow, and it is necessary to look for them only here. From that day until the day of departure (March 9), I took part in the search every day with a probe in my hands. At first, he participated as a leader of his own, out of five people, a group, and then, when some tourists left for Ivdel, as the leader of the entire civilian part of the search group. The search tactic was not established from the very beginning. Initially, the search groups went with a broad search, rarely and shallowly penetrating snow cover with ski poles from tent to cedar (1500 m) and then the tactics changed elbow to elbow, walked along or across the slopes of the valley of an emergency, deeply piercing the snow with metal probes.

This method gave the results: on March 5, under a snowy one, the thickness of which was at least 350 mm, one of the participants of the dead group Rustem Slobodin was found. He was lying belly down, arms outstretched, on one of which - the right one, was a joint of the thumb joint. On the same hand was a watch. On the head there is a cap, on the basis of which I believe that at the time of the death of a particularly strong wind there was not, because he would inevitably have blown the cap off his head, if not alive, then dead, Slobodina. One leg, the right one (I could be mistaken) was in a felt boot, the left one without it, pulled up under the right leg. Calm, no trace of violence during this external examination was visible. Under the knees, breasts, i.e. the parts of the body to which the weight of the lying man was distributed were a half-snow semi-snow layer about 70 to 80 mm thick, which allowed me to conclude that Slobodin did not die instantly, but <inaudible>, after the fall, some other period of time . The corpse was located approximately in the middle between Kolmogorova and Dyatlov. As you know, 2 corpses were found near the cedar: Krivonischenko and Doroshenko, but a careful study of the campfire suggests that the fire had more people. I have the following reasons for this: 1.) Judging by the work done, two of them are not able to cope with the amount of work that has been done there. 2.) A small burnt, obviously women's scarf was found near the fire. 3.) A dark-colored ragged sweater cuff found

What, on the basis of my personal impressions, is the picture of the death of the group drawn to me? February 1, the group got up late. It's late because, judging by the diary, the group was very tired the day before, or because in the morning, or already after the diary was written, it was decided to do a storage shed late in the evening so that at least three days to free the shoulders weighed by the previous campaign , increase the speed of movement. In the morning the group got up at 11 o'clock and proceeded to the construction of a warehouse. While they were doing a storage shed, while they were sorting out what to take with them and what to leave (on the eve this was not done, because the device of the warehouse was questionable), breakfast was ready.

It was about 2 o'clock in the afternoon. And I believe that the group left no earlier than half past two and set one of two tasks: 1) To transfer from the forest to the forest, from the Auspii valley to the Lozva valley, or the fact that for several days now the group has been walking on extremely deep snow, the movement in which is extremely tiring. Considering that the group had a good rest at this noon, she ate late, move as far as possible along the forest border, without going into the forest (deep snow, towards Otorten so that the next evening will be at Otorten itself). A group with lightweight backpacks enters the route, but at a relatively late time - hours 5, poor visibility, more precisely, the lack of it makes the group stop for the night outside the forest. This does not exclude any of the options offered here. Was the decision to spend the night in a bare place (I deliberately avoid the word slope, because I believe that the slope, as such, did not play any role in their death) was justified? In my opinion, yes. Why? Last year, in the Subpolar Urals, we had four such overnight stays. All of them were in such conditions, when security considerations of the group dictated the need to stop where there was a place, while there was still light time to put up a tent. It was in strong (-25 - 30 ° C) frosts and there was no reason to admit that this decision was tactically wrong. So Dyatlov had precedents, and they stopped for the night without indulging, not blindly submitting to the forces of nature. It should be noted that the practice of high-altitude mountaineering is the night only snow, only in extreme cold and, often, in a blizzard and snowstorm. It is not excluded that while the group was putting up a tent, 2-3 people went on reconnaissance. Tent set. The tent is weather-proof. They are tightly stretched <unclear>, backpacks are laid on the windward side inside, a "barricade" of stoves and backpacks is arranged at the entrance so as not to blow. In the tent, of course, the temperature is below zero and you need to exercise too much endurance and composure in order to write and fill your diaries with stiff hands at 25-30 ° C. The only thing that had enough strength and humor - it was the release of "Evening Otorten." It is the evening, not fun, or something day or another. It is the work of their collective efforts, instead of writing personal diaries. Personally, the letters seem angular to me, and the handwriting is like Zolarevsky, but with significant changes. In the cold it is possible. By the way from the diaries it appears that Zolotarev liked to draw and comrade, judging by the photos, not without humor. Having laughed a lot, the group rested during the day (only 2-3 kilometers were practically covered with lightweight backpacks), the group goes to bed. The tent is quiet, only the wind howls around. For 8 of nine overnight stays in such conditions is a new thing. One of them hoped for his hardening and relative warmth, and he didn't put stockings lined with cat fur on his feet, or maybe he just laid them out of his backpack and could not find them later. The second lay in his felt boots, but at night one leg was frozen, and he, to rub, removed one felt boot, or, on the contrary, put a felt boot on the foot that had begun to freeze. Awakening was scary.

My firm conviction that nothing and no one from the inside could inspire panic in the guys. From the inside in the sense of the tent itself. So, they were forced to flee by the manifestation of some kind of external forces. If the tent is sleeping, closed, then it is either a very bright light, or a very strong sound, or a combination of the two. It may be that one of the comrades who came out to urinate gave a signal to escape, dropped the surprise from surprise. At the entrance, only a few zippers are unzipped. The triangular end of the tent is stretched well, and therefore it is not easy for one person to crawl through. Crush, crush. Maybe at this time not knowing what to grab Slobodin puts on his boots (is it his?). Someone falls into the hands of a saving knife. Not the first time, so from the third the tent is cut and the stampede begins, down the wind, to the place where it is easier to run. The fact that there is a forest, they guess only later.

I stood with a group of tourists for a long time on the site of a tent with a group of tourists (Sogrin, Korolev, Baskin, Shuleshko) and we came to the unanimous conclusion that if they had only one chance to return, they would return and return with any wind. The group is running. But these are not animals, but young, energetic, Soviet people. They run in one 2 groups. Somewhere on the ridge of stones Slobodin breaks his head and soon falls.

But the tent is not visible, legs burns cold snow, and maybe Slobodin closes the group of fugitives, and he remains lying on the snow. And somewhere else, she broke away and lost sight of the last Zina Kolmogorova. For a long time, and she falls on the snow. The rest of them reach the forest, deep snow and begin to struggle for life by inhuman efforts. At the cost of a long time of frostbitten arms and legs, the fire was lit and Woodpeckers, the head of the group, a faithful companion, goes in search of the stragglers and freezes there. And maybe after him goes looking for Dyatlov and Slobodina Kolmogorov. It has not yet come to her that it is a matter of life and death, that the group cannot be broken up, but it has always been in a team (first vocational school, then school, institute, tourist section) and for it the tourist slogan "Die for yourself, and comrade help out "is not an empty phrase. She goes into a blizzard up and falls exhausted into the snow and freezes. By the fire a few people. They decided to collect more lapnikas for cedar, bury themselves in it and wait out the bad weather, especially since there is no close firewood, they cannot break thick ones, and their hands and feet are already frozen. They understand that they will not return to the tent. Two, Krivonischenko and Doroshenko, falling asleep, die, and the rest in the last attempt to save life rush either to the labaza or to the tent. On this path, death overtakes them. and the rest in the last attempt to save lives rush either to the labaza or to the tent.

Begin the search group. Found a tent. While they were digging into it, crackers and a piece of fat that had not been eaten by someone earlier could have fallen out of the bag and blankets. Hardly anyone will come to he got up early for the night, having a lot of time left without finishing dressing up without having finished releasing the newspaper to sit down for dinner.

Separately, you should express your opinion on the organization and technology searches. The organization of searches from the moment of arrival in Ivdel Maslennikov (throwing of assault forces on the route at several points) does not cause any objections. There is also no doubt that by the end of my stay at the site of the search, the practice of methodically probing the most likely locations ("safe" - twice crossed out, approx. Status) of frozen tourists. I believe that this method in the conditions of a snowy winter and the existing gap in time between the death of the group and the beginning of the search was the most rational. Naturally, if the search began 2 days after the death of tourists, the best would be a free search. Now you can only talk about

The question arises whether the existing method of preparing tourist groups for hiking does not have any potential danger. Unfortunately yes.
And here's why:
1. Unfortunately, we have neither the Rospromsovet's system nor the light industry set up the production of appropriate tourist equipment for winter hikes of great difficulty, such as: 1. Glued wide skis with a metal edging. 2. Insulated storm suits. 3. Special boots. 4. Special tents, <inaudible>, etc.

2. In each separate region of the Union, tourism ("given up" - twice crossed out, approx. Status) was put to chance. The current situation is such that the route through the Urals can be approved in Moldova, and the Moldovan route in Sverdlovsk. In my opinion, it would be necessary in each district to create a route commission, which would have the right to approve hikes in this area. This, by the way, will lead to the fact that groups will start preparing for campaigns in advance.
3. For each large tourist area, follow the pattern of mountaineering, create rescue groups with an emergency food supply, equipment, and a permanent composition of people.
4. It would be necessary to assign the task to construct lightweight radios, through which it would be possible to keep in touch by airplanes sent by the chief of the district rescue unit over the places of the groups' routes.

M. Axelrod (signature)
24 / IV / 59.
Prosecutor-criminalist
Ivanov (signature)

252

Discovery of Luda, Nicholas, Alexander, and Simon- Official Report

PROTOCOL inspect the place where the body was discovered. On May 6, 1959, the prosecutor of the Ivdel town of the Sverdlovsk region Jr. Counselor of Justice TEMPALOV, in the presence of witnesses Dilevich Yuri Davydovich, residing in Kiev, st. Comintern house 12 square meters. 11, Fedorov Vadim Ivanovich, prozh. Sverdlovsk, st. Strike house 19, apt. 222 (first two crossed out - approx. Comp.) And Artyupov Georgiy Semenovich prozh. Sverdlovsk .... compiled the present protocol of the site for the detection of corpses in the amount of 4 people. On the slope of the western side of the height of 880 from the famous cedar 50 meters in the creek pass 4 corpses were found, three of them are men and one woman. The corpse of a woman identified - this is Dubinina Lyudmila. The corpses of men can not be identified without raising them.

All the corpses are in the water. They were excavated from under the snow with a depth of 2.5 meters to 2 meters. Two men and a third lie heading north along the stream. The corpse of Dubinina lay in the opposite direction with her head against the stream. Dubinina is wearing a head -gear on her head, a yellow T-shirt on her body, a cowboy shirt and two sweaters; one gray is another dark color; dark leg pants and brown ski pants are on her legs; on the back of the head and on the back there are traces of damage by the probe from the words of Mr V. Astenadze, who recognized Dubinin. Her corpse has decomposed. The first corpse of a man wearing a khaki storm jacket on his hands is on the first two watches of the Victory and Sports watches show - a victory of 38 minutes and 9 hours, and sports watches 15 minutes 9 hours, the head and legs of this corpse are not visible, since not all the corpse excavated from under the snow. And two corpses lie embracing, there is nothing on the heads of both, there is not all hair on the head, one of them is dressed in a storm, the same is true and the second one, in which you can still be identified after lifting the corpses out of the stream. The legs are not visible, because not excavated until the end and are under the snow.

The corpses have decomposed. The corpses are photographed.

Corpses should be immediately removed from the stream, as may further decompose even more and may be carried away by the stream, because the current is very fast. Up the creek six meters following the tracks, a flooring was found at a depth of 3 to 2.5 meters. The flooring consists of I4 charge and I birch peaks in the snow. Things found on the floor. Half beige sweater found 15 meters from the stream (gaps - approx. Comp.) under a tree. Half of the ski trousers were found at the place where vertices were cut for flooring, and from the flooring 15 meters to the forest, under the snow at the place of detection, the Dyatlov group tents found ebony sheaths for the knife and a tablespoon of white metal. On examination of the place of detection, Vladimir M. Asenadze, prozh. Sverdlovsk, st. Lenin 66, apt. 303, and Kuznetsova ("a" crossed out - approx. Comp.) Nikolai Igorevich, prozh. st. Lenina, d (?) 66, kv. (in the handwritten version of "room") Prosecutor of the mountains. Ivdel Ml. counselor of justice

Understood: 1. Kuznetsov- signature
2. Astenadze - signature

3. Artyukov - signature
4) Gilev - signature
5) Fedorov - signature

Protocol

Inspection of the place of detection of corpses.

On May 6, 1959, the prosecutor of the Ivdel city of the Sverdlovsk region, ml. Counselor of Justice Tempalov, in the presence of witnesses Dilevich (or "Gilevich"? - approx. comp.) Yuri Davydovich, living in Kiev, ul. Comintern house 12 square meters. 11, Fedorov Vadim Ivanovich, prozh. Sverdlovsk, st. Strike house 19a, apt. 22 and Georgy Semenovich Artyukov prozh. Sverdlovsk .. _ _ _

I made this protocol of the location of the detection of corpses in the amount of 4 people.

On the slope ("north" - crossed out, approx. Comp.) Of the western side of height 880 from the famous cedar 50 meters in the first stream, four corpses were found, three of them were men and one woman. The corpse of a woman identified - this is Dubinina Lyudmila. The corpses of men can not be identified without raising them. All the corpses are in the water. They were excavated from under the snow with a depth of 2.5 meters to 2 meters. Two men and a third lie heading north along the stream. The corpse of Dubinina lay in the opposite direction with her head against the stream. Dubinina is wearing a cap comforter, on the body is a yellow jersey, a cowboy shirt and two sweaters; one gray and another dark light on the legs; leggings; dark and brown ski pants. 2 woolen socks on one leg, polo Askinadze V.M., recognizing Dubinin. Her corpse has decomposed.

The first corpse of a man wearing a storm jacket light khaki on his hands are on the left two watches of the mark "Victory" and "Sports" watches show - a victory of 38 minutes 9th hour, and sports 15 minutes (this is not visible, note). the corpse is not visible because not all the corpse excavated from under the snow. And two corpses lie embracing, there is nothing on the heads of both, there is not all hair on the head, one of them is dressed in a storm, the same is true of the second one, in which you can still be dressed only after lifting the corpses from a stream. The legs are not visible, because the excavations are not fully completed and are under the snow. The corpses have decomposed. The corpses are photographed. Corpses should be subject to immediate withdrawal from the stream, because they can be further decomposed (further the word is illegible - approx. Comp.) Even more and can be carried away by the stream, because the flow is very fast.

Up the creek at six meters in the footsteps of lapnika found flooring at a depth of 3 to 2.5 meters. The flooring consists of 14 fir and 1 birch peaks on the (second "on" crossed out, approx. Comp.) Snow. Things found on the floor.

(drawing reflecting the layout of things on the floor:

Upper left corner: Trouser leg from ski pants in black

Upper right corner: whole Chinese sweater. white Colour.

254

Lower left corner: a warm woolen brown whole sweater

Lower right corner: brown trousers from the ends are not intact

Right upper side, closer to the upper corner: - 6 m - corpses
The second half of the beige color sweater. found 15 meters from the stream (added: "southern stream" - approx. comp.) under a tree. (on the side of the sheet is a postscript, poorly discernible, perhaps "second in the stream" - approx. status) Half of the ski trousers were found at the place where vertices were cut for flooring, from the flooring 15 meters to the cedar just under the snow at the spot where the Dyatlov group tents were found riveted sheath for a knife and a tablespoon of white metal

At survey of a place of detection participated also witnesses Askinadze Vladimir Mikhaylovich, prozh. Sverdlovsk, st. Lenin 66, apt. 303, and Kuznetsova ("a" crossed out - approx. Comp.)

Nikolay Igorevich, prozh. st. Lenina, d (?) 66, room 338.

Prosecutor of the mountains. Ivdel
Ml. counselor of justice

(signature)

The Understood: 1) Artyukov (signature)
2) Kuznetsov (signature)
3) Askenedze (signature)
4) Gilevich (signature)
5) Fedorov (signature)

Zina- Official Autopsy Report

Kolmogorova corpse investigation report
FORENSIC-MEDICAL INVESTIGATION OF A CITIZEN TROUGH
KOLMOGOROVOY Zinaida Alekseevna, 22 years old

March 4, 1959, according to the decision of the Prosecutor 's Office of the Sverdlovsk region of March 3, 1959 forensic experts of the Regional Bureau of Forensic Medical Examination of the Sverdlovsk Region REVIVED VA. and Laptev II. in the presence of the public prosecutor of the Sverdlovsk region, the state counselor of justice of the third class, Klinov NI, prosecutor of the criminal prosecutor of the regional prosecutor's office of the junior counselor of justice IVANOV LI and comrade-in-arms. Comrade. The SD GORDO and NASKICHEV the KVIn the morgue room of the central hospital of the control room No. H-240 in daylight and sunny weather, a corpse of a 22-year-old citizen of KOLMAGOROVA Zinaida Alekseyevna was investigated to determine the cause of death and answer the questions indicated in the resolution.

The circumstances of the case

255

On January 23, 1959, an amateur group of tourists consisting of 10 people went to a ski resort along the route Ivdel - Mount Oorten. From the site of the 2 nd Northern in the ski trip went 9 people. On February 1, 1959 the group began the ascent to Mount Oorten and in the evening broke the tent near the height of 1079.

On the night of February 2, under unclear circumstances, all 9 people died.

a / Exterior inspection

On the sectional table is the female corpse ???? and the corpse: both upper limbs are bent at the elbow joints. The left lower limb is more unbent in the knee and hip joint. Both limbs are connected together and touch the lower third of the right shin and the inner surface of the left knee joint. The toes are extended and lowered downwards.

Clothes on the corpse: on his head a red wool cap tied on the chin to the bow, beneath it a blue wool knitted hat, a blue woolen sweater attached to the hair, a blue cuff cut off, dressed on the left side, under it a cotton cowboy with a long sleeve and one left pocket is unbuttoned, the left sleeve is ripped at the cuff. Color cowboy, green, red cells, under the cowboy on the left side of the chest found a protective mask of a military sample. Under the cowboy, the wigone sweaters are light red in a blue cross stripe, dressed on the left side, on the left and right sleeve there are two patches, one of the brown sock, the other of cotton cloth of blue color; knit shirt with a long sleeves in blue ; black sateen bra buttoned on two buttons; Ski trousers,sports black in color with bikini with fasteners on the sides, buttons are unbuttoned, in the bottom of the cuffs of the trousers are not fastened to the buttons, on the cuff of the right leg there are three discontinuities with a depth of 0.5 cm 1.2 cm and 0.3 cm; blue cotton sports pants with? -th inner pockets, fasteners on the sides are unbuttoned, the right pocket is turned out of it exposed races

Brown color with two broken teeth, in the black pocket; underneath * yuki on an elastic band; ladies' knitted trousers with a fleece of color; ladies' cotton tights of black color on an elastic band; shorts of cotton smelting on four buttons; on legs woolen brown skis with fur insoles , beneath them blue and brown wagon socks.

The length of the corpse is 162 cm. Good nutrition, with well developed muscle groups . Cadaverous spots of cyanotic-lilac color are located on the posterior surface of the trunk. The rigor mortis was resolved in the muscle groups of the joints. On his head dark-haired hair braided in two braids, connected by two silk red ribbons, the length of the hair is up to 30 cm. The forehead is high sloping posteriorly; the skin of the face and hands of lilac red color, in the area of the right frontal hillock a dark red color scab 2 x 1.5 cm in size, dense to the touch, next to it is a section of pale-colored color measuring 3 x 2 cm, reaching the right eyebrow, in the right temporal- the zygomatic area of the skin is an irregularly shaped brownish-colored skin of the size?x 5 cm. Eyebrows narrow black. In the upper eyelid of the left and right eye, the area of dark red coloration is 5 x 1 cm and 0.5 x 0.5 cm. The left eye crack is half-open , the cornea is cloudy, the iris is light-brown in color; on the cornea of the left eyeball Lärsche spots. Mucous period of reddish color. The back of the nose is slightly arched , on the dorsum of the nose there is a bruise-colored abrasion in the size of 1 x 0.7 cm, at the tip of the nose there is the same abrasion of the parchment density of 2 x 1 cm. In the area of the zygomatic arches, cheeks and chin a number of abrasions of various shapes and sizes under dry Brown colored crusts from 6 x 2 cm in size to? x 1 cm and less.The lips are cyanotic red, swollen, the mouth is slightly ajar, teeth are even white, the tongue in the mouth is behind the teeth; gums of cyanotic mucous pink on the back of the nose, a brownish-colored abrasion measuring 1 x 0.7 cm, at the tip of the nose the same abrasion of a parchment density of 2 x 1 cm.

colors. The opening of the mouth, nose and ear aisles are clean. Ear shells oval in pink, neck without features. The thorax is cylindrical, the mammary glands are of medium size, and the testes. The nipples protrude above the surface of the mammary glands, nipples and nipple circles of pale gray color; the abdomen is located at the level of the thorax. The external genitalia are formed correctly, their mucous membranes are cyanotic-pink in color. The hymen is annular, its free edge is fringed, the natural opening of the hymen allows the tip of the adult's little finger to pass. There are no vaginal discharge.

On the back of the right and left hand in the region of the metacarpophalangeal and interphalangeal joints, bruise-colored abrasions are dense to the touch, measuring from 1.5 x 1 cm to 0.3 x 3 cm. In the rear of the right hand, at the base of the third finger, the wound is irregularly shaped, angle facing the terminal phalanx with dimensions of 3 x 2.2 cm with uneven edges and scalp skin graft. End phalanges of the left hand 1-5 fingers dense to the touch, dry, brownish-colored; The venous network is well defined in the region of the inner and outer surfaces of both upper limbs. Lower limbs without traces of visible damage pinkish -red.In the lumbar region of the right lateral surface of the trunk, right side of the abdomen, a skin of bright red color in the form of a strip measuring 29 x 6 cm. The rest of the surface of the trunk and extremities is pale red,

b / Internal Research

Skin flaps of the scalp from the inner surface are moist, juicy, glistening red.

The bones of the arch and the base of the skull are intact. The dura mater is cyanotic-gray, full-blooded, the soft dura mater is turbid, swollen. Cortex and fissures of the brain are flattened , flattened. The contours of the lateral ventricles of the brain are not distinguishable, the gray matter of the brain is hardly distinguishable from white. The substance of the brain is a jelly -like mass of cyanotic-reddish color, the pattern of the cerebellum is poorly discernible. Vessels of the base of the brain without features. Subcutaneous fat tissue of the trunk is well developed. The position of the internal organs is correct , the lungs lie freely in the pleural cavities.In the near-cardiac bag contained about 30 cm3 of amber liquid, a heart size of 12 x 10.6 cm, coated with fat on the surface. The heart muscle on the cut is dark red. The right and left halves of the heart contained up to 150 cm3 of liquid dark blood, the valves of the heart of the aorta and pulmonary artery are smooth, thin, brilliant, the coronary vessels of the heart are free, passable, the inner surface of the aorta smooth, clean; the width of the aortic arch over the valves is 8 cm.

Lungs from the surface of the cyanotic red color, testovaty to the touch, on the cut tissue of light dark red color, when pressed from the surface of the cut, bloody liquid and liquid dark blood drip abundantly, the larynx and bronchus lumen is free . The mucous esophagus of the trachea and bronchi is cyanotic red. The sub-lingual bone is intact.

Thyroid gland on the incision is cyanotic red . In the cavity of the stomach contained traces of foamy mucous mass of dirty yellow color, the gastric mucosa of grayish-red color with well expressed folding. On the upper surface of the folds of the mucosa of the stomach, small bleeding spots Vishnevsky. Pancreas on a section of lilac-colored small-lobed. Liver with smooth shiny surfaces liver size 24 x 15 x 11 x 8 cm on the cut liver tissue burovishnevogo color with poorly discernable pattern hepatic blooded sharply .; gallbladder contained up to 30 seet3 olive colored fluid, mucous gallbladder velvety, brown. Spleen is loose to the touch, the capsule is wrinkled, on the cut fabric, temnovishnevogo, its color from pulp gives a large cut surface scraping. spleen size 9 x 6.2 x 2 cm. The lumen of the small intestine mucosa contain gryaznozheltogo mass color, intestinal mucosa bluish-red color. In the lumen of the colon fecal burokorichnevogo color colonic mucosa bluish-gray color.Kidneys with smooth surface, brilliant, the capsule of the kidneys are removed easily on a kidney tissue section temnovishnevogo color, cerebral cortical kidney layer discernible bad. adrenal well distinguishable layers, the size of the right kidney 8 x 5 x 3 cm., left 8 x 5 x 2.5 cm. The uterus is small, dense feel, on the cut fabric blednoserogo its color, uterine lumen traces pale red slime. Appendages on the cut without features. The bladder 300 contained seet3 turbid yellowish fluid bladder mucosa blednolilovogo color.

For the chemical and histological examination, a part of the internal organs is taken from this corpse. In the study of the corpse, the presence of alcohol is not established.

COURT OF MEDICAL EXPERT OF THE REGION

BUREAU OF SUDMEDEXPERTISY - / signature / / REVIVED /

SHUD.MED.EXPERT OF THE CITY

SEVEROURALSK - signature / LAPTEV /

PROSECUTOR OF THE SVERDLOVSK REGION

STATE ADVISER

JUSTICE OF THE IIIrd CLASS - signature / KLINOV /

PROSECUTOR OF THE REGIONAL CRIMINALIST

PROSECUTORS ML. ADVISER OF JUSTICE - signature / IVANOV /

CONCEPT - signature / GORDO /

CONCEPT - signature / NASCICHEV /

Sheet 134

CONCLUSION

Based on these studies the corpse of a citizen Kolmagorova Zinaida Alekseevna, 22 years, and given the circumstances of the case, believe that the death of Kolmogorov was the result of low temperature / freezing / as evidenced by swelling of the meninges, the sharp plethora of internal organs, liquid dark blood in the heart cavity, Vishnevsky spots on the gastric mucosa, the third fourth-degree frostbite terminal phalanges of the fingers; found injuries on the body in the form Kolmagorova osadneniya abrasions and skin wounds caused by a blunt instrument, resulting drop contusion against rocks, ice, snow.

The above injuries were caused by Kolmogorov during his lifetime, as well as in the agonal state and posthumously.

These studies corpse Kolmogorov suggest that the meal had for 6-8 hours until death. The presence of alcohol in the study were found, preserved virginity Kolmogorov. Violent death, an accident.

SUD.MED.EKSPERT REGIONAL

BUREAU forensic - Signature / Renaissance /

SUD.MED.EKSPERT CITY

Severouralsk - Signature / Laptev /

Rustem- Official Autopsy Report

ACT number 5

Forensic medical examination of corpses CITIZEN
Slobodina Rustem Vladimirovich '23

March 8, 1959 according to the decision of the prosecutor's office of Sverdlovsk Region 7 March 1959 the forensic experts of the Regional Bureau of the Sverdlovsk Region Renaissance forensics BA in the presence of the public prosecutor of the Sverdlovsk region of the state counselor of justice Ivanova LN tov.tov and witnesses. PROUD SD and NASKICHEVA KV in the room of the morgue of the central hospital management p / H-240 in daylight and sunny weather made the study of the corpse of a citizen Slobodina RV, to determine the cause of death and the responses to the questions listed in the decree.

Circumstances of the case :

January 23, 1959 amateur group of tourists of 10 people went to ski tour route gorIvdel - Mount Otorten. From phase 2 nd North went 9 people in the ski trip. 1st February 1959 the band began the ascent to the mountain Otorten yesterday and pitched tents at the height of 1079.
On the night of 2 of February under mysterious circumstances has occurred the death of 9 persons.

and External examination:

On the table lies the corpse of a man in a pose: a corpse's head tilted somewhat backwards, chin forward and to-top, right hand on the right shoulder joint more reserved, bent at a right angle at the elbow, fingers clenched into a fist. The left arm is drawn back and the side, straighten the elbow. On hand watch "Star", which features 8 hours and 45 minutes. The right leg in the hip joint is bent at an angle of 120 degrees and the knee joint at right angles. The left leg in the hip joint is bent at a right angle and the knee joint at an angle of 60 degrees. Both legs adjoin each other in the inner surface of the lower thigh and the lower third of the leg.

On the corpse's clothing: a black cotton svitr, beneath a black cowboy shirt red cell, fastened by 3 buttons and cuffs fastened each in the 2 buttons. Cowboy has left buttoned patch pocket on a safety pin. In his pocket was found: / passport in the name of Rustem Slobodina Vladimirovich, money - 310 rubles / one hundred, 4 x 50 and 10 rubles / pen ink. Between svitr and cowboy on his chest, felt insole 2 of the shoe. Under cowboy breeches warm fleece sweatshirt, fastened with two buttons under her blue knit shirt with long sleeves. Ski pants, dark, fastened with a button and strap. In pockets: a box of matches from 48 matches, a pocket knife on a long rope, comb in a case, two strings and a pencil, x / paper sock. Beneath blue satin sweat pants, in the back pocket which on January 20, 1959 letter to the trade union of the year. Under sweatpants pants, warm light gray fleece buttoned / steam from (?) Shirt / Under pants blue satin pants with an elastic band on the right foot black boots under it: x / paper socks, then gray vigonevye socks, x / paper sock vigonevy brown sock. On the left leg missing boots and socks in the same order.

At the head of dark brown curly hair length up to 8 cm. High forehead sloping backwards. Skin Face bluish-reddish color. Cadaverous sinyushnokrasnovatogo spot colors abundantly located on the back of the neck and trunk and extremities. Rigor mortis was resolved completely in the muscle groups joints. In the area of ??the forehead in the middle of the small abrasions burokrasnogo parchment color density slightly depressed. Above them, two scratches linear form under dry brown crust up to 1.5 cm, located parallel to the superciliary arcs at a distance from each other by 0.3 cm. Thick brown eyebrows. Eyes half-open. In the area of ??the right upper eyelid abrasion burokrasnogo color measuring 1 x 0.5 cm. In the abrasions and scratches on his face marked hemorrhage in the soft tissues to be. The cornea is cloudy, serovatokorichnevogo iris color, the pupils are dilated. In the area of ??the cornea Lyarshe spots. Bridge of nose straight, in the bridge of the nose and the nose apex soft tissue burokrasnogo color. At the tip of the nose soft tissue area under dry crust burovishnevoy measuring 1.5 x 1 cm. The lips are swollen. The mouth is closed, the openings of the nasal secretions traces of dried blood. The border color of the lips burovishnevogo wrinkled and dry. Teeth are smooth, white. Language in the oral cavity for teeth. The mucous membrane of the mouth and gums blednose cerned color. The right half of the face a few swollen, her many small abrasions irregularly shaped parchment density under the dry crust, passing in part on the chin. On the left half of the face minor scratches of the same nature, among them one abrasion measuring 1.2 x 0.4 cm below the dry brown crust in the left zygomatic tuber. Auricles oval sinyushnokrasnovatogo color on the outer edge of the right auricle soft tissue burovishnevogo color touch dense parchment density of the same character soft tissue in the left auricle. The opening of the mouth and the ear passages clean. On the neck of small abrasions on the left dark red color, the chest of a cylindrical shape, the stomach is located at chest level. The skin of the trunk and upper extremities to the wrist joints and lower limbs [cyanotic?] Pink. Soft fabric rear and palmar surfaces of both hands burolilovogo color. In the metacarpal-phalangeal joints of the hands osadnenie protrusions of soft tissue in areas measuring 8 x 1.5 cm, covered with a dry crust with parchment density below the skin. On the left hand edge of the elbow portion osadneniya burovishnevogo parchment color density measuring 6 x 2 cm. Osadneniya with the transition to the side surface at the left hand finger. Palm surface brushes sinyushnolilovogo color. In the area of ??the terminal phalanges of both hands wrinkled soft tissues are dense to the touch. The lower third of the right forearm on the back surface with two sections of the epidermis lack measuring 2.5 x 3 x 3.5 cm and 1.5 cm. Irregular edges blednokrasnogo color. The front internal surface of the upper limbs well defined vein pattern. External genitalia are formed correctly. The head of the penis lilovokrasnogo color, dense to the touch wrinkled. The opening of the anus clean. In the area of ??the stop well defined vein pattern, soft cloth feet have the form "bathhouse" skin. soft tissue osadnenie dark red color 2.5 x 1.5 cm. and 4.5 x 1.5 cm on the outer surface of the lower third of the left tibia.

b / Domestic research

Skin patches of the scalp with the inner surface of the moist, juicy, brilliant. Accordingly lobnovisochnoy right area, the right and left temporal muscles spilled hemorrhage impregnation with soft tissue. From the front edge of the left temporal bone scales toward anteriorly and upward portion of the frontal bone is a bone fracture with the divergence of the edges up to 0.1 cm, the crack length up to 6 cm. The crack is located at a distance of 1.5 cm from the sagittal suture. In addition, there is a discrepancy in the joints temporo-parietal suture on the left as well as right / postmortem /. The dura mater cyanosis, poor blood supply to the vessels of it. Under the dura mater it contained up to 75 cm3, bloody fluid, pia cloudy, krasnozelenovatogo color. brain substance is a shapeless mass zelenovatokrasnogo color contours indistinguishable ventricles, and gray and white matter. In the upper left edge of the pyramid site hemorrhage under bone plate measuring 0.3 x 0.4 cm. The bones of the skull base intact.

Subcutaneous fat body developed satisfactorily correct the position of the internal organs. The pleural cavities contained up to 1 liter of bloody fluid / exudate /. The pericardium contained 30 cm3 of bloody fluid. Heart 11 x 10 x 6 cm. Cardiac muscle dark red color in the section, the left ventricle muscle thickness of 1.5 cm. 0.5cm right. The left and right halves of the heart contained up to 100 cm3 dark liquid blood. The valves of the heart, the pulmonary artery aortic smooth, thin, dark red color unclear. Coronary heart freely passable. The inner surface of the aortic smooth and clean. Light surface color sinyushnokrasnogo testovatoy to touch on the cut lung tissue dark red color when pressed with the cut surface liberally dripping bloody foamy fluid and fluid dark blood. The lumen of the larynx and bronchi free. Esophageal tracheal bronchus lilovokrasnovatogo colors contained in the stomach mucous mass burozheltogo color in an amount of about 100 cm3. The mucous membrane of the stomach swollen, serovatokrasnogo color with well-defined folding. On the surface of mucosal folds melkotochechnye hemorrhage Vishnevsky spots. Horns pod"yazychnoy bones intact. The thyroid gland in the red section. Pancreas on lilovokrasnogo color section. The liver surface is smooth, shiny, liver size of 23 x 16 x 12 x 7 cm, on the section of liver tissue burovishnevogo color, full-blooded sharply, with poor hepatic discernible pattern. The gallbladder contained up to 30 (or 80 - approx compiler.) Cm3 brown fluid, mucous burozheltogo its velvety color. Spleen loose to the touch, the cut fabric of her temnovishnevogo colored pulp with a cut surface gives big scrape. Spleen size 7 x 11 x 3 cm.

In the lumen of the small intestine contained a slimy mass gryaznozheltogo color. In the lumen of the colon poluoformlenny cal. The mucous membrane of the intestine sinyushnoserogo color. Kidneys from the surface smooth, brilliant, right kidney size 11 x 5 x 3 cm, left 10 x 5 x 3 cm. On the cut fabric kidney temnovishnevogo color, cortical and medullary layer of kidney discernible well. The layers of the adrenal glands to distinguish good. In the area of ??the right adrenal hemorrhage in the medulla. The bladder contained up to 200 cm3 hazy pale yellow liquid. The mucous membrane of the urinary bladder cyanosis. For chemical and histological examination of the corpse is taken from the specified portion of the internal organs and part of the pyramid of the temporal bone.
In the study of internal organs presence of alcohol is not detected.

print
SUD.MED.EKSPERT REGIONAL
BUREAU forensic - / signature / / Renaissance /
PROSECUTOR the Sverdlovsk region

counselor of state
JUSTICE ??? - CLASS - / signature / / KLINOV /
REGIONAL PROSECUTOR criminologist

PROSECUTION ML. Counselor of Justice - / signature / / Ivanov /
Concepts: - / signature / / PROUD /

- / Signature / / NASKICHEV /

CONCLUSION
Based on these studies the corpse of a citizen Slobodina Rustem Vladimirovich, 23 years, given the circumstances of the case believe that the death Slobodina come from the action of low temperature / freezing / as evidenced by: swelling of the meninges, congestion of internal organs, spots Vishnevsky on the mucous membrane of the stomach, frostbite the fingers of the upper extremities of the third, fourth degree.

Discovered at an internal study of the left frontal bone fracture could occur in the fall Slobodina citizen or contusion of the head against hard objects, what could be a stone, ice and more. Said closed cranial trauma caused by a blunt instrument. At the time of occurrence, it certainly caused a state of momentary stun Slobodina and contributed to the rapid freezing Slobodina. The lack of explicit bleeding under the meninges gives reason to believe that death is Slobodina came as a result of frost.
The injuries found on the body of a citizen Slobodina, due to abrasions, scratches, osadneniya caused by a blunt instrument as a result of a fall or injury on the rocks, ice and more.
Damage had been caused during his lifetime, as well as in the agonal state posthumously.

262

These studies corpse Slobodina suggest that meal he had for 6-8 hours until death. Alcohol is not detected during internal investigations.

In view of the above injuries SLOBODIN in the early hours from the moment of their infliction could move and crawl.
Death Slobodina violent - an accident.

SUD.MED.EKSPERT REGIONAL
BUREAU forensic - signature / Renaissance /

Igor- Official Autopsy Report

Mortem examination CITIZEN
Igor A. Dyatlov, 23 years old

March 4, 1959 according to the 4th March 1959 according to the decision of the prosecutor's office of the Sverdlovsk region of the 3rd March 1959 the forensic experts of the Regional Bureau of Forensic Medicine of the Sverdlovsk region Renaissance VA and Laptev Yu in the presence of the public prosecutor of Sverdlovsk Region State Counselor of Justice Class III Vee-NI, the prosecutor criminologist regional prosecutor's office junior counselor of justice Ivanova LN tov.tov and witnesses. PROUD SD and NASKICHEVA KV in the room of the morgue of the central hospital management n / box number 240 when examined with the corpse of a citizen Dyatlova daylight and sunny weather, IA 23 years, to determine the cause of death and the responses to the questions listed in the decree.

Facts:

January 23, 1959 amateur group of tourists of 10 people went to ski like the route Ivdel - Mountain Otorten. From phase 2 nd North went 9 people in the ski trip. February 1, 1959 the group began to climb the mountain and in the evening Otorten pitch a tent at a height of 1079.
On the night of February 2, under mysterious circumstances, there was the death of 9 persons.

and / external examination

The body of the man right physique is on the dissecting table, the corpse pose: hands laid in the shoulder joints, the forearm bent at the elbows and are in a horizontal position. Fingers of hands flexed into fists and are located on the chest. the corpse's head tilted slightly backward, legs bent at the hip and knee joints, toes are turned inward and touching each other with your thumbs on the left forearm in the lower third of wearing watches brand "Star", the clock shows "5:00 31 minutes."
Clothes on the body: a fur sleeveless jacket covered with cotton blue material on the dark gray fur, blue vigonevy svitr, cotton cowboy shirt red in the dark gray square with three buttons, two upper undone. The cuffs buttoned one button. In the breast pocket was the packaging "streptocid" with 4 tablets, blue sleeveless jersey. Ski pants brown knitted fleece with an elastic band, beneath bumazeevye sports trousers blue-green

color, with elastic, black satin pants. On the right foot wearing white woolen sock underneath cotton brown socks on his left foot cotton socks brown, like golf.

corpse length 175 cm, good food, with well-developed muscle groups. Cadaverous spots bluish-reddish color on the rear surface of the trunk of the neck and limbs. Rigor mortis was resolved in muscle groups joints. At the head of light brown hair. hair, up to 7 cm, trimmed at boxing, high forehead, sloping posteriorly, in the forehead on the frontal mounds minor abrasions dark red color in the left brow ridges graze the brown-red color, parchment density rises above the surface of the skin, eyebrows bushy svetlorusye, skin facial sinyushnokrasnovatogo color, eyes half-open, on the upper eyelids minor abrasions brown-red, the cornea is the eye is cloudy, iris gray, dilated pupils, nasal bridge straight to the bridge of the nose and the tip portion of the brown-red color of parchment density, size . 2 x 1.5 cm in both cheeks abrasion brownish-red color under dry crust 3 x 1.5 x 1 cm x 0.5 cm 3, -. the left and right small abrasions. Lips bluish-purple, covered with dried blood, mucous membrane of the gums pale gray. On the upper jaw teeth are white, even, rare, mandibular central incisor is absent without changing the mucous gums. Auricles bluish-pink oval in left cheek minor abrasions dark brown parchment density, nose and mouth openings clean neck unremarkable. The rib cage is cylindrical in shape, the stomach is situated below the chest level. External genitalia are formed correctly. The opening of the anus clean.
In the area of ??the knee right and left bruises dark red, the size of 1 x 0.5 cm.? 0.5 to 0.5 cm. Parchment density without bleeding into the underlying tissues. In the area of ??the left ankle susutava on the front side and rear surfaces in the areas of both ankles abrasions brown-red color depressed over the surface of the skin, as well as on ???? skin measuring 1 x 0.5 cm, 3 x 2; 5 cm., with bleeding into the underlying soft tissue. In the visible scratches one incision in the lower third of the right tibia skin osadnenie 4 x 2 cm, the outer-side surface in the lower third of the right forearm on the palmar surface of minor abrasions dark red parchment density. Rear right hand purple-gray. In the metacarpal-phalangeal joints and inter-phalangeal joints, soft tissue brown-purple, covered with parchment density dry parched skin with hemorrhage into the underlying tissues. The left hand burolilovogo Sadin color with brownish-red color, parchment density, the size of 1 to 0.5 cm to 0.2 cm 2. ???? Ix skin in the area of ??the rear surface of the 2nd 4th ?? tsev. In the palmar surface of the 2nd 5th finger skin wound wrong-linear form with smooth edges, arranged transversely dlinniku fingers wound surface to a depth of 0.1 (or 0.2 -.. Ed note) see bone and cartilage skeleton. while feeling safe.

b- The internal investigation

Skin patches of the scalp with the inner surface of the moist, juicy, shiny pale red color, a set of bones and skull base - intact, dura cyanotic red-blooded, pia muddy, swollen, gyrus and sulcus of the brain ????? enes flattened, veschevstvo brain is jelly-like mass of green-red color. Grey matter of the brain poorly distinguishable from white, ventricles of the brain circuits are not distinguishable, the substance of the cerebellum pattern discernible bad vessels base of the brain without features, the subcutaneous fatty tissue of the body is well developed, the position of the internal organs proper, pleural cavity free, in the pericardium contained up to? 0 cm3 amber-colored liquid. ? Heart 2 x 7 x 10 cm, with a surface slightly charged to fat, cardiac muscle on the cut dark red; left ventricular muscle thickness 2 cm, 0.7 cm of the right, the right heart and the left half 250 contained sm.m3 dark liquid blood, heart valves, pulmonary and aortic smooth, thin light brilliant red mouth of the coronary arteries of freedom, arterial lumen expanded, well pass. The inner surface of aortic smooth, clean, width aortic arch over valves 8 cm. The light from the surface of bluish-red testovatoy to touch the cut lung tissue deep red color, when pressed with the cut surface flows in a large amount, the liquid dark blood and foamy bloody fluid lumen of the larynx and bronchi free, mucosa of the esophagus, trachea and bronchi bluish-red color. Horns pod"yazychnoy bones intact. The thyroid gland is the cut fleshy red. The stomach contained about 100 cm. 3 liquid slimy mass of brown-reddish color, the gastric mucosa purplish-red, swollen, with a well defined folds, on the upper surface of the mucous membrane of the stomach folds to have large numbers of small bleeding spots Vishnevsky. The sense of smell of the contents of the stomach felt sour smell, the pancreas on the cut shallow-lobed purplish-red color. In the lumen of the small intestine contained a slimy mass of reddish mucous ???? echnika bluish-reddish color. In the large intestine poluoformlenny feces light brown, slimy ???? chnika pale purple, spleen loose to the touch, her wrinkled ???? ula, the spleen size of 13 x 7 x 2 cm on the cut fabric spleen dark cherry color, pulp gives ??? cut large surface scraping, liver surface is smooth, shiny, liver size of 26 x 16 x 11 x 10 cm ?? section of liver tissue brown-cherry color, full-blooded, drawing liver slightly differences in the gallbladder contained up to 30 sm.m3 liquid olive green, gallbladder mucosa velvety mud color, kidneys ?? The surface is smooth, brilliant; capsule with a kidney removed easily, right kidney size 10 x 5 x 3.5 cm left kidney ?? x 5 x 3.5 cm. In the context of kidney tissue dark cherry color, cortex and medulla discernible bad distinguishable layers of the adrenal well. The bladder contained ?? liters of turbid, light-yellow liquid-colored, bladder mucosa pale gray. When the corpse study the presence of alcohol is not established.

For the chemical analysis of said corpse and taken for histological examination of the internal organs.

SUD.MED.EKSPERT REGIONAL
BUREAU forensic - signature / Renaissance /

SUD.MED.EKSPERT CITY
North Ural - signature / Laptev /

PROSECUTOR the Sverdlovsk region
counselor of state
JUSTICE III-CLASS - signature / KLINOV /

REGIONAL PROSECUTOR criminologist
PROSECUTION ML. Counselor of Justice - / signature / / Ivanov /

CONCLUSION

Based on these studies the corpse of a citizen Dyatlova Igor Alekseevich, 23 years considering the circumstances of the case believe that the death of Dyatlov was a result of low temperature / freezing / as evidenced by: swelling of the meninges, the sharp hyperemia of internal organs, overflow liquid dark blood cavities of the heart, the presence of stains Vishnevsky in the gastric mucosa, overflow bladder, limbs frostbitten fingers III and IV degree.

discovered (the word is entered by hand -.. Ed note) For external damage in the form of study osadneniya, abrasions and skin wounds caused by a blunt instrument that could arise as a result of a fall or injury on the rocks, ice and more.

The above injuries were caused during his lifetime, as well as in the agonal state posthumously. By the nature of injuries, damage to the above belong to the category of light without health disorders.

These studies corpse Dyatlova suggest that meal he had for 6-8 hours until death. The presence of alcohol is detected in the investigation. Death is violent, an accident.

SUD.MED.EKSPERT REGIONAL
BUREAU forensic - signature / Renaissance /

SUD.MED.EKSPERT CITY
North Ural - signature / Laptev /

George- Official Autopsy Report

Forensic medical examination of corpses CITIZEN
KRIVONISCHENKO George Alekseevich, 23 years old

March 4, 1959 according to the decision of the prosecutor's office of the Sverdlovsk region of the 3rd March 1959 the forensic experts of the Regional Bureau of Forensic Medicine of the Sverdlovsk region Renaissance VA and Laptev Yu in the presence of the public prosecutor of Sverdlovsk Region State Counselor of Justice Class III Vee-NI, the prosecutor criminologist regional prosecutor's office junior counselor of justice Ivanova LN witnesses and comrade. Comrade. PROUD SD and NASKICHEVA KV indoor central morgue n / box number H-240 control hospitals in daylight and sunny weather made a citizen cadaver study KRIVONISCHENKO GA 23 years, to determine the cause of death and the responses to the questions listed in the decree.

Facts:

January 23, 1959 amateur group of tourists of 10 people went to ski like the route Ivdel - Mountain Otorten. From phase 2 nd North went 9 people in the ski trip. February 1, 1959 the group began to climb the mountain and in the evening Otorten pitched tents at the height of 1079.

On the night of 2 of February under mysterious circumstances has occurred the death of 9 persons.

and / external examination

On the dissecting table is a man's body; corpse pose: head assigned to the left, right arm bent vloktevom joint and assigned to the top, right hand fingers touch the head, left arm bent at the elbow, and brought to the shoulder, wrist bent, and the hand fingers touch the chest. Straighten right leg, left leg slightly reserved in the hip joint and bend at the knee. Clothes on the body: cotton cowboy shirt, blue in red ink on the cell 3 buttons / dvepugovitsy undone /, cuffs fastened with two buttons, a pocket in the outer coil of copper wire ishelkovaya pink ribbon. To the left on the inside surface of the pocket is sewn from white matter. Under kovboykoyhlopchatobumazhnaya breeches white shirt, white pants from the material "Grizbon". The left lower half missing pants to the knee level, edge of the fabric pants in areas with uneven obryvakalson tissue charring under pants blue satin trunks on 2 ??? Kach. On the left nogehlopchatobumazhny sock torn edges of his charred.

The corpse of a man in length 169 cm., The right physique, good food, well razvitymimyshechnymi groups of the trunk and extremities. Cadaverous bagrovolilovogo spot colors, located nazadney surface of the trunk of the neck and limbs. Rigor mortis was resolved in muscle gruppahsustavov. On the head temnorusye curly hair up to 10 cm. Cut under poluboks. Forehead vysokiypokaty posteriorly. Eyebrows dark brown, thick, skin face cyonatic gray color. On average

(corrected by hand - approx ed.).

her portion of the forehead osadneniya round shape the size of 0.3 by 0.3 cm. of brown-red color pergamentnoyplotnosti. In the left temporal region two abrasions brown-red color of parchment density razmerom1,2 on? 3 cm and 1 cm. By 0.2 cm. The eyes slightly open, right eye gap larger than the left, in the right eye and rogovitsylevogo Lyarshe spots. Corneal cloudy, Iris gray-green color, dilated pupils, pale mucous century gray. Bridge of nose straight. In the middle third of the nose graze the brown-red color, parchment density passing in the wound in the area of ??the tip of the nose and wings of defective soft tkaneyrazmerom 1.8 x 2 cm, the bottom of the wound are the cartilage of the nasal septum, with the right-nostril; on the bottom (the first part of the word is not quite legible - approx ed.). lip and chin hair length 0.5cm pepelnogotsveta..

The mucous membrane of the lips dark cinnamon-colored parchment density, closed mouth, lips swollen. For the lower epidermis zubamiloskut pale gray with papillary lines of the flap size 1.8 to 0.6 cm. The teeth are straight sbeloy enamel, opening the mouth and nose are clean, bruises on his cheeks dark brown leather osadnenie pergamentnoyplotnosti and this same color. Auricles swollen bluish-red, neck bezosobennostey, thorax cylindrical shape; external genitalia are formed correctly, the opening of the anus clean, the skin of the chest, neck and limbs to luchezapyastnyhsustavov krasnovatolilovogo color with marked venous pattern on the extremities. On the right side of the chest at armpit abrasion pale krasnogotsveta size of 7 by 2 cm, without bleeding into the underlying tissues.

- 4 - (corrected by hand - approx ed.).

At the edge of the rib on the right hypochondrium middle clavicular line abrasions pale red tsvetapergamentnoy density measuring 2 x 1.2 cm. 1 x 1.2 cm, without bleeding into the underlying tissues. Rear right hand Patriotic. In the metacarpal-phalangeal joints, soft tissue belesovatoserogo color fingers burolilovogo color terminal phalanx dry dark brown, on the rear of the small finger skin abrasions dark brown parchment density. Palm surface of the right hand bluish-red skin with Ranko with jagged edges dark brown color at the base of the thumb. Nasredney third phalanx (forwarded with the "average" - approx ed.). Epidermis finger defect in shape irazmeram coinciding with the detected in the oral cavity. The terminal phalanges of all fingers ?? sohshie dark brown. In the left wrist abrasions dark red color parchment density of 5 x 2.5 cm, the rear left hand swollen. Along the entire diameter of the rear-left kistiskalpirovannaya wound to exfoliate the epidermis dark brown parchment density of 8 x 2 cm., Left rear 2-5 fingers black with a wrinkled epidermis 5 finger ipodsohshimi terminal phalanges. On the palmar surface of the soft tissues of the terminal phalanges of the dried, dense. The middle phalanx of the fingers 4-5 cutaneous wound measuring 1.5 x 1 cm. And 1 x 0.5 cm. Korichnevogotsveta dark, dense to the touch from the charring. On the outer surface of the left buttock and left thigh - uchastkimyagkih tissue pink color and the color of parchment burokrasnogo density by sliding the epidermis in the area of ??10 x 3 cm, 6 x 2 cm and 4 x 5 cm on the front, inner thigh ssadinytemnokorichnevogo.dark red color density measuring parchment? x 2 cm. x 1.5 cm 1 and smaller. On vnutrenneypoverhnosti the upper third of the left thigh three skin lesions ??? eynoy shape with smooth edges do0,3 depth cm. With acute angles measuring 1.5 to 04 cm. The left shin and ??? and swollen. On the entire outer surface of the leg burn on a plot size of 31 x 10 cm. Parchment density. In the lower third of the left ????? burochernogo color with charring of tissue and skin cover for bursting - ??? in the middle third iverhney thirds burn surface ???? red and light brown color. On zadnevnutrenneypoverhnosti left shin abrasions dark brown parchment density measuring 8 x 1.3 cm.? x 1.5 cm and 2 x 1 cm. The rear left foot burokorichnevogo color with patches of peeling of the epidermis 10 x 4cm. ??? second finger charred dark brown color fabric ????? dense to the touch. On peredneypoverhnosti right thigh and shin bruises dark brown parchment density of 5 x2 cm. 3 x 8 cm, 7 x 1 cm and 2 x? cm.

b / Internal research

Skin patches of the scalp with the inner surface of the juicy, brilliant, red, right ?? chnoy region and occipital region of diffuse bleeding from impregnating the right temporal muscle. The bones of the cranial vault base intact. The dura mater Xin ???? full-blooded, myagkayamozgovaya shell muddy, swollen, gyrus and sulcus of the brain are hard to distinguish. The substance of the brain is a jelly-like mass

- 6 - (corrected by hand - approx ed.).
krasnovatozelenogo color. The gray matter of the brain poorly distinguishable from white. The contours of the lateral ventricles of the brain poorly distinguishable layers of the cerebellum distinguish good base of the brain vessels without osobennostey.Podkozhno-fatty tissue of the body is well developed, correct the position of the internal organs; pleural cavity free. The pericardium contained up to 20 cm3 turbid yellowish liquid, heart size of 12 x 10 x 5.5 cm, cardiac muscle dark red color in the section, the left ventricle muscle thickness 1.8 cm. Right 0.5 cm. In the right and left side of the heart It contained up to 200 cm3 liquid of dark blood, heart valves, aortic, pulmonary artery thin, smooth, brilliant. Coronary heart free, smooth, walkable. The inner surface of the aortic smooth and clean. Light from the surface purplish red testovatoy to touch on the cut of their cloth is dark red, the pressure-sensitive section spoverhnosti profusely dripping liquid dark blood and frothy bloody fluid, throat bronchi lumen is free, mucosa of the esophagus, trachea and bronchi bluish-reddish color. Thyroid zhelezana fleshy section, dark red color. Horns for 'lingual bone intact. The stomach contained sledyslizistoy mass burozheltovatogo colors gastric mucosa bluish to reddish horoshovyrazhennoy folding; on the surface of the stomach many small hemorrhages folds - pyatenVishnevskogo, swollen mucous membrane of the stomach; Pancreas on the cut melkodolchataya dark red. The liver with a smooth surface, brilliant. liver size 26 x 16 x 14 x 9 cm. in the section of liver tissue burovishnevogo color, full-blooded sharply with poor liver distinguishable pattern. The gallbladder contained

30sm3 xxxxxxxxx brown liquid color. The mucous membrane of the gall bladder velvety greenish color. Spleen size 9 x 6 x 3 cm section of spleen tissue is dark -. ??? Nevogo color, spleen feels flabby, wrinkled kapsulaee, pulp to the cut surface gives a great scraping. In the lumen of the small intestine weight soderzhalasslizistaya burozheltogo colors in the lumen of the colon fecal burokorichnevogo tsveta.Slizistaya bowel sinyushnokrasnovatogo color. Kidneys from the surface smooth, brilliant on the cut kidney tissue temnovishnevogo color, kidney layers are hardly distinguishable. right kidney size 10 x 6 x 3.5, left 10 x 5 x 3 cm. Cortical and brain ???? adrenal well distinguishable. The bladder contained up to 500 sm3mutnoy yellowish liquid. The mucous membrane of the urinary bladder cyanosis. To study the chemical isssledovaniya igistologicheskogo of said corpse is taken of the internal organs.

SUD.MED.EKSPERT REGIONAL
BUREAU forensic - signature / Renaissance /

SUD.MED.EKSPERT CITY
North Ural - signature / Laptev /

PROSECUTOR the Sverdlovsk region
counselor of state
JUSTICE III CLASS - / KLINOV /

REGIONAL PROSECUTOR criminologist
PROSECUTION ML. Counselor of Justice - the signature / Ivanov /

Concepts: - Signature / Gordo /
Signature / NASKICHEV /

CONCLUSION

Based on these studies the corpse of a citizen KRIVONISCHENKO George Alekseevich, 23 years iuchityvaya circumstances of the case believe that the death KRIVONISCHENKO was caused by frost / freezing / as evidenced by swelling of the meninges, the sharp polnokrovievnutrennih bodies overflow liquid dark blood cavities of the heart, the presence of Vishnevsky spots naslizistoy stomach, full bladder, limbs and fingers frostbite burns II - III degree / campfire /.
found (inscribed by hand, approx. Ed.) For external study of damage in the form osadneniya, abrasions and skin wounds can result from a fall or injury on the rocks, ice and more.
The above injuries were caused KRIVONISCHENKO both in life and in the agonal state posthumously.
These studies corpse KRIVONISCHENKO suggest that meal he had for 6-8 hours before death. The presence of alcohol is not detected in the investigation. Death is violent, accidental.

SUD.MED.EKSPERT REGIONAL
BUREAU forensic - signature / Rojdestvensky /

SUD.MED.EKSPERT CITY

North Ural - signature / Laptev /

(corrected by hand - approx.
Yuri- Official Autopsy Report

Forensic medical examination of corpses CITIZEN
Doroshenko, Yuri Nikolayevich, '21

4th March 1959 in accordance with the decision of the prosecutor's office of
Sverdlovsk region from the 3rd March 1959 the forensic experts of the Regional Bureau
of Forensic Medicine of the Sverdlovsk region Renaissance VA and Laptev II in the
presence of State Counselor of Justice Class III Vee-NI, the prosecutor criminologist
Ivanova LI, and clear tov.tov. PROUD SD and NASKICHEVA KV in the room of the
morgue of the central hospital management n / box number H-240 in daylight and sunny
weather made the study of the corpse of a citizen Yuri N. Doroshenko 21 years, to
determine the cause of death and the responses to the questions listed in the decree.

Facts:

January 23, 1959 amateur group of tourists of 10 people went to ski tour route Ivdel -
Mount Otorten. From phase 2 nd North went 9 people in the ski trip. 1st February 1959
the group began to climb the mountain and in the evening Otorten pitched tents at the
height of 1079.
On the night of 2 of February under mysterious circumstances has occurred the death
of 9 persons.

and / external examination :

The corpse of a man, the right body; corpse pose: upper limbs laid in shoulders upwards
towards the head, flexed at the elbows, as well as in the joints of the fingers. The lower
limbs are stretched. His head turned to the left.
Clothes on the body: shpatelnaya cowboy shirt with short sleeves blue to the red cell,
with two patch pockets on the 2 buttons, cowboy shirt buttoned all six buttons. Mike
sleeve - knitted, salad color, shorts and swimming trunks blue satin, blue knit pants
fastened with two buttons. In the middle third of the inner femoral surfaces on the left
and right on the front surface discontinuities are pants, size 22 x 33 cm. X 13 right and
13 cm. Left. On left leg two pairs of knitted socks light brown, with breaks in the rear
foot and ankle; white wool socks, lined with the heel, in the region of the forefoot on the
toe has obozhzhonny plot measuring 2 x 5 cm. dark brown. On the right leg remains of
cotton socks with elastic sock color is the same as on the left. Wool socks white. The
inner surface of the pant has a marking label with the inscription 5P1513.

corpse length 180 cm, good food, with well-developed muscle groups.; cadaveric
bagrovolilovogo color spots arranged on the rear surface of the neck of the trunk and
extremities. Truponoe mortis dispersed in the muscle groups of the joints; temnorusye
color hair length up to 6 cm. cut under the "poluboks".

In the right temporo-parietal and occipital region has a lot of calcined hair ends, hair stained remnants of moss and needles of coniferous trees, the skin color of the person burolilovogo, facial contours are smoothed. Eyebrows bushy temnorusye, eyes closed, cloudy cornea, iris brown, pupils dilated, mucous pale pink color century. Bridge of nose straight. At the back of the nose area, the tip of the nose and upper lip traces of dried blood separation. Upper lip swollen, in the red border of the upper lip bleeding dark red color in the size 1.5 x 2 cm. Mouth slightly open s , even white teeth, gums and mucosa of the buccal cavity blednokrasnogo color, tongue in the mouth shut. In the area of the right cheek, soft tissue covered with a layer of gray foamy liquid color, from the opening of the mouth traces of discharge liquid gray. Auricles oval sinyushnokrasnogo colors in the tragus and lobule of the right shell dense regions burokrasnogo color 6 x 1.6 cm., On the left ear in the tragus portion of the same color 4 x 1 cm. Parchment density, ears with inner surface bright red color. Neck xxxx unremarkable. In the inner surface of the shoulders and upper arms of both extremities is well defined vein pattern. The soft tissues of the upper extremities bluish-red color on the inside surface of the right shoulder in the middle third of two abrasions 2 x 1.5 cm. Burokrasnogo parchment color density of irregular shape, without bleeding into the underlying tissues. Two cuts are made ??in the field of linear abrasions. The front edge of the right axillary line osadneniya skin dark red color of 2 x 1.5 cm. The front face of the right shoulder minor abrasions burokrasnogo color in strips measuring 4 x 1 cm., 2.5 cm x 1.5 cm., And 5 x 0.5 cm., and minor abrasions in the lower third of the right forearm. In the rear of the right hand soft tissue swelling and small abrasions. On the back of the hand, respectively, of the second metacarpal bone the size of a scratch 2 x 1.5 cm. Burokrasnogo color bleeding into the underlying soft tissue. Soft hand fabric and fingers especially terminal phalanx temnolilovogo color. On the inner surface of the left shoulder in the lower third color burokrasnogo abrasion measuring 3 x 0.5 1.5 x 0.7 x 1.5 and 1. On the side surfaces of the left elbow minor abrasions burokrasnogo parchment color density and abrasion of the same color 2 x 3 cm. With sliding tracks in the form of parallel strips. On the inner surface of the left forearm on the border of the middle third and the bottom third of a skin wound irregular oval shape measuring 0.6 x 0.5 cm., Its edges slightly podmyaty and covered with dried blood, under Ranko traces of dried blood. It makes an incision in the area of ??the wound, which was found to be bleeding in the soft tissue. The soft tissue in the rear of the left hand slightly swollen burokrasnogo color. The terminal phalanges temnolilovogo colored hands. The rib cage is cylindrical in shape, the stomach is slightly below the chest level. In the right iliac region cutaneous scar whitish linear form 8 cm. The external genitalia are developed correctly, in the foreskin and the glans penis bright red color fabric. The opening of the anus and urethra clean. The muscle groups of the lower limbs are well developed. On the back, inner thighs and lower legs venous pattern is well defined. On the front surface of each of the drums in the middle third osadnenie blednokrasnogo skin parchment color density measuring 8 x 4 cm. On the left, and 5 x 1.5 cm. On the right shin. Soft tissue in the terminal phalanges stop temnolilovogo color. Bones and cartilage skeleton with feeling safe.

B / Internal study

Skin patches of the scalp from the inside ???? pressor moist, juicy, shiny, blednokrasnogo color. The bones of the skull base and vault - intact, dura cyanotic, full-blooded, pia muddy, swollen. Brains and Brain furrow smoothed, flattened, the brain substance is a jelly-like mass zelenovatokrasnogo color. The gray matter of the brain poorly distinguishable from white, ventricles contours indistinguishable matter of the cerebellum pattern discernible bad. ?? Tzu base of the brain without features. Subcutaneous adipose ????? TKA trunk and limbs ("limb" culled or fixed - approx ed.). Well developed. The position of internal organs proper, pleural cavity free. The pericardium contained up to 40 cm 3. The amber-colored liquid. Heart 13 x 10 x 6 cm., The heart muscle is cut to dark red color, the thickness of the left ventricular muscle of 2 cm., 0.7 cm right., In the right and left side of the heart to contain 270 cm 3 of liquid blood dark, ?? ??? s heart aorta and pulmonary artery smooth, thin, shiny, blednokrasnogo color; the mouth of the coronary arteries are free, arterial lumen expanded, well pass; vnnutrennyaya aortic surface smooth, clean, aortic arch width ?? valves .. 8.5 cm from the surface Light sinyushnokrasno ??? color testovatoy touch, on sections of lung tissue dark ???? bit color, with pressure from the cut surface ste ???? in large quantities and the liquid dark blood yanistaya ??? foamy liquid; the lumen of the larynx and bronchi free; mucosa of the esophagus, trachea, bronchi sinyushnokrasnogo color. ???? pod'yazychnoy bones intact. The thyroid gland is the cut ??? flock, reddish color. The contained about ventricle? 50 cm 3 of the liquid mass of mucous burokrasnogo colors gastric mucosa lilovokrasnogo color, swollen, with well-defined folding; on the upper surface of the gastric folds have large numbers of small hemorrhages - spot Vishnevsky. The sense of smell of the contents of the stomach felt sour smell. The pancreas is a sectional melkodolchataya lilovokrasnogo color. In the lumen of the small intestine mucosa contain the mass of reddish color, intestinal mucosa sinyushnokrasnogo color. In the large intestine poluoformlenny light brown feces, intestinal mucosa blednolilovogo color. Spleen loose to the touch, her wrinkled capsule, the size of the spleen? 1 x 7 x 3 cm., On tissue sections temnovishnevogo its color, pulp gives a cut surface slight scraping. The liver surface is smooth, shiny, size of the liver? 9 x 12 x 10 cm., On the section of liver tissue burovishnevogo color, full-blooded, drawing liver tissue slight differences, gall bladder contains up to 30 cm 3 of liquid olifkovogo color, gallbladder mucosa velvety brownish colors. Kidneys from the surface smooth, shiny, capsule with them easily removed, the size of the right kidney 11 x 6 x 4 cm., Left kidney 11 x 5 x 3.5 cm., On the section of kidney tissue temnovishnevogo color, kidney layers are hardly distinguishable. The layers of the adrenal glands to distinguish good. The bladder contained about 150 cm 3 turbid light yellow liquid colors; bladder mucosa pale color ??? cerned. In the study of internal organs presence of alcohol is not detected.

For chemical analysis and histological examination of the corpse of the test is taken of the internal organs, which are sent to the laboratory of the Regional

Bureau of Forensic Medical Examination for research.

SUD.MED. REGIONAL EXPERT
BUREAU forensic - signature / Renaissance /

SUD.MED. CITY EXPERT
North Ural - signature / Laptev /

PROSECUTOR the Sverdlovsk region
State Counselor of Justice Class III - Signature / KLINOV /

REGIONAL PROSECUTOR criminologist
PROSECUTION ML.SOVETNIK JUSTICE - signature / Ivanov /

Concepts: Signature / PROUD /
Concepts: Signature / NASKICHEV /

CONCLUSION

Based on these studies the corpse of a citizen Yuri N. Doroshenko, 21 and in the circumstances of the case believe that the death was caused by the action DOROSHENKO low temperature / freezing / as evidenced? swelling of the meninges, the sharp hyperemia of internal organs, blood, dark liquid overflow cavities of the heart, the presence of Vishnevsky's spots on the mucosa of the stomach, full bladder, as well as frostbite fingers extremities III and IV degree.

For external investigations in the form of damage osadneniya, abrasions and skin wounds caused by a blunt instrument that could arise would result from a fall or injury ?? stones, ice, and so forth.

The above injuries were caused during his lifetime, as well as in the agonal state posthumously. The nature of damage to the above lesions are classified as light without health disorders.

These studies corpse DOROSHENKO suggest that meal he had for 6-8 hours until death. The presence of alcohol is not detected in the investigation. Death is violent, an accident.

SUD.MED. EXPERT REGIONAL OFFICE forensic - signature / Renaissance /

SUD.MED. CITY EXPERT
North Ural - signature / Laptev /

Alexander- Official Autopsy Report

forensic examination of the corpse.

May 9, 1959. According to the decision the prosecutor criminologist Sverdlovsk regional prosecutor's office on May 7, 1959 forensic scientist region. Bureau of forensics for the Sverdlovsk Region Renaissance, in the presence of the prosecutor criminologist Sverdlovsk regional prosecutor's office ml. Counselor of Justice LN Ivanova, expert criminalist Churkina GA, indoors infirmary morgue n / I 240, in daylight investigated the corpse c. Kolevatova Alexander , 24 years, to determine the cause of death.

Circumstances of the case:

23.I.59, a group of tourists consisting of 9 members went to ski tour route Ivdel - Mount Otorten.
I.II.59, the group began to climb and in the evening stood at the height of "1079".
On the night of February 2 this year All trip participants died.

A. External examination:

273

On the dissecting table lay the corpse of a male right physique, clothes: ski jacket made of black fustian on a zip, unbuttoned, the left and right chest pockets and cuffs undone, buttons intact. The left sleeve of the jacket on the upper side has a tissue defects in the area of ??25 x 12 x 13 cm., The edges of the tissue in the designated area of ??deification. On his right elbow jacket has minor tears tissue 7-8 cm in length. Above brown jacket with fleece knit svitr, then underneath the second svitr gray, worn, cotton cowboy shirt in blue, red and black check pattern, with two breast pockets. On the right pocket of safety pin, it was flat on the key lock gate and cowboy cuffs undone. In the left pocket a piece of wrapping paper, wrap the package "Codeine with soda."
Underwear shirt with fleece, pale gray, worn. Canvas trousers - overalls khaki straps with elastic. In the right pocket of his trousers Soaked box of matches at the bottom of trousers on metal buckles with anguish, beneath a blue ski pants bikes with side buckles, pocket their handkerchief. The feet woolen socks dirty, white, home-knitted with portions of the calcined, brown cotton socks. On the left leg wearing three brown cotton socks under them on the ankle gauze bandage. Pants pale gray paired with a shirt, dark blue satin panties.
corpse length 174 cm. right body, a satisfactory supply.
Cadaverous bagrovolilovogo spot colors are located abundantly on the back right side surface of the trunk and extremities. Rigor mortis was resolved in muscle groups joints. Skin of face, trunk zelenovatoserogo color with a purple hue.

On the head temnorusye hair up to 10 cm.
In temennozatylochnoy area of ??land with a lack of hair (hair slide rigor).
The forehead is low, straight. The eyebrows are absent. In the area of ??the eye sockets and brow absence of soft tissues exposing the facial bones, soft tissue around the edge of the outcrop flabby bones, flattened, slightly raised. Eyeballs wrinkled, sunken into the cavity of the eye sockets. Bridge of nose straight, nose cartilage, soft to the touch, unusual mobility. The base of the nose flattened. The nasal openings are compressed. In the area of ??the right cheek soft tissue defect in the area 4 x 5.5 cm. Oval wrong with podmyatymi smooth, thinning margins. The bottom soft tissue defects are the bones of the lower jaw. Mouth wide open, straight teeth, white. Language in the oral cavity. The soft tissues of the face thinned flabby, dirty-gray color. For the right auricle, in the mastoid wound indefinite shape measuring 3 x 1.5 x 0.5 cm., Penetrating to the mastoid process. Around the defect located on the right cheek and the lower jaw, the soft tissue bagrovozelevatogo color. The neck is long, thin, deformed in the area of ??the thyroid cartilage. The rib cage is rectangular in shape, the skin of the chest with the slipping of the surface layer of the epidermis. In the field of bone fingers' skin bath "blednoserovatogo color. His fingers half-bent brushes. The stomach is located at chest level. The right thigh is given to the left. In the area of ??the outer surface of the right thigh section of soft tissue depressions 25 x 15 cm. Without bleeding into the underlying soft tissue. External genitalia are formed correctly, without features. The opening of the anus clean. In the stop "bath skin" blednoserovatogo color. Limb bones are safe to the touch. In the left knee joint, on the inner surface of diffuse hemorrhage in the underlying tissues.

B. The internal survey.

Skin patches of the scalp with the inner surface of the wet, blednokrasnovatogo color. The bones of the skull base and vault intact. The dura mater cyanosis, a satisfactory blood supply. Pia thin, hazy. Brains and brain sulcus poorly distinguishable. The gray matter of the brain poorly distinguishable from white. The contours of the ventricles of the brain are indistinguishable. The substance of the brain is a jelly-like consistency of the base of the brain vessels without features. Subcutaneous fat body developed satisfactorily. The position of internal organs proper.

(not inscribed paper)
The pleural cavities contained up to 500 cm3 of bloody fluid. The pericardium contained up to 13 cm 3 of an amber-colored liquid.
Heart with surface slightly charged to fat. heart Size 13 x 12 x 5 cm. The heart muscle in the dark red color of the cut. The thickness of the left ventricular muscle 1.5 cm, right -.. 0.5 cm on the right and left half of the heart contained up to 100 cm 3 of liquid of dark blood.. The valves of the heart, the aorta and the pulmonary artery slightly thickened on the closing line. Coronary heart freely passable. The inner surface of the aortic smooth and clean. The width of the arch of the aorta valves 7 cm. Light from the surface sinyushnokrasnovatogo colored fluffy to the touch. In the context of the fabric of their dark red color. When pressed with the cut surface of a large amount of frothy bloody fluid. The lumen of the larynx and bronchi free. The hyoid bone is intact. Neck muscles and intervertebral cervical spine are minor soft tissue remnants zelenovatoserogo color (putrid changes). The stomach contained up to 100 see 3 slimy mass of pale red color. The mucous membrane of the stomach swollen sinyushnokrasnogo color, loose, with a well defined folding. Pancreas on melkodolchataya sectional zheltovatosinyushnogo color. Liver surface dull, smooth, liver size of 23 x 15 x 12 x 7 cm .. In the context of liver tissue burokorichnevogo color with a bad liver discernible pattern. The gallbladder contained up to 5 see 3 brown liquid. Mucous burovatozelenogo its color. In the lumen of the small intestine contained a slimy mass blednokrasnovatogo with a yellowish tinge. In the lumen of the colon fecal burozelenovatogo color. The mucous membrane of the intestine sinyushnokrasnovatogo color. Spleen loose to the touch. In the context of the fabric of her temnovishnevogo color. The pulp from the cut surface provides a small scrape. spleen size 9 x 7 x 2.5 cm. The buds from the surface smooth, brilliant, capsule kidney removed easily. In the context of kidney tissue temnokrasnovatogo color. Cortical and medullary layer distinguishable well. The layers of the adrenal glands to distinguish bad. The bladder contained up to 700 see 3 turbid yellowish liquid. The mucous membrane of the urinary bladder cyanosis.

The medical examiner - the signature (revived)
Prosecutor criminologist - signature (Ivanov)
The expert criminologist - (Churkin)
in Sverdlovsk

CONCLUSION :

Based on the research of a corpse Kolevatova I believe that his death was caused by exposure to low temperature. Discovered Body Kolevatova injuries in the head - soft tissue defects, as well as the "bath" skin are postmortem changes of the corpse that was in the last time before it is detected in the water. Death Kolevatova violent.

The medical examiner - the signature (revived)

Nicholas- Official Autopsy Report

Forensic examination of the corpse.

May 9, 1959. According to the decision the prosecutor criminologist Sverdlovsk regional prosecutor's office of the city medical examiner 7.U.59 regional forensics for the Sverdlovsk Region Restored Bureau, in the presence of the prosecutor-criminalist of the Sverdlovsk regional prosecutor's office ml. Counsellor of Justice LN Ivanova, an expert forensic Churkina GA, indoors infirmary morgue n / I 240, in daylight investigated the corpse gr. Thibault-Brignoles Nikolai, 23 years, to determine the cause of death.

Circumstances of the case:

January 23, 1959 a group of tourists in the composition of 9 people left in the ski trip from the mountains. Ivdel - Mount Otorten. I.II.59 of tourists began to climb and in the evening stopped at the height of 1079.
At night I.II.59, all trip participants died.

A. External examination:

On the dissecting table is the corpse of a male clothing: wearing on his head and tied tightly knitted wool, green, sports cap with three holes round shape measuring 3 x 3 cm, located in front.. Canvas fur color khaki helmet with Velcro zipper, lace hat is tightened. Canvas green fur jacket with sheepskin, on a zip, two patch pockets. In the right pocket woolen, grayish gloves, metal coins in the left pocket 10 kopecks, 20 kopecks.. and 2 kopecks., two folded pieces of paper, comb. Wool worn suites, dressed to the left side. Blue worn knitted jersey that has the right and the bottom of damage breaks oval tissue measuring 2 x 3 seen from a left forearm, two hours: sports watch that show 8:00 14 minutes 24 seconds. Watch "Victory" show time chas.39 8 minutes. The feet dressed almost new gray boots. On the right foot toe white wool hand-knitted, on the left leg the same sock. Brown crumpled wool socks in boots and is accordingly footbed. On the corpse wearing warm woolen [winter] of trousers, buttoned cuffs which, a leather belt with a metal [tyazhe] Loy buckle. Under these pants wearing, cotton, blue sports pants and black satin pants. In the bag xxxxx top trousers found a white button and a metal chain from a wall clock.
After removing the clothes found:. Corpse male, correct body, satisfactory food, length 174 cm Cadaverous spots lilovozelenovatogo color is on the back-side surfaces of the chest, neck and extremities . Rigor mortis was resolved in muscle groups sustvov. Skin of face, trunk and limbs ?? rozelenovatogo color with slipping surface layer of the epidermis. At the head of black hair length up to 8 cm. The forehead is high, sloping backwards. Eyebrows black, thick. Eyes closed. Eyeballs far sunk into the eye socket. The cornea is cloudy, dry. Iris dark green, slimy century blednoserogo color. Bridge of nose straight. Xxxxxxxxxxxxxxxxxxx nasal bones are safe to the touch. In the area of the upper jaw on the left defect soft tissue irregular oval shape measuring 3 x 4 cm. with thinned slightly podmyatymi edges, exposing the alveolar edge of the upper ??? STI.

The teeth are smooth, white. Mouth open. Lips blednoserogo color. Language in the oral cavity. The mucous membrane of the mouth and tongue gryaznovatozelenogo color. On the cheeks, chin and upper lip black hair up to 1 cm. The openings of the mouth, nose and ear passages clean. The neck is long, thin. The rib cage is cylindrical in shape. The stomach is located below the chest level. Dorsum of the hand and fingers blednokorichnevogo color, parchment density, half-bent fingers. In the areas of fingers "bathhouse skin" color blednoserovatogo rejection of nail plates. In the area of the right shoulder in the anterior-internal surface - spilled a bruise the size of 10x12 cm zelenovatosinego color at the middle and lower thirds. In the area of the bruise to be bleeding in the soft tissue. External genital organs without features. The opening of the anus clean. In the toes "bath skin" blednoserogo color.

B. The internal investigation.

Skin patches of the scalp with the inner surface ???? e, juicy, dull. In the right temple area marked diffuse hemorrhage in the right temporal muscle with diffuse impregnation. ???? ie excision of the right temporal muscle is determined by the depressed fracture of the right visochnotemennoy area on a plot measuring 9 x 7 cm defective bone and temporal bone measuring 3 x 3.5 x 2 cm. This area of bone is pushed into the cranial cavity and is located on the dura mater. After removing the brain substance in the middle cranial pit discovered multisplintered fracture of the right temporal bone and the transition to a discrepancy of bone fracture in the anterior cranial fossa on ??? th supraorbital region of the frontal bone, the second crack runs along ????? days sella surface area wedge otsrostka, venturing into the thick of the underlying bone, then moves to the middle cranial ??? on the left, with the divergence of the bone edges 0.1 -. 0.4 cm to the dura, respectively place of fracture sharply ???? okrovna with congestion of the brain substance of the right hemisphere of the brain, ??? oro? It has a more zelenovatobagrovym staining. Brains and ??? hells of the brain to distinguish bad. The gray matter of the brain poorly distinguishable from white. ???? urs ventricles are not distinguishable. The brain is a jelly-like mass gryaznokrasnogo color. Overall length of the crack in the ??? to the base of the skull is equal to 17 cm. In addition, there is asymmetry ???? Thu compression fracture of the area. Subcutaneous fatty tissue of the body is developed satisfactorily. ???
APPENDIX internal organs proper. Pleural cavity free. The pericardium contained up to 10 cm3 reddish muddy liquid. Heart size 13h12h 5.5 cm. From the surface lightly oblo- ??? fat. Cardiac muscle on a cut dark red color, dryablovata touch. The thickness of the left ventricular muscle 1.8, right -. 0.6 cm on the right and the left half of the heart contain a liquid dark blood vvide ??? s "dry heart." The valves of the heart, aorta and pulmonary artery smooth, ??? tyaschi slightly thickened. Coronary heart free, passable. ??? rennyaya surface aortic smooth and clean. The width of the arch of the aorta above the valve stem ??? E 8.5 cm. The light from the surface sinyushnokrasnogo ("cyanotic" imposed on top of other text?) Color, fluffy ??? schup. In the section of lung tissue dark red color. When pressed with the cut surface liberally allocated foamy liquid. Clearance ???? Ani and bronchi free. The hyoid bone is intact. The mucous membrane of the esophagus, trachea bronchi bluish-red color. The ventricle contained up to 100 cm3 slimy mass krasnovatozheltogo color. The mucous membrane of the stomach sinyushnokrasnogo color, with well-defined folding. Pancreas on melkodolchataya sectional sinyushnokrasnogo color. The liver surface is smooth, shiny, on the cut fabric of her burozelenovatogo color with yellow tint .. Liver pattern discernible bad. The

gallbladder contained traces of brown liquid. The mucous membrane of the gall bladder velvety brown. Liver size of 24 x 16 x 14 x 8 cm. The spleen is loose to the touch, the capsule it is wrinkled, spleen size 9 x 5 x 3 cm. In the context of tissue spleen, dark red color, the pulp yields a thick scraping. In the lumen of the small intestine contained a slimy mass of yellowish a brown tinge. In the lumen of the colon poluoformlennaya stool. The mucous membrane of the intestine sinyushnokrasnovatogo color. Kidneys from the surface smooth, brilliant, capsule kidney removed easily (? "? EHKO"), on the cut fabric kidney dark red color, cortex and medulla of the kidneys distinguishable. Right kidney size 9 x 6 x 6 cm, left -. 10 x 6 x 3 cm cortical and medullary layer nadpochenikov discernible bad. The bladder is empty. . Mucous his cyanotic for chemical and histological examination of the internal organs are taken, a part of the temporo-parietal bone on the right.

The medical examiner - the signature (revived)

Prosecutor criminologist - signature (Ivanov)
oblprokuratury
ml. Counselor of Justice

Forensic Expert (Churkin)

Conclusion:

Based on the research of a corpse c. Thibault-Brignoles NV I believe that his death was the result of a closed comminuted? pressure change in the region of the roof and base of the skull, with profuse bleeding under the meninges and the brain substance in the presence of the low temperatures. The above extensive multisplintered bone fracture roof and base of the skull in vivo origin and is a result of a large force to the subsequent fall, cast and injury Thibault-Brignoles. Injuries of soft tissues of the head region and the "bath skin" limbs are postmortem changes cadaver Thibault-Brignoles, was in recently, before finding water. Death Thibault-Brignoles violent.

The medical examiner - the signature (revived)

Simon- Official Autopsy Report

forensic examination of the corpse.

May 9, 1959 According to the decision the prosecutor criminologist Sverdlovsk regional prosecutor's office on May 7, 1959 sud.med.ekspertom oblbyuro forensics for the Sverdlovsk Region Renaissance, in the presence of the prosecutor-criminalist of the Sverdlovsk regional prosecutor's office ml. Counsellor of Justice LN Ivanova, an expert forensic Churkina GA, indoors infirmary morgue n / I number 240, in daylight investigated the corpse gr.Zolotareva Alexander, 37 years, to determine the cause of death.

Circumstances of the case:

January 23 a group of tourists in the composition of the 9 participants went to ski tour route Ivdel - Mount Otorten. I.II.59, the group began to climb and in the evening stood at the height of 1079. On the night of February 2, all participants of the march were killed.

A. External examination :

On the dissecting table lay the corpse of a male clothing: cap on his head wearing ear flaps, black, trimmed with black fur, sporting woolen knitted cap in red, with three light stripes. Wool scarf in a cage of brown and blue with unbuttoned pin, scarf Ponos. Travel tales mask and green tarpaulin with elastic bands. Fur vest on a black sheepskin, Ponos much. Brown sports flannelette jacket buttoned. The left breast pocket without buttons. They are three buttons in the top two gates undone. The sleeve on the left arm fastened to one button, while the right unbuttoned. Black cotton svitr slightly Ponos. Sport cotton with blue-sleeved T shirt, cotton knitted cherry-colored shirt. Canvas khaki pants overalls with two patch pockets. In the right pocket of the bulb and coins in three, five and fifteen cents. Black quilted cloaks, they brown woolen socks, and on the right foot and a sock on the left two darned sock, a wool, the other cotton. In the inner breast pocket of the overalls were a comb and a ball of yarn. In the back pocket of the overalls rolled up newspaper. Under the coverall torn flannel blue ski pants with buttons, three buttons on the belt is not fastened down buttons on the cuffs buttoned. Inside his pockets empty, underneath the second pants are the same, but on the gums. In the pocket of the pants pieces of paper and five coins, two to 15 kopecks, two for 2 kopecks.. and 10 kopecks. Grey cotton trunks dressed to the left side over the blue satin panties. On the left hand wearing a compass.

After removing the clothes found:. Corpse of a male, a satisfactory supply of correct body length 172 cm Cadaverous lilovoserogo spot color, richly arranged on the back of the neck, trunk and extremities, and on the side of the rib cage on the right. Rigor mortis was resolved in muscle groups joints. The fronto-parietal region of balding site. Available scalp to the touch slides, remnants of hair black color up to 10 cm in the right parietal region -. Soft tissue defect of irregular shape with a thinned size of 8 x 6 cm, slightly podmyatymi edges, exposing the parietal bone.. Skin Face zelenovatoserogo color. The forehead is low, sloping backwards. The eyebrows are absent. In the brow and eye sockets soft tissue defect rounded shape at the site 7 x 6 cm. With thinned edges, exposing the facial bones. Hollow gape. The eyeballs are absent. Bridge of nose straight. The bones and cartilage of the nose to the touch intact. The nose is flattened at the bottom. nose holes are compressed. On the upper lip on the right-preserved remains of a brown mustache, lips blednoserogo color. Teeth are smooth, white. On the right side of the upper jaw tooth and two crowns of white metal, four crowns of white metal on the lower jaw. Mouth wide open. The mucous membrane of the mouth zelenovatoserogo color (putrid changes). The openings of the mouth and the ear passages clean. The neck is long, thin. The rib cage is cylindrical in shape. The stomach is located below the chest level. External genitalia are formed correctly. From traces of the anus release the stool. In the area of ??fingers and toes "bath skin". Covers the trunk and extremities serovatosinyushnogo color with slipping surface layer of skin, the epidermis. His fingers half-bent brushes. At the rear of the right hand at the base of the big toe tattoo "Gene". At the rear of the right forearm in the middle third of the tattoo with the image of " beet and letters + C "on the rear of the left forearm tattoo with the image of" GS

279

"DAERMMUAZUAYA" five-pointed star and the letters "C", the letters G + C + C = D "and figures 1921".

B. The internal survey :

Skin patches of the scalp with the inner surface of the wet, dull, blednokrasnogo color. The bones of the skull base and vault intact. The dura mater sinyushnozelenovatogo color, poor blood supply. Pia thin, muddy. Brains and brain sulcus poorly distinguishable. The gray matter of the brain poorly distinguishable from white. The contours of the brain ventricles are not distinguishable. Vessels base of the brain without features. The subcutaneous tissue of the body is developed satisfactorily. The position of internal organs proper. The pleural cavities contained up to I liter of liquid of dark blood. The pericardium contained up to 15 cm 3 turbid, amber-colored liquid. Heart size of 13 x 10 x 6 cm. The heart muscle in the dark red color of the cut. The right and left half of the heart contained up to 50 cm3 dark liquid blood. The valves of the aorta and pulmonary artery of the heart somewhat thickened by closing the line. Coronary heart free, passable. The inner surface of the aortic smooth and clean. Light from the surface sinyushnokrasnogo color fluffy to the touch. In the context of lung tissue temnovishnevogo color. When pressed with the cut surface in multiple flows foamy bloody fluid. The lumen of the larynx and bronchi free. The hyoid bone is intact. The mucous membrane of the esophagus, trachea and bronchi sinyushnokrasnogo color. The stomach contained traces of a slimy mass blednokrasnovatogo color. The mucous membrane of the stomach bluish-red color with a barely visible folds. Pancreas on melkodolchataya sectional krasnovatozheltogo color. The liver surface is smooth, dull. In the context of the fabric of her burokrasnogo color with a bluish tint and poorly distinguishable pattern liver. liver size 26 x 15 x 10 x 7 cm. The gallbladder contained traces of brown liquid. Mucous its brown color. Spleen loose to the touch. Capsule her wrinkled. spleen size of 10 x 7 x 3 cm. In the context of the spleen tissue of dark cherry color. Pulpas cut surface gives a great scraping. In the lumen of the small intestine contained a slimy mass of dirty yellow color. The mucous membrane of the intestine sinyushnozelenovatogo color. In the lumen of the colon fecal burozheltovatogo color. The mucous membrane of the intestine sinyushnoserogo color. Kidneys from the surface smooth, dull, capsule kidney removed easily. right kidney size 10 x 6 x 3 cm., Left 9.5 x 6 x 3 cm., and cerebral cortical kidney poorly distinguishable layers. kidney tissue in the dark red color of the cut. Cortical and medullary layers of the adrenal gland discernible bad. The bladder contains 500 cm3 turbid yellowish liquid. After removing organocomplexes of the thoracic and abdominal cavity defined fracture II, III, IV, V, yi ribs on the right okologrudnoy and mid-axillary line with hemorrhage into adjacent intercostal muscles.
For chemical and histological examination of the corpse is taken from the specified portion of the internal organs.

The medical examiner - the signature (revived)
Prosecutor criminologist - signature (Ivanov)
oblprokuratury
Ml. Counselor of Justice
Forensic Expert (Churkin)

CONCLUSION :

280

Based on the research of a corpse c. Zolotarev, 37 years old, I believe that his death was caused by multiple rib fractures on the right to internal bleeding into the pleural cavity in the presence of the low temperatures. The above multiple rib fractures in Zolotarev with the presence of bleeding into the pleural cavity appeared during his lifetime and are the result of a large force to the chest area Zolotarev at the time of his fall, or compression of the drop. Injuries of soft tissues in the head Zolotarev, and the presence of "the skin of bath" in the fingers, upper and lower extremities are the postmortem changes of the corpse Zolotarev, who was in the last time before it is detected in the water.

Death Zolotarev violent.

The medical examiner - the signature (revived)

Luda- Official Autopsy Report

forensic examination of the corpse.

May 9, 1959 According to the decision the prosecutor criminologist prosecutors Sverdlovsk region on May 7, 1959 the regional forensic medical examiner for the Sverdlovsk Region Restored Bureau, in the presence of the prosecutor-criminalist oblprokuratury ml. Adviser Justice GN Ivanova, expert criminalist Churkina GA, indoors infirmary n / I number 240, in daylight, studied the corpse gr. Dubinina Lyudmila Alexandrovna, 20 years old, to establish the cause of death.

Circumstances of the case:
January 28 a group of tourists in the composition of the 9 participants went to ski tour route Ivdel - Mount Otorten. I.II.59 the group began climbing in the evening stopped at the height of 1079.
On the night of February 2, all participants of the march were killed.

A. External examination :

On the dissecting table is a female corpse in the clothes: color knitted knitted hat. Wool gray-brown svitr worn, underneath wearing beige wool svitr, plaid cowboy shirt? Ority whose sleeves fastened with buttons. Yellow jersey T-shirt with short sleeves, white cotton bra on the three buttons buttoned. On the corpse dressed ragged cotton pants are dark, with a belt with an elastic band. Pants torn badly and sometimes deified.
The left leg - the area partially leg and foot wrapped in a gray shestyanoy deification of the flap jackets with sleeves. On the left leg wearing a ragged brown woolen sock. On both legs, cotton blue, torn socks. Beneath gray woolen socks machine knitting. Black cotton tights torn in the crotch area, in poyasa- with an elastic band. On the feet of the corpse light brown cotton stockings. With his left foot stocking launched, right stocking is held eraser. Grey waist with elastic bands ??? MSCI-garter. Satin masculine cut pants. Belt fastened on the black buttons.
After removing the clothes found: a female corpse, correct body, good nutrition, length 167 cm Cadaverous spots bluish-gray in color, richly arranged on the back and side surfaces and ??, trunk and extremities.. At the head of blond hair, braided into a single

plait up to 50 cm. The braid is woven blue silk ribbon. Forehead straight, sloping backwards.

Skin Face zheltovatoskorichnevogo colors, soft tissue in the brow, the nose, eye sockets and left temporo-malar area missing exposing the facial bones. Gaping orbits, the eyeballs are absent. Bones of the nasal bridge are intact, the cartilage of the nose flattened. The absence of the soft tissues of the upper lip on the right with the thinning of the edges and the exposure of the alveolar edge of the upper jaw and teeth. Teeth are smooth, ?? lye. Language in the mouth is missing. Oral mucous gray-greenish in color. Auricles oval. The openings of the mouth, nose and ear passages clean. The neck is long, thin. Soft tissue of the neck area of ??the touch flabby. When the feeling of the neck is determined by an unusual mobility horns of the hyoid bone and thyroid cartilage. The rib cage is cylindrical in shape. The mammary glands of average size, elastic. Nipple and areola blednokorichnevogo color. The stomach is located at chest level. External genitalia are formed correctly. Hymen annular shape with a high roller, fleshy. Natural orifice hymen passes the tip of the little finger of an adult. The mucous membrane of the vagina lilovokrasnogo color. On the outside and the front surface of the left thigh, in the middle third, diffuse bruising bluish-purple on a plot size of 10 x 5 cm., With hemorrhage into the thickness of the skin. The back of the hands soft tissue, dense to the touch, the fingers half-bent arms. The terminal phalanx of hands covered with "skin of bath", which slides along with the nail plate. In the feet and toes "bath skin" blednoserogo color and a violet hue. When the feeling of the chest is determined by the unusual mobility of the ribs. In the area of ??the left parietal bone defect of soft tissue, the size of 4 x 4 cm., The bottom of the defect is naked parietal bone.

B. The internal survey.

Skin patches of the scalp with the inner surface of the moist, juicy and brilliant. The bones of the skull base and vault intact. Brain membrane cyanosis, poor blood supply. Brains and Brain furrow distinguished bad. The gray matter of the brain is different from the bad white. The contours of the lateral ventricles of the brain to distinguish bad. Vessels base of the brain without features. Subcutaneous fatty tissue of the body is well developed. The position of internal organs proper, in the pleural cavity contained up to one and a half liters of liquid of dark blood. The pericardium contained up to 20 cm 3 of a yellowish clear liquid. Heart 12 x 4 x 5. In the right ventricle of irregular oval shape size 4 x 4 cm hemorrhage., Impregnation with diffuse right ventricular muscle. The thickness of the left ventricular muscle 1.4 cm right -. 0.5 cm .. In the right and left half of the heart contained up to 50 cm liquid dark blood.. heart valves of the aorta and pulmonary artery smooth, thin, brilliant. Coronary heart available passable. The inner surface of the aortic smooth and clean. Light from the surface sinyushnokrasnogo color fluffy to the touch. In the context of lung tissue dark red color when pressed with the cut surface liberally dripping bloody foamy fluid lumen of the bronchi free. The horns of the hyoid bone XXXXXXXX unusual mobility, soft tissue adjacent to the hyoid bone gryaznoserogo color. Aperture mouth and tongue missing. The upper edge of the hyoid bone is exposed. The mucous membrane of the esophagus, trachea bronchi sinyushnokrasnovatogo color. The stomach contained up to 100 see 3 slimy mass temnokrasnovatogo color. The mucous membrane of the stomach is loose, sinyushnokrasnogo color. Pancreas on melkodolchataya sectional sinyushnokrasnogo color. The liver surface is smooth, dull. liver size 23 x 12 x 10 x 6 cm.section of liver tissue korichnevokrasnovatogo color ??? plohorazlichimym night pattern. The

282

gallbladder soderzhalosb to 5 cm. Of brown liquid, gallbladder mucosa velvety brown. Spleen loose to the touch, the channels still wrinkled. spleen size 7 x 5 x 2 cm. In the lumen of the small intestine contained a slimy mass gryaznozheltogo color. In the lumen of the large intestine contained fecal ?? landscaped colors. The mucous membrane of the intestine sinyushnokrasnovatogo color. ??? Ki from the surface smooth, brilliant. Capsule with kidney removed easily. In terms of kidney tissue dark red color. Right kidney size? x 5 x 2 cm., left kidney 9 x 5.5 x 2.3 cm. The cortical and medullary layer ??? ek well distinguishable. The cortical and adrenal medulla distinguishable ???? ho. Uterus on the cut blednoserogo color, lumen traces ??? tovatoy pale mucus. The ovaries and appendages without features. After removing organocomplexes of the thoracic and abdominal cavities found multiple broken ribs on the right sided II, III, IV, V by mid-clavicular line, and ?? ednepodmyshechnoy left fractured II, III, IV, V, yi, VII ribs in the midclavicular line. has spilled bleeding in the intercostal muscles in places ribs fracture. In the area of ??the handle to the right of the sternum diffuse hemorrhage.

For chemical and histological examination of the corpse said to take some of the internal organs.

The medical examiner - the signature (revived)

Prosecutor-criminologist
prosecutors Sverdlovsk region
Ml. Counselor of Justice - the signature (Ivanov)

Criminal expert (Churkin)

CONCLUSION:

Based on the research of a corpse c. Dubinina LA I think ??? Dubinin's death was the result of extensive hemorrhage? ravy ventricle, multiple bilateral rib fractures, ??? ceiling elements of internal bleeding into the chest cavity. These injuries may occur as a result of the impact of a large force, which entailed grave closed deadly ??? BMY chest at Dubinin. And the nature of the damage in vivo and are the result of a large force to the subsequent drop, throw or field of thoracic injury Dubinina cells. The injuries of the head area of ??the soft tissue and "skin bath 'limbs are posthumous changes (decay and decomposition) Dubinina corpse, which was recently before finding water.
Death Dubinina violent.

The medical examiner - the signature (revived)

Histological (Microscopic) Examinations
These tests were to look for the presence of hemorrhages in the skin of Alexander, Nicholas, Simon, and Luda. Microscopic hemorrhaging indicates the injuries happened while the individual was alive. Lack of hemorrhaging indicates the wounds happened after the individual died.

Nicholas
Histological Analysis No. 66/602 358

Due to the attitude of the court. honey. expert Revived in the histological department of the Sverdlovsk Region. Court. Honey. examination made a histological examination of pieces of skin, bones and internal organs from the corpse of Thibault-Brignol NV, 23 years old, to resolve the issue of hemorrhages. Coloring g / e and picrofuxin.

Microscopic examination:

soft tissues - In soft tissues hemorrhages are not visible, red bone marrow in a state of putrefaction.

Rib - Between the bone beams blood is in a state of putrefaction.

Skin - Epidermis is absent, in the dermis of hemorrhage with the presence of brown pigment.

Thyroid gland with surrounding muscles - In soft tissues hemorrhages are not visible, iron in a state of putrefaction.

Conclusion Hemorrhages in the skin (in the dermis).

29 / V 1959 honey. expert Ganz

Alexander
Histological analysis No. 64/600 359

Due to the attitude of the court. honey. expert Revived in the histological department of the Sverdlovsk Region. Court. Honey. examination carried out a histological examination of pieces of skin, bones and internal organs from the corpse of A. Kolevatov, 24 years old, to resolve the issue of the presence of hemorrhages. Coloring g / e and picrofuxin.

Microscopic examination:

A part of the costal bone with surrounding soft tissues - Bone - the usual structure, in surrounding soft tissues hemorrhages are not visible, pronounced putrefactive decomposition.

Skin - The epidermis is flattened, visible only along the edges of the drug, it is not visible in the derma of hemorrhages.

Kidney - Putrefactive changes.

Heart - The presence of gaps between the fibers of the myocardium

Conclusion In the sent pieces of skin, bones and internal organs from the corpse of Kolevatov, hemorrhages were not detected.

29 / V 1959 honey. expert Ganz

Simon
Histological Analysis No. 65/601 360

Due to the attitude of the court. honey. expert Revived in the histological department of the Sverdlovsk Region. Court. Honey. examination made a histological examination of pieces of skin, bones and internal organs from the corpse of Zolotarev

AA, 37 years old, to resolve the issue of the presence of hemorrhages. Coloring g / e and picrofuxin.

Microscopic examination:

Part of the sternum with surrounding soft tissues - Hemorrhages are not visible.

Part of the rib with the surrounding soft tissues - Putrefactive changes, in the soft tissues are visible bone fragments and hemorrhages.

Skin – Absence of superficial layers of the epidermis (eye sockets), in places its complete absence, in the dermis of hemorrhage with the presence of brown pigment and shadows of cells, putrefactive changes.

Muscle - Putrefactive changes.

Heart - The gap between the fibers of the myocardium, the fullness of the vessels, diapedemic hemorrhages.

Conclusion Hemorrhages in the skin (in the dermis), heart muscle and soft tissues, in the region of the rib fracture.
29 / V 1959 Honey. expert Ganz

Luda
Histological Analysis No. 67/603 361
Due to the attitude of the court. honey. expert Revived in the histological department of the Sverdlovsk Region. Court. Honey. examination carried out a histological examination of pieces of skin, bones and internal organs from the corpse of L. Dubinina, 21, to solve the question of the presence of hemorrhages. Coloring g / e and picrofuxin.

Microscopic examination:

Rib - A transverse fracture of the rib with a hemorrhage at the site of the fracture.

Sublingual bone - Hemorrhages not seen

Skin - The epidermis is completely absent in places (eye sockets), hemorrhages with the presence of brown pigment and shadows of cells are visible in the dermis.

Heart - The gap between the fibers of the myocardium, small hemorrhages in the myocardium.

Conclusion Hemorrhages in the skin (in the dermis), hemorrhage at the site of the rib fracture, small hemorrhages in the myocardium.
29 / V 1959 Honey. Expert Ganz

The Radiation Report

DECISION
(on the appointment of examination)
May 18, 1959. city of Sverdlovsk The prosecutor criminalist of the Prosecutor's Office of the Sverdlovsk region Ivanov having examined the criminal case on the death of students of the Ural Polytechnic Institute and taking into account that to determine the reasons for the death of tourists it is necessary
to make radiological studies and solve the issue of radioactive contamination of tourists' clothing, guided by Articles 63 and 171 of the Code of Criminal Procedure of the RSFSR ,

IT WAS RESOLVED:

to assign physical and technical expertise in the present case to resolve the following issues:
1. Is there a radioactive contamination of clothing and parts of corpses of dead tourists.
The expertise of the expertise is entrusted to the Chief Radiologist of Sverdlovsk Levashov.

At the disposal of the expert, to present all the clothes of Zolotarev, Dubinina, Kolevatova and Thibault Brignol, as well as part of their corpses.
Prosecutor criminalist
Junior Counselor of Justice (SIGNATURE) / Ivanov /

Subscription
Given this subscription is that I am warned of the responsibility under articles 92 and 95 of the Criminal Code of the RSFSR
(Signature of Levashov) 18.V.1959g

In the examination report, all objects of investigation are numbered from No. 1 to No. 4

No. 1 Kolevatov

No. 2 Zolotarev

No. 3 Thibault Brignoles

No. 4 of Dubinin

Conclusion
Samples of solid biosubstrates and clothing, which were sent to the radiological laboratory of the Sverdlovskaya Gorshenepidstadt, were examined for the content of radioactive substances, and dosimetric measurements of clothes were carried out on the Tiss device, which revealed an overestimation of the natural background for 200-300 imp / min Further, with radiometric measurements without ashing in a lead cottage with cassette counters STS-6 in the number of 4 pieces, maximum contamination was established in some sections

of deshdy:
1) a brown sweater from No. 4 -

-9900 rpm with 150 cm2.

2) the bottom of the bloomer from No. 1

- 5000 rasp / min with 150 cm2
3) belt of sweaters from No. 1 -

5600 rpm with 150 cm2

Table 2 shows the contamination of different types of clothing.

Table 2 Contamination of clothes

№ 1 / №6	Name	Area in cm ^{2}	Total score in cpm.	Activity of contaminated section	Activity of the loading zone in terms of 150 cm ^{2}
1	Land from №1	-	96	-	-
2	Belt of a sweater from №1	70	384	2600	5600
	(after washing)		306		
			244	1280	2700
			218		
3	Bottom of the breech from # 1	55	297	1840	5000
			265		
	(after flushing)		210		2600
			184	970	
4	from №2	60	182	820	2000
			160		
	(after flushing)				
			182		1400
			163	560	
5	Sheepskin quilts from No. 2(after washing)	60	176	770	1920 940
			156	370	
6th	The bottom part of trousers № 3	66	120	270	600 230
			111	100	
	(after flushing)				

287

No.	Sample			
7th	Jacket from No. 4	88	210	1070	1800 1160
8	(after flushing) Black trousers from No. 4 (after flushing)	77	177 164	690 660	1280 700
9	Sweater white from No. 4 (after washing)	63	140 185	360 850	1840
10	Brown sweater № 4 (after washing)	75	163 640 390	560 4900 2600	1340 9900 5200

Recalculation was carried out on the B-2 installation in a lead house with a cassette counter STS-6 in the number of 4 pieces.

Conversion factor of the installation B-2 k = 8,9

background in lead house (before flushing) 90 pulses / min

background in lead house (after washing) 100 pulses / min

Experimental washing of clothes showed that the contamination is removed, the percentage of washing ranges from 30% to 60% (washing clothes was done in running cold water for 3 hours).
When determining the type of radiation, it is established that the activity takes place due to beta particles . Alpha particles and gamma quanta were not detected.

The absence of appropriate instruments and conditions in the laboratory made it impossible to perform radiochemical and spectrometric analysis to determine the chemical structure of the emitter and its radiation energy.
Radiometric measurements of solid biosubstrates were carried out in a B-2 facility (No. 2554) in a lead house with a BFA-25 meter. The
unit was tested using a strontium preparation with the following activity:

1) 7,000 rpm

2) 2000 rpm

The results of sample measurements from No. 1,2,3,4 are summarized in Table No. 1

Table №1

№ п/п	Name	Hitch in gr.	Weight of crude sample in gr	Weight of ash in gr	Background in imp / min	Account over the background in cpm	Sample activity in decays per kg per min	Curie activity / kg
1	Intestine #1	0.2	24.42	0, 670	23	3	2000	0, 9 * 10^{-9}
2	Liver №1	0.2	19,130	0, 690	22	3	3000	1, 35 * 10^{-9}
3	Brain # 1	0.2	42,820	0, 710	26th	4	1850	0, 85 * 10^{-9}
4	Heart number 1	0.2	8,500	1, 300	24	2	**8400**	3, 8 * 10^{-9}
5	Leather №1	0.25	1,400	0.025	24	-	-	-
6th	Intestine #2	0.2	20,470	0, 350	23	6th	2800	1, 25 * 10^{-9}
7th	Liver №2	0.2	13.590	0, 480	29	6th	5800	2 , 6 * 10^{-9}
8	Brain # 2	0.2	41.00	0, 840	26th	4	2200	1 , 0 * 10^{-9}
9	Stomach number 2	0.2	24,460	0, 480	29	3	1600	0, 85 * 10^{-9}
10	Breast No.2	0.2	4,170	0,740	24	-	-	-
eleven	Breast, rib number 2	0.2	4,300	0.390	24	-	-	-
12	Thigh skin №2	0.022	6,500	0.300	24	-	-	-
13	Bowels # 3	0.2	21,770	0, 740	23	3	2800	1 , 25 * 10^{-9}
14	Liver №3	0.2	33.00	0, 920	20	6th	4600	2 , 0 * 10^{-9}
15	Kidney №3	0.08	10.10	0.080	26th	-	-	-
16	Leather №3	0.014	1,150	0.040	24	-	-	-
17th	Breast 3	0.2	7,200	1,300	24	-	-	-
18	Guts number 4	0.058	14.10	0.100	23	-	-	-
19	Liver №4	0.2	18,830	0, 490	34	7th	5000	2 , 2 * 10^{-9}

№	Name	Weight in gr	Weight of crude sample in gr	Weight of ash in gr	Background in imp/min	Account over background	The activity of the sample in the dose/kg in min	Curie activity/kg
20	Kidney №4	0.2	18,470	0, 330	27th	4	2000	$0,9*10^{-9}$
21	Leather №4	0.09	11,910	0, 100	27th	4	900	$0,4*10^{-9}$
22	Skin of Thigh # 4	0.2	7,600	0, 280	24	2	2000	$0,9*10^{-9}$
23	Skin of lower leg №4	0.1	3,840	0.150	24	-	-	-
24	Heart number 4	0.2	12,720	0, 350	24	4	3000	$1,4*10^{-9}$
25	Rib number 4	0.177	1,300	0.180	24	-	-	-

Conversion factor of installation = 5,5

The results of the measurements from the control samples are summarized in Table No. 3

Table No. 3
Control samples

№ п/п	Name	Weight in gr	Weight of crude sample in gr	Weight of ash in gr	Background in imp/min	Account over the background	The activity of the sample in the dose/kg in min	Curie activity/kg
1	Lungs	0.2	23,100	0.700	24	+3	2500	$1.1*10^{-9}$
2	Bud	0.2	30,200	0.920	24	+1	-	-
3	Liver	0.2	26,030	0.960	24	+1	-	-
4	A heart	0.2	19,640	0.950	24	+6	**8000**	$3.6*10^{-9}$
5	Leather	0.2	28,200	0.690	24	+3	2000	$0.9*10^{-9}$
6th	Edge	0.2	13,800	1,180	24	+2	4700	$2.1*10^{-9}$

Control samples were obtained from the forensic medical expert of Dr. Renaissance. The samples of the tissues of a person who died in the accident of a motor vehicle in the city of Sverdlovsk, also showed the presence of a natural radiological element of potassium-40 in approximately the same amounts as in Table 1.

Thus, the results of the studies in Tables 1 and 3 do not exceed the averaged data on the content of radioactive substances in human organs and can be attributed to naturally-radioactive Potassium-40. Radiation by type refers to the Beta- particles; Alpha particles and gamma quanta were not detected.

CONCLUSIONS:

1) The solid biosubstrates studied contain radioactive substances within the natural content determined by potassium-40.

2) The individual samples of clothing examined contain several inflated quantities of radioactive substances or radioactive
material, which is a beta emitter.

3) Detected radioactive substances or radioactive substances when washing clothing samples tend to flush, i.e. are caused not by a neutron flux and induced radioactivity, but by radioactive contamination with beta particles.

Chief radiologist of the city

27.V.1959 (Signed) / Levashov /

The investigations were carried out in the radiological laboratory from 18 / V-59 to 25 / V-().

ADDITIONAL QUESTIONS TO EXPERTS:

1. Should there be (can it be) increased contamination of clothing with radioactive substances under normal conditions, i.e. without being in a radioactive contaminated environment or place?

Answer: It should not be perfect.

2. Was there any contamination of the objects you are researching?

Answer: As stated in the conclusion, contamination of radioactive substances / substance / beta emitters of selected samples of clothes of the samples sent is contaminated. For example, the notch from No. 4 - brown sweater at the time of the study had 9.900 decays of beta particles per minute at 150 cm2, and after washing / for 3 hours, we / he gave 5,200 decays per minute of beta- particles from 150 sq. cm.

For example, according to the sanitary rules in our country, the contamination in the beta particles from 150 square centimeters per minute should not exceed the purification / washing / 5.000 decays, and after cleaning / washing / there should be a natural background, e. as much as it gives cosmic radiation to all people and all objects in a given locality. This is the norm for workers with radioactive substances.

Cutting from No. 1 - the sweater belt shows up to a wash of 5.600 decays, and after washing - 2.700. The bottom of the bloomer from No. 1 shows 5,000 decays before washing and 2.600 after washing. In your data it is indicated that all these objects were in the flowing water for a long time before the study, i.e. have already been washed.

3. Is it possible to consider that this clothing is contaminated with radioactive dust?

Answer: Yes, clothes are contaminated or radioactive dust dropped from the atmosphere, or this garment has been exposed to contamination when working with radioactive substances, or on contact. This pollution exceeds, as I have already indicated, the norm for persons working with radioactive substances.

4. What do you think, what could be the degree of contamination of individual objects, if you take into account that prior to research they had been in the running water for about 15 days.

Answer: It can be assumed that the contamination of individual garments was many times greater, but here one must take into account that clothes could be washed unevenly, that is, with varying degrees of intensity.

Expert Levashov

Chief radiologist of the city of Levashov (Signed) 05/29/1959

Fireballs- Official Witness Statement

Witness the interrogation report
April 15, 1959 The public prosecutor of the investigation department prosecutors Sverdlovsk Region mL. Counselor of Justice Romanov in regional prosecutor's office as a witness st. Art. 62-168 Code of Criminal Procedure
1. Last name, first name Karelin, Vladislav
2. Born in 1932 Born 3. Place of birth city of Kamensk-Uralsky, Sverdlovsk Region.
4. Nationality Russian.
5. Partisanship ... Nonpartisan
6. Education ... Higher - in 1956 graduated from nat-tech. Faculty UPI.
7. Lesson: a) at the moment - the place of work and position mL. Researcher VNIIMT
b) at the time, which includes readings: the same.
8. permanent residence (detailed address and telephone ?) mountains. Sverdlovsk, ul. Lenin, 101, Apt. 47, to serve. tel 2-1 89-07.
9. Passport ... -
11. In what ways is the accused -
12 On the responsibility .... Warned
V.Karelin (signature)

I, VG Karelin in the public tourist worker in the Sverdlovsk leisure club (the club's deputy chairman), have 1 sports category Tourism.
Preparations for the campaign group Dyatlov I learned at the beginning of January 1959 Dyatlov came to me for the card hike the area and told about the route. In addition, through me Dyatlov took the paper from gorkomfizkulta with a request to leave one of the comrades working in the factory. The full composition of the group, I did not know. Before leaving on a campaign I knew that Dyatlov went Kolmogorov, Doroshenko, Kolevatov, Slobodin. These people on the tourist qualification in its stowed

experience fully satisfy the requirements of the participants of the III Cat hiking difficulty. All of them were physically strong, mentally stable.

In preparation I met Dyatlova twice in the tourism club, where he came for the approval route.

Dyatlov group route seems to me normal "average" campaign in difficulty could be completely gone in the month of February. This statement is based on personal experience. From 9 to 24 February 1959 I grppoy tourists in Sverdlovsk took place in the same area as that of a group of Dyatlov, but 50-60 km to the south, in the campaign and III categories of difficulty. We climbed to the city Oyko-Chakur, which was supposed to come up artist Dyatlov at the end of the route. It was and we have bad weather, but it is not an insurmountable obstacle. With traverse region and its features Djatlova group was familiar.

May 1957 Woodpeckers led the march a group of tourists UPI in an area where we are today. We took them a note from a mountaintop Yalking-Nyeri (molebens stone). In 1957, together with Dyatlov went Kolmogorov and Thibault-Brignoles.

In connection with the death of group of Dyatlov must tell about an unusual celestial phenomena that we have seen in his campaign February 17, 1959 in the watershed ridges and rivers Sev.Toshemki Vijay. Around 7:30 am I was awakened by the Sverdlovsk time cry duty preparing breakfast: "Guys Look, look What a strange phenomenon".!.

I jumped out of the sleeping bag and the tent without shoes in some woolen socks and standing on the branches, saw a big bright spot. It was spreading. At its center there was a small star, which also began to increase. All this spot moved from the northeast to the southwest, and fell to the ground. Then it disappeared behind the ridges and woods, leaving the sky bright band. This phenomenon is produced on the different people different impression: Atmanaki argued that it seemed to him that now Zamli explode from a collision with a planet; Shevkunov this phenomenon seemed "not so scary" to me it made no particular impression - the fall of a large meteorite, and nothing more. All of this phenomenon occurred a little more than a minute.

In the search for a group our group Dyatlov came from Serov, where we came back from his trip. Serov of the disaster, we learned in the dining room from the casual visitor, who asked us. "Not from UPI Do we?" He told us that he had lost some group of tourists UPI By phone, we contacted the Sverdlovsk and Ivdel and were ordered to arrive. in Ivdel, where we arrived by train on February 25 at 11 pm. February 27, we have been abandoned by helicopter to the discovery on the eve of the tent. we leave the backpacks at the pass, where we landed the helicopter, FEB of us went down to the valley Lozvy looking for a place to camp, and two with two conductors and two dogs went to the n alatke and then continue to look for on this day, four bodies were found:.. Kolmogorov, woodpeckers, and Doroshenko Krivonischenko latter we initially confused with Zolotarev, because his face was covered with snow.

The next day, the tent was dismantled and removed a group of Dyatlov Pass on three corpses.

Dogs are no longer found nothing.

Further searches were using metal probes. During the detailed survey of the area involves finding the remaining bodies was found Slobodin.

March 10, our group has been removed from search operations.

My subjective thoughts on the death of the group are as follows.

A breakdown of the tent above the forest is an error group, its reluctance to descend to the forest and then climb back to go on an ice crust, which greatly facilitated the movement.

Pitch a tent group became settle for the night and prepare a cold supper. At this time they something frightened, they all rushed out of the tent barefoot. These people were in the group of Dyatlov could scare phenomenon, out of the ordinary. Wind whistling noise celestial phenomenon, even a single shot they could not scare. Although I can not say in this and vouch for Zolotarev, because he did not know. In general, its appearance in the group Dyatlov seems unnatural to me. Traces fled from the tent, we have clearly seen on the hillside. At first there were about 8-9, and then they became less and soon they disappeared altogether.

Probably the people in the dark and confused by the fire is not sobrlis all. Making an attempt to start a fire that could not save them because of the low availability of firewood, they decided to make their way to the tent. Poses Dyatlov, Slobodina Kolmogorova and say that they went to the tent.

The other four probably were not near the fire or come to him later, when Krivonischenko and Doroshenko already frozen. Go far these four could not without skis.

The mystery of what happened can be possibly explained after finding four people is not found.

In conclusion, I wish to note that, in principle at least 10 people, although the scene is no evidence of presence of strangers not only discovered an armed group of people could scare a group of Dyatlov.

The protocol was written by me personally, .V.Karelin (Signature)
The interrogation ... (signature)

Rempel- Official Witness Statement

March 7, 1959 Investigator Ivdelsky district of Sverdlovsk region Lawyer 1 cells. Kuzminih questioned indoors Vizhayskogo lagotdeleniya POB 240
As witness to meet Articles 162-168 Code of Criminal Procedure
1. Last name, first name and patronymic Rempel Ivan Dmitrievich
2. Year of birth 1906
3. Place of birth Dnipropetrovsk region hortinsky Ra-n to. Morozovo
4. Nationality German.
5. Partisanship b / n.
6.Obrazovanie 9 classes.
7.Zanyatie a) at the moment - Vizhayskogo forester forestry.
B) at the time, which includes readings: the same.
8. Conviction: do not judge.
9. Domicile: Pos. Vijay Ivdelsky area.
10.Pasport 738 685, 16/02/1956, at Ivdelsky GOM.
11. In what ways is the accused: -.
On the responsibility of the first part of Art. 92 of the RSFSR Criminal Code for refusing to testify and under Art. 95 RSFSR Criminal Code for giving false testimony.
Rempel (signature)

The witness testified: January 25, 1959 to me, as head of the forest approached by a group of tourists who showed their travel route and get advice how best to get them up the mountain Ottorten and asked to familiarize them with our plan of the place where they go. When I learned about their route he has expressed the opinion that it is dangerous, so there are a large ravine, pit into which you can sink and in addition there are rampant strong winds, demolishing people in the winter to go in the Ural ridge. This fear I expressed to them because I was the area of ??the Ural mountain range known from the words of a local resident, I myself have not been there. On my statement, they said that it is for us to be considered as a first class constraints. Then I said, yes, first you have to pass it. I gave them a ground plan they did vykupirovku your route and struck the border afforestation Ural Mountains planned route. Here I have advised them that they may go closer by one of our forest glades. To this they replied resolve this issue when we arrive at the second North mine. Then they went away from me, and on January 26 at a passing car left in the village. 41 quarter.

My personal opinion about the death of the tourists is that they can only be killed by the disaster of the climatic conditions. The fact that neither x attacked Mansi and had an interest in their deaths, I think this is not could be because with Mansi I often meet and hostile statements from them to other people heard and they are very hospitable when they happen or occur .veteran I know from stories that cases of deaths in passing through the Urals occurred before.

The peoples of Mansi living in the territory of our forest and in the area where the tourists were killed sacred places or molebens stones are not available. From the stories of the locals I know that Mansi molebens stones are in the upper Vizhaya for 100-150 km from the place of death of tourists.

More show can not do anything with my words properly recorded and read by me.

Questioned pom. Attorney Ivdel, lawyer class I
Kuzminih

Afterword

Several clues are found through the many official files and statements. Many researchers around the world continue to study and analyze this complex case and despite the mystery being 60 years old, there is a continual flow of new information.

This book is not meant to be an end, but rather a stepping stone in providing a clear path into further research. While the evidence points to murder, we still don't know who or why. We can only hope that all the answers are someday known.

It's been an honor and a pleasure sharing this journey with you. I'm humbled by this experience and forever grateful that you've shared your time with me.

Thank you,

Launton Anderson

Printed in Great Britain
by Amazon

34741963R00182